Self-Education is Greater than Higher Education
A Great Guide to Learning and Living Your Life Purpose

Written by <u>Miles Goodloe</u>

ImproveYourRetention.com
@ProfessorMiles_
(Instagram & Twitter)
DM me your feedback

2

"It takes a village to raise a child."
-African Proverb

To My Guardian Angels, thank you for caring for me and setting a great example. I love you all so much. This book, my first of many to come, is dedicated to you:

Dr. Sharon E. Jackson, Ed.D.
Lemonde Goodloe
Grandma Mary
Grandpa Sylvester
Valerie Goodloe
Aunt Darlene
Uncle Tim

GOD

4

Copyright

Miles Goodloe wrote this book. Contact Professor Miles at milesrgoodloe@gmail.com , @ProfessorMiles_, or at ImproveYourRetention.com

All images are original concepts that he created and envisioned.

Azani Pinkney digitized all images and the cover of this book. He was compensated for all images and has granted the rights to Miles Goodloe to use and reproduce the images as Miles Goodloe sees fit from this November 1, 2016 and hence forth.

The copyrights of this book and all its content belong to Miles Goodloe.

10% of the proceeds will be used to as academic scholarships for college students overcoming financial and academic barriers.

All rights are reserved. This book is copy written by Miles R. Goodloe.

No parts of this book may be reproduced, stored in a retrieval system, or transmitted in any form or by any means, electronic, mechanical, photocopying, recording or otherwise, without the prior proper and written consent of the author, Miles Goodloe.

All Rights Reserved, © 2016.

About the Author

Miles Goodloe is a career development expert with a focus on retention. He grew his skills at UCLA teaching high school students how to succeed in school despite financial hardships, single family homes, and academic support at the age of 18. As a graduate of Crenshaw High School, Miles experienced a lot of these challenges first hand. He taught others how to succeed in school.

After helping over 100 students gain access to college, he graduated UCLA at 21 years old and entered the University of Pennsylvania to earn his Master's of Science in Higher Education with a concentration on Affordability, Access and Retention. He led the Dana How Scholars Mentoring Program at the age of 22.

Upon completion of his graduate degree, Miles Goodloe began working as a Program Coordinator at Drexel University. He focused on improving the academic advising and career development of students. He improved academic support by co-founding a tutoring program and leading over 100 workshops across the nation at multiple universities on academic and professional success. He became a thought leader in academic retention and professional development by the age of 23.

His consistent and passionate efforts earned Miles an adjunct faculty position at Drexel University in the Pennoni Honors College when he was 24 years old. He taught classes on the business and finance of higher education. He soon became known on campus and across the nation as "Professor Miles" for his retention expertise and high energy presentations.

Today, Miles serves as the National Program Manager of Advancement and Instruction for LeadersUp. He consults community college districts seeking to improve their access and retention for stackable credentials. He also consults employers seeking to improve retention by using his multimedia instructional programs to professional develop entry-level employees and designing career pathways to mission-critical positions because advancement and mentorship serves as the greatest retention efforts a company can implement to improve retention. Lastly, Miles bridges the skills gap for employees by teaching the habits and skills necessary for professional success.

Miles still travels the nation to teach his personal philosophy, B.E. G.R.E.A.T., found at the end of this book that serves as the basis of his professional and personal development philosophy. How B.E. G.R.E.A.T. helped him to excel in his life, school, and profession follows in the pages to come.

Prologue

Why did I write this book? There is a problem in American Higher Education. The problem is, you can go to college, get a degree, and still have no idea what your passion is. Therefore, you will not care about the degree you got. You earned a degree just to say you earned a degree. You should graduate from college and know who you are and what impact you want to make in the world. That is the best way for you to pursue a career that you love and enjoy.

The next problem that exists is that you have to live your life in order to know what you like to do. Do something. You will not find your passion just going with the flow in life. You will find your passion when you make an intentional effort to create it. It takes thought, practice, and everyday engagement. This way, you know your best passions, talents, skills, and knowledge. You take the previous knowledge of self and implement it in the world to make change. Make change in the world and make change in your pocket!

College provides a great space for you make changes in your life and start over. Take this time to explore your interest and pursue your deepest passions. Unfortunately, most of us do not know how to navigate universities in a manner that benefits us directly. Colleges are getting more difficult to maneuver as a student because we stress about getting a job.
Pursue a career instead. A job is for right now. A career is for tomorrow and the next day because you will be able to grow in an industry and thrive. Put yourself in the best position to succeed in creating your career is to create your passion and act on it right now!

This book will be your guide to finding yourself in a college setting so after graduation you can thrive as a professional. Colleges have so many options that can overwhelm you but when you know who you are, you can dominate your college environment and professional life after graduation. It is super easy to go to class and go to parties and call it a day but that will not make you a better person and professional. That is far from enough to figure out who you truly are and what you are best at. There is some trial and error but those willing to fail are more likely to succeed if they have the perseverance to continue to create themselves despite difficulty. Life is not easy so don't take the easy approach. Go hard or go home!

Life may require certain experiences for you to flourish in your passion. The earlier you start to create yourself, the better. The world belongs to the young, dedicated, and focused individuals who use their strengths to dominate their lane. You can do that. I believe in you. If you believe in you, then you can achieve anything your mind can conceive.

I wrote this book to help you outline your passion, talents, skills, and knowledge so you know who you are and who you want to be. Then, it is up to you, to engage in the activities outlined in this book that will allow you fill the gap between who you are and who you want to be. Enjoy!

-Miles Goodloe

TABLE OF CONTENTS

p. 13	01 – **INTRODUCTION** – Your Self-Education is Greater than Your Higher Education
p. 26	02 - **ACADEMICS** – The Process of Learning in School
p. 49	03 - **CO-CURRICULAR** – Out of Classroom Commitments
p. 72	04 – **EXTRACURRICULAR** – What You Really Like to Do
p. 83	05 – **SOCIAL** –You Are Who Your Friends Are
p.100	06 – **PROFESSIONAL** – Your Passion Is Your Profession
p. 128	07 – **NETWORKING** – Friendships Are Two Way Streets
p. 143	08 – **RELATIONSHIPS** – Love Is an Ocean
p. 160	09 – **DIVERSITY** – No Two People Experience the World the Same Way
p. 180	10 – **TEACHING** – Every Day You Teach Others
p.210	11 – **ADVISING** – Personal Trainers for Higher Education Success
p. 220	12 – **PROGRAMMING**- The Power of Understanding
p. 224	13 – **MENTORSHIP** –You Know What I Don't Know That I Don't Know That I Don't Know
p. 229	14 – **REFLECTION** – It's All About You
p. 245	15 - **IMAGINATION GAP** – Where You Are vs. Where You Want to Be
p. 258	16 – **RESOURCES** – Control Your Assets
p. 270	17 – **SELF-EDUCATION** – Be Great! You Already Are.

01
Introduction

Your self-education is >
your higher education.

To my students, I love you. I want to help you as much as I can but I cannot change your life. ONLY YOU CAN MAKE YOUR LIFE GREAT! Change your life today. It is your responsibility and no one else's. As you learn more about who you are, life will become clear. Decisions will become easier and you will discipline yourself to become who you want to be. Therefore, your education is your responsibility. You must learn what you need to learn to become who you are supposed to be. Do not stop learning when you leave the classroom. Higher education is a great place for prosperity, but we are missing a lot self-education within the grander education system. I wrote this book because I believe the current structure of education in the United States of America is incomplete and needs to evolve. The system may take hundreds of years to catch up to the many different learning styles we have, so I place the responsibility to educate yourself, on *you*. This book teaches you how to maximize your education by taking control of your life while you attend college. Learning never stops. Learning is forever. However, schools and colleges are not designed to teach you forever. They teach you the discipline necessary for you to learn on your own. Self-education is one of the greatest loves. Self-education is self-love. Schools are decent instruction until we can grasp on our own how to teach ourselves what we need to know to become our best selves.

Colleges have forgotten their truest purpose: teaching self-education. Self-education becomes difficult when you do not understand why you should self-educate in the first place. The best reason to excel in school is to master self-education. You wake up every day to achieve in your classroom because someone else demands you to learn what he or she determines to be important. Demand from yourself that you self-educate yourself. Establish what you think is important and learn from life. In life, class is always in session. Through self-education, self-love, and self-awareness, you can empower yourself by critically analyzing your environment to understand your best route to success. It's imperative to acknowledge our passion(s) to learn, or we will learn aimlessly and without truth. As we hold laptops on our thighs, we contemplate dreams and grand achievements, but the journey along the way to success will test us many times. We dream dreams of our deepest passions coming true. We look for others to make these dreams come true, including higher education. College is not designed to make your dreams come true. It is designed to give you access to the information and resources you will need to make yourself successful. College helps you develop the tools necessary to learn, analyze, and convey proof of your education. Not just the degree you earn at graduation but also in your personal and professional development. Nonetheless, higher education serves as a supplement to your life's studies.

Our greatest aspirations live outside of the classroom, especially when there is a boring professor dragging on about a topic no one, not even the teacher, enjoys. Each day, the broken podcast of academia repeats itself. Many times, the information is not appreciated because it is not directly correlated with your life. School distances itself from speaking about where in the world this information came from and how it applies today. The students' souls scream due to the passion for life that is omitted from the college classroom. The love for learning does not live.

Love pushes our best pursuit of knowledge. The pursuit of knowledge is everything we need in life to conquer our dreams. Schools are not designed for everyone's dreams to be achieved on campus. School is designed to expose your mind to knowledge discovered and created by our ancestors. Humanity's relentless pursuit of knowledge should encourage us all to achieve similar triumphs to push our human race forward. Within education, post-secondary institutions remain the most creative and intellectually progressive learning industries on the planet. Most of the creativity is left inside of research and does not factor into the teaching practices of the classroom. It serves as an intriguing home to eclectic minds. The university encourages people from around the world to unite in their pursuit of information; information that the professor believes will change the world.

The world will be changed by actions carried on outside of the classroom. Self-education will provide the greatest satisfaction and fulfillment one can find in learning. The best lessons learned come from failure that leaves memories. A hot stove leaves a mark, a physical reminder of the incident. I failed to realize the intensity of the heat. It is okay. For next time I remember how to succeed by not touching the stove without an oven mitten. I wear the oven mitten every time. Every time I win. Winning becomes normal.

I love to teach students through activities, writing on the board, talking, discussions, multimedia, and performance art. As I teach my students, I entertain them. I am an edutainer. I enlighten while informing people. The brain learns better when it is having fun. Imagine math and physics being completely relevant to your life in ways beyond basic measurements. Making the normal essays we write in school about our fantasies, dreams, or experiences. Always express yourself in creative and intriguing manners. Make yourself have fun in every second of the day and life will become more fun. Make learning more fun for you every day and learning will become easier to you. The current teaching format should evolve with the various learning styles of the students. As education research progressed to understand cultural, mental, and psychological differences in learning, there seems to be a strong lack of transferring educational research and teaching knowledge into practice. Exposure to various styles of learning, reflection, building and deconstructing knowledge in the "real world" becomes a great advantage in life as we develop our best selves. We must learn to process what we know about life, education, and the world we live in.

We know what we know and we don't know what we don't know. You know what success looks like to you, but you do not know what success means to others. If you do not know what success means to you, take a break from reading right now, get an unruled composition book, and define success for yourself. **What is your definition of success?** I challenge you to answer every question I ask you in this book. Take a minute to write down the questions and your answers in an unruled composition book. I define success as designing a life and executing your dream to the best of your ability. Conquer every challenge set before you in your pursuit of achievement. If you fail, you will reflect and discuss your efforts. Then you will fall into your dream more by giving it your all. If your desire and discipline is great enough, you will be successful in college and life. You can always try harder, especially when you can see the lesson of the experience and adjust your approach. Once we know our passions, the directions we need to take in life are easy to follow like a GPS. We may not know the destination but the turns and exits we need to make on the road of life are much easier to understand. Believe in having multiple dreams and passions. You are one being, so unite those passions into the beautiful person you are. Define your own success. Only you know who you are and who you are to become. **No one else can tell you or define your success appropriately.**

Unfortunately, success is often defined by the tangibles of a career and the accumulated money earned in the process. Money is representation of your production value. It is not the only one. Loved ones, people, natural resources, and opportunities also represent production value. The education industry is designed to coalesce with the corporate culture. We are given one format of living and if we do not conform, we are marked early, as young as third grade, to be in jails and prisons instead of colleges. At the surface of the K-12 education system, the hours of operation for a school align with the assumed work schedule of your parents, corporate employees. The adults who thrive in the economic workforce as employees push our nation ahead.

Assignments of duty and purpose promote these individual workers to collaborate to make our nation's services and products continue to be economically positive. This is the mindset of America. We work hard to produce better and faster than everyone else on the planet. We lead by example. Work hard and you will be adequately rewarded for your efforts. This mindset must be proven to us at a young age for us to believe in it for a lifetime. It serves as the nucleus of the American Dream. Thus, schools serve to preserve the U.S.A.'s mission by cultivating the mindset of rewarded achievement. Achievement confirmations are granted to the greatest conformist of the day who can excel in the desired behavioral pattern. The mindset of education in regards to the American Dream slightly alters with each school in order to adapt to the community. Schools are a reflection of their communities. Communities are a reflection of their schools. It is important to read the mission of the college you attend to know what the school intends to develop within you as a contributing citizen of the United States. Success in school often requires confirmation of the school's values. Confirm the school's intentions and you will be rewarded at the school as a great student. Success in your job requires confirmation of its values. Likewise, success in the U.S.A. requires confirmation of its values. The definition of success, when left to an external force, will be nothing but a confirmation of that entity's values. **What are your values? What do you live to do? What is most important to you? What is your mission statement? In order from 1-5 with 1 being most important, can you recite your values?**

Memorize your values and compare them to the institution you are interested in attending. Make sure your school and your personal mission share the same commitment. Do not waste your money on a college if the school is not designed for your success. You have a choice. You are a consumer purchasing the service of disciplined learning of knowledge from teachers. The books you buy in the bookstore can be bought on your own online. The ideas in the book do not change, but you need the discipline and guidance of these expert institutions. Or maybe you don't. Make sure the values of your major's department align with your preferences as well. The specifics of what you want to study should definitely speak to your interest and goals.

    The values written and the values acted upon in an institution may not always be in accordance, either. Be sure to visit the college and talk to random students. Email and have phone conversations with students. Have a list of key components you want to experience. Ex. 1) smaller classroom sizes 2) early registration for classes 3) exposure to sporting events and theater. 4) Pre-professional training 5) Summer Internships or Co-operational learning. Make sure to ask directly about these academic experiences you prefer. I called a friend of mine attending the University of Pennsylvania before choosing to enroll. I would not be able to get my $60,000 loans cleared once I agreed to attend. It is a costly decision. Therefore, I made sure to speak to official representatives and people who were not given incentives to advocate for the university. I learned character traits and habits of the faculty, staff, and student culture prior to enrolling. Choosing a graduate school was a very serious process. It shed light on how I did not ask myself my own values, intentions, and goals of attending college when looking for an undergraduate institution. Something I thought was a poor decision in retrospect but luckily UCLA was a great experience.

I saw college as the destination instead of seeing it as a short time in my lifetime of learning. I did not contemplate my passions and talents in great detail to see what life I wanted. I lived day to day. I never questioned whether or not college was enough. Now I know that college at any level is just a new beginning, a stepping-stone to the life I am creating.

I attended the University of California, Los Angeles (UCLA) for undergraduate school. The primary purpose of my alma mater focuses on "...the creation, dissemination, preservation, and application of knowledge..."[1] Knowledge stands as the most valuable possession in the university's hands. It speaks a lot to the charge and focus of the leaders. The administrators aim to implement this mindset. The leader will take charge first. The leaders in the classroom begin with the teacher. **The teacher, according to Paulo Freire, should be everyone.** In an open dialogue, everyone can learn from each other. We are all teachers, advisors, and students in life. You can learn. You can teach. You can advise. We do it every day with our friends. In common conversation we often give advice to friends. Every day we learn, even if all we do is scroll on Instagram. Every day we teach others how we want to be treated by the actions we take upon them. Without accepting all three of these roles, we cannot become our destiny. These words are self-evident. I refer to this triad as the Trinity of Knowledge.

I look at the current state of American education wondering where the Trinity of Knowledge needs to expand in order for us to create more love in the classroom as we all embrace the responsibility of information, knowledge, and wisdom. Higher Education has a mission to create and disseminate knowledge. No other industry in the world is more dedicated to the development

---

[1] http://www.ucla.edu/about/mission-and-values

of humanity. School culture is supported with the longest institutional series in our foundational development as children.

We learn one pattern of success and apply the standards to everyone. We embrace the college culture academically and socially. We are given information inside and outside of the classroom on how we should conduct ourselves. Schools today set up a structure where the teacher will tell us all we need to know. That is not true if everyone is the teacher. School will prepare us for many challenges laid before us. This is our safe house to learn about how we learn. Our sanctuary of knowledge will transcend the human race into great achievements, which requires great learning. Learning is constant and does not stop. We will learn to accomplish our dreams by embracing all that life has to give us in the Trinity of Knowledge. This pursuit of knowledge is the ultimate key to happiness. Thus, the education system serves as a great opportunity for people to enhance their passions and purpose by learning what other humans have done before us to achieve happiness. Every subject is a history lesson of how someone journeyed to discover happiness in their own unique way. Experiencing education daily without passions and purpose will provide a great disservice to many students.

The great professors at your institution know much more than you in their field but they don't know you. **No one knows you better than you know you.** Being at a university provides a great opportunity for guidance to learn all the school offers to aid you in your efforts to better yourself. They will teach you things you have never known. The development and care you will receive in college is unparalleled when you create a family atmosphere yourself and utilize the support of student services.

Intellectually, the conversations with professors, professional educators, and student leaders will enlighten you on your journey to become the best *you* if you apply what you learn outside of the classroom to your life. Learn to apply what you learn from school to life and from Dr. Bernard A. Harris, MD attended the University of Houston. He became an astronaut. NASA is headquartered in Houston, Texas. He studied the stars in the same city as the nation's greatest rocket scientists. [2] He pursued his dreams beyond the university and made himself available to learn from those who achieved his dream before him. He studied physically near his dream and created a route to success for himself with the help of others along the way. He embarked upon his dream and learned inside and outside of the classroom to achieve it. Dr. Harris is a great American scientist. A scientist is a person who studies one of the sciences (natural, mental, social, physical, and/or spiritual). A scientist studies a specific field by creating questions and pursuing the answer to his question through the creation of research, data collection, observations, and discussion with colleagues. I think a scientist needs to experience something special in the journey itself. The finish line is the start of another race in life. Keep running forever. For when we have nothing to run for, we do not run anymore. I ran this morning until I was filled with sweat and panting. I ran after my fitness goals each and every day. Bit by bit I begin to, sculpt the physique I seek. The chase for knowledge is no different than running.

Gaining knowledge requires *reflection, inspiration, and motivation*. By reflecting, a scientist can critically analyze their experience. "What happened? Why did it happen? If I encountered that situation again, would the same events happen again?" This often makes a scientist want to consider their decisions in great detail. The experiment may also be to inspire what scientists engage in the same scenario with different techniques. We may gain new insight in our reflection that promotes us to take more risk or yield to caution. When we take action, we motivate ourselves to become better people. We trade in our fear of positive results for

---

[2] http://www.theharrisfoundation.org/sitecontent/603/.aspx

faith in our ability to trust the process necessary to achieve our goals.

You are the scientist of your life! **You must embark upon a quest each day to answer your own questions about who you are to be. Why you are the way you are? How will you become who you are meant to be?** Place yourself in the best position to know what you need to know to accomplish your goals. That may be higher education and it may not be. Higher education is a great practice facility for trying out your goals. Dr. Harris studied for his dream to be an astronaut in the same city as NASA's Houston headquarters. He placed himself in the vicinity of his dreams. You may be closer to your dreams than you think. As your own personal scientist, you must discover the best qualities you have that support your ability to achieve your goals. I call your personal scientific quest method a RIM shot. Through Reflection, Inspiration, and Motivation, you can identify what you need to learn from your experiences and life observations in order to succeed. The RIM shot provides you with the power to understand yourself by reflecting on your life. In reflection, you will find your inspiration to achieve, change, or develop yourself. Your inspiration may be a negative or positive catalyst, but let it motivate you to succeed. There is no greater scientific journey than the one you develop to understand yourself. Not just finding your purpose, but putting it into use. Through self-comprehension, we can truly grasp the knowledge of the world. We are microcosms of the universe. To understand our purpose within the world and education, we must practice RIM every day to become our best self.

Find your purpose by putting it into use

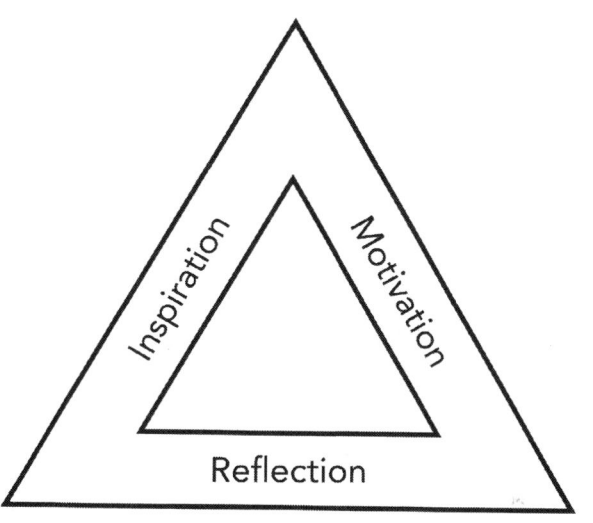

R.I.M. Shot

We learn all we can in school, but forget to pull the lessons out of life that would teach us the most about who we are and who we are to become. Life is about becoming the best you can be. Life is a journey, not a destination. School is structured here for us to learn the discipline it takes to master what we are supposed to learn in life. You are guaranteed to live, today. You are not guaranteed life tomorrow, but today, we can live. We do not go to school to find our purpose. We go to college *with* purpose. A purpose discovered outside of the classroom that influences the decisions we make to learn inside the classroom. The classroom itself is in the real world, but we often belittle higher education as free time to party before we go to employment. It is the greatest time in an educational setting to discover your path to greatness. Every decision is a life decision. The classroom is a microcosm of life and how we choose to place value on the lessons taught. Higher education is not excluded from the real world but a result of the real world. We travel from all around the world to attend these great institutions of higher learning and do not have an understanding of how to manifest our best selves within higher education because we never place the time and effort we put in school into our own lives.

The higher education environment is much more unique than a series of buildings closely together to present information to your liking. It is a home of exposure and inclusion to see what values and morals you hold true to in times of peer pressure and conflict. In college, you are exposed to the greatest ideas of the greatest minds from the past.

A genius is a scientist who leads experts in a specific realm of study. Every professor on campus is an expert in his or her field, the best at what they do on campus. It is imperative you learn from your peers while you are in school because the social environment provides opportunities to meet people who are the experts of being themselves. Everyone in college has a plan to achieve a goal. That goal is graduation. Graduating symbolizes that you mastered the discipline necessary to fully understand the most recent developments of your field. But in truth, your most important field of study is *yourself*. Become a genius of yourself. Know yourself better than anyone else. You hold the greatest advantage to being a genius of you. The goal of college is not just a degree but to know a better version of yourself who learns to constantly improve and advance your passions and purpose.

College lessons teach you to interact with people from different cultures, communities, and thoughts, but you must know and value what you bring to the table: you! We all think differently for we can only remember and see our own experiences from life. College will provide a lot of pressures for groupthink, but groupthink is a decision to join the majority, not a requirement. In those moments of peer pressure, you find out who you really are. You make decisions every day that shape your next day. Every decision we make is a life decision. Decide to live for your dreams. We need them. You need them. You are most happy when you excel on the path to your dreams. College is a great place to excel and pursue your dreams, but only if you create the life you dream.

Every decision we make is a life decision

02
ACADEMICS

Academics is about understanding the process of learning and replicating it for yourself so you can learn what you truly desire to know and apply it to life.

Your life is your academics. Your subconscious is always taking in information. Your subconscious is the part of your brain that you do not control. It controls you. It tells your heart to pump blood without you telling it to. Your subconscious is extremely powerful. It takes in information your entire life. You use this information for your subconscious influences your conscious decisions. Have you ever sang along with a song and realized you knew more words to the song than you thought you did? I went to the first Made in America festival. Before the concert started, I told my friends Jay-Z was my 7th favorite rapper. When the concert started, I realized all the songs Jay-Z made when I was younger, I knew. I heard them over a decade ago, but my subconscious filled in many of his raps once I began singing along with the crowd. Whether I wanted to consciously admit it or not, I was influenced by Jay-Z's lyrics. He later made it into my top 5 list of favorite rap artists. My brain had already decided I was a fan of his music.

Every decision and thought creates a neural pathway of what patterns you repeat in your life. To be brave while young is to be brave when old. Every time you do the right thing, it becomes easier to do the right thing next time. The same goes for decisions that are not so great for your life and humanity. What you study the most is what you tell your brain is the most important subject to learn in college. Your major in college does not have to be your final profession. It is definitely an advantage if your major directly correlates with your career interest. It is definitely an advantage if your career directly correlates to your passion. It is definitely an advantage to become your passion and receive an abundant compensation from multiple sources. To be paid to live your passion is the greatest achievement in life. Use academics as a way to learn more about your passion and create the neural pathways needed for you to lead yourself toward your dreams.

Fulfillment lives where passion and achievement meet on a consistent basis. In higher education, fulfillment is relevancy of your major to your passion. All the time you spend studying a subject must be relevant to your life's interests. For those who are pursuing medical studies, your bachelor's degree is very important, but shadowing physicians and volunteering for a research lab are the best hands-on experience to see how your coursework correlate to your pursuit of becoming an MD. No matter your career or academic interests, shadowing a professional works best to enlighten you on the professional requirements you must be ready for to actualize your passion.

The purpose of academics, as defined by the best institutions of higher education in the United States, is to create and disseminate knowledge. It has been proven throughout the history of humanity that knowledge is the most powerful force on the planet. In fact, knowledge serves as a critical component to the evolution of humanity, when knowledge is applied. Knowledge is not solely created to transfer information from one to person to the next. Knowledge demands application. We know what you did, not what you say you did. Thus you must prove your information is relevant, not only to you, but to others. Knowledge is designed to emerge from life experiences and influence the behavior of others. The information you receive in school comes from another person's journey through life experiences, their observations and analysis.

We read the efforts of people in the past for what they did outside of a classroom.

      Every class subject is history when you consider we focus on the knowledge discovered by people before us who uncovered a mystery of Earth. A scientist is defined as a person who has a method to obtain knowledge hidden in the universe. The academic system we have today honors the great minds of the past to serve as our intellectual foundation. Information is the prior knowledge a scientist has gained and conveyed from their hunt to discover another mystery of Earth. We often engage information through various forms of communication. Academics have the ability to engage the mind through all of the senses. We express our history of action and thought in a multitude of ways. Storytelling is a long-time tradition of transferring knowledge in humanity. We continue storytelling in books, multimedia, blogs, news articles, social media, music, and film. The transaction occurs when you tell another person the information you discovered. From information, you gain perception. Perception is powerful, for it influences your thoughts heavily. Our classrooms and textbooks provide perception into humanity's experiences through story telling. We learn to see the world through the eyes of the authors of the text. It is not an all-inclusive education. Intentionally, the education system desires to present a specific perspective. The information held mostly valuable is presented before us in our education system. The rest is up to you to discover on your own when you learn how to acquire and apply knowledge to your life. School provides the skills of note-taking, discipline, consistency, and analysis. Take those skills and apply it to your life's work. **What is your story? Do you tell your story? What is the story of your life's work thus far? If you could accomplish all of your goals, what would they be? Prioritize those on paper.** Tell me.

Perception is powerful

What is yesterday?

I am from _____ & I love my life because...

How do you tell your story?

Goals	Life's Work	Priorities
_____	_____	_____
_____	_____	_____
_____	_____	_____
_____	_____	_____
_____	_____	_____
_____	_____	_____
_____	_____	_____
_____	_____	_____

The information is presented in the perception of the teller. The person who conveys the knowledge holds the pen. The author recites the story in the preferred tone. Power is attached to the information. The author provides perspective. The view of history's value and importance is contributed to the eyes we all learn to see through. School is not designed to teach you everything. It is a place to learn the basics of learning so you can educate yourself on what you really want to know beyond the university. For example, inside of history class, the authors inform you of what they believe are most valuable for you to know about the time and era. Consequently, there are over 7 billion pairs of eyes, each holding their own perspectives, who would tell the same history in a different way. The historical fiction movie, Roots, conveys that African-Americans' roots are slavery. In my perspective, the roots of African-Americans are African civilizations. Roots convey the Africans killed and kidnapped in the middle passage were savages but I see the roots of Africans as the first kingdoms established in the world. The genesis of all creation, power, hierarchies, and humanity were developed in African civilizations, such as spoons, knives, agriculture, chemistry, and spiritual conceptions. History is subjective and in constant evolution so one perspective is never enough. School usually only presents one perspective of history, science, math, and language. School, even at the university level, is still, just a starter kit for your educational success. You will make history with inventions and decisions you make outside of school.

You are history in the making. Record it for the world to treasure.

The reader may set the tone of the textbooks. If your mindset is positive, enthusiastic, and confident while reading, the story will read better. The same is true if you read the same words in a sad, pedantic, and depressive mindset. Written communication can be interpreted in many different ways. Many a times, in texting conversations, you receive a message and perceive it differently than the sender intended. The message, "hey babe", can be perceived in many ways. There are certain phrases that are used by people differently with a myriad of intentions. The notions and body language of the sender is not there, so you cannot depend on it to define the meaning of the text. Body language is 87% of communication. In text communication, there is no human body. 7% of communication is tone. You cannot hear the tone of voice for the words sent in text communication. Verbal communication comprises 6% of communication. In text communication, there is only verbal/written communication. My friend Tina says "babe", quite often. She calls everyone she meets "babe". Often times, when she sees me, she says, "hey babe". I don't think anything of it because I know Tina. It means the same as brother, sister, or friend to her. My good friend David picks up my phone and sees Tina wrote, "hey babe. wyd" (what are you doing?). He instantly interprets the situation romantically instead of platonically. He says to me, "Who is Tina? Why didn't you tell me you had a new babe?" David used babe to convey lover or romantic interest. Tina's use of babe differed from David's use of babe. This gives babe multiple meanings. The context was not provided, and the written text was left to the readers' interpretation for the tone and intention. Information can hold many written and spoken truths to the eye of the beholder, much like beauty.

<u>Beauty</u>
By Miles Goodloe

Beauty
It is in my eye
For I am the beholder
I told her
I come from a long line of hugs and holders
Guns, shooting the triggers of older

Soulful Soldiers of the Sahara's Buffalo

I am smart, rich, & loud
Smart for the books rooted in me
Rooted in creativity, scream through brass
Obscene stories of old
Challenging Joseph Hayden's concertos

I am smart, rich, & loud
Rich, for the books in my library are free
To enter my mind a world
Greater than every city
Not filled with James Baldwin's inceptions

I am smart, rich, & loud
Loud, for my voice sends beats into hearts
Pumping blood of enlightenment
Down your spine
And in time you will see my divine

Beauty
It is in my eye
For I am the beholder
I told her
I come from a long line of hugs and holders
Guns, shooting the triggers of older
Soulful Soldiers of the Sahara's Buffalo

What does beauty mean to you?

We can conclude that textbooks are only 6% of the true story conveying the unique perspective of the author because we do not have the body language and tone of the author while reading.

Much of the information we announce as beautiful artworks of literature are in books. Libraries are everywhere. In buildings and phones, books live on! Books are the mental explorations of the authors' minds. Their truth and perception become a display for other minds to travel. It is the result of their journey through a quest for knowledge to become wise. They gathered so much information that they must share it. It is truly valuable. These storytellers are scientists, authors, entrepreneurs, mathematicians, professors, and analysts of the world. We take heed to the truths they express. It may be through visual or performing art, literature, athletics, and S.T.E.M. (science, technology, engineering, and math) but nonetheless, expression of knowledge comes in many fields. From ancient civilizations to present day, humanity appreciates the free expression of people's thoughts. We resist many ideas as well. The fear we grow inside from the unknown is often perceived as a threat. To conquer that fear, we must learn more about it. School requires us to open our mind to new ideas, people, and academic stories.

The oldest and most prestigious collegiate institution in the United States, Harvard, was founded in 1636. It sets the benchmark for educational advancement and research. In its inception, it focused on classrooms teaching students to become lawyers, clergy, and businessmen. The institutions would soon expand forever and always since its inception. Many schools began to spring up afterwards in the 18th and 19th centuries. The United States government supplied Moore Land Grants to build agricultural and technical colleges in the 19th century. Many of these universities wanted to be focused on building a solid American workforce of free and educated people. The schools received the Moore Land Grants to begin with, but needed to find other ways to sustain themselves. During the 20th century, universities became a great source of military and defense research, giving higher education a purpose beyond knowledge acquisition.

The Information Age used the academic structure as a playground for learning styles and access to resources. Once we learn how to read, listen attentively, reflect, and test the information of the past, we have the opportunity to catch up to the most current and prevalent knowledge available. Everything a scientist or person has dedicated their life to developing, we can read ten times faster than she wrote. The best researchers in academia develop new knowledge constantly. Their convictions may require writing because of the detailed understanding they have of a single subject. This information is thus processed and given power. The power of the information depends on the meaning we assign to the convictions delivered. These written convictions are called *research*. The research enables a professor to convey their findings along with the methods used to gain the information. Discovering and developing research is the most valuable commodity the university has. Knowledge from the researchers at a university gains monetary, human, and academic capital. When a researcher obtains a grant, the university may utilize up to 60% of the grant funds to cover the operation cost of the school's facilities. The school is paying for lights, security, and other amenities necessary to have a physical and safe researching environment.

Research is a great revenue generator for professors, colleges, and the university as a whole. For a school within the Revenue Center Management (RCM) system, this is most advantageous. The RCM model challenges each college within a university to compete for student enrollment and attendance to acquire funding. It makes each school (engineering, biology, law, etc.) become entrepreneurial academic hubs for marketing, recruiting, teaching, and professionally advancing students. To reduce the financial pressure of tuition as a funding source, the colleges hire great researchers who can acquire grant funding to support their academic initiatives. Funding is then utilized for the operational cost of the school and the research intended. Many a time this places pressure for researchers to apply for grants to gain funding opportunities and fiscal favor with the dean and administration of their specific school. Having multiple grants allows for the researcher to feel more at ease about the funding options they have access to. Access to money for research development provides the opportunity for research to advance the present knowledge of the universe. The term *university* means an institution that studies the universe. The universe is a collection of knowledge and consciousness developed into physical matter. We do not completely understand how the universe operates, but **our research on Earth conveys what we have discovered.**

    Universal data collected and analyzed becomes new pedagogy and praxes. New developments in comparison to the prior information may warrant intense dialogue on the concepts presented. Many universities created peer review journals allowing researchers from across the globe to compare and contrast information to gain confidence in the field of study. Through academic journals (magazines), an entire culture of educators highlighting the strengths and weakness of American education travel throughout the higher education system between interested philosophers. Within humanity's short time here on the planet, we see each piece of new philosophy as a quantum leap forward in humanity's intellectual transcendence. A treetop with roots of infinite fruit to bear.

    Unfortunately, money is finite for research funding. The 3,400 higher education institutions in the United States cannot all participate in receiving grant funding for research development. Only 60 to 65 universities actually obtain most of these research grants. These research institutions thread the needle of the educational research fabric molding and analyzing each generation of people and new developments. This cloth warms our minds with new ideas with aims to progress the human race in the soft and hard sciences. We take these ideas as pieces of gold. Each golden nugget of information becomes a wealth of consciousness. The golden pieces of knowledge allows us to dance throughout the world for we know more about how to excel in this world due to the learned knowledge of researchers who spend years analyzing problems and solutions. Our music, DJ Knowledge on the ones and twos, shows us the rhythm of the world. DJ Knowledge conveys the rhythmic patterns of the universe and how we can be on beat to make the best moves at the best times. The complexity of a song is comprised of many single notes (nuggets of information), composed together in a musical cadence for our benefit. The college classroom was designed in American education to be our intellectual dance floor. It had every intention of allowing knowledge to emerge. Each student would not only dance with knowledge, but also become a choreographer if they dared to create their own researched conceptions of the universe and convey it to others (**Write a book**). **The classroom chose to be a harmonious room for creating, expressing, and disseminating knowledge.**

As schools continued to present prior knowledge gained from humanity's ancestors, the classroom emerged as a transactional engagement of teachers depositing information instead of dancing with students to the composed collections of information's notes. The teachers became restricted to statewide standards in the K-12 education system so dancing to DJ knowledge became an after thought to the fear of being fired for not having students reach a cookie cutter approach of imposed academic standards.

In higher education, we witness the teachers being replaced with researchers. The researchers are required to teach students at the university as a secondary focus. These teachers profess their knowledge to the students as a mandate of their researching commitment and employment contract. The students receive information in lecture form an expert but not necessarily a willing and able professor. The professor communicates the necessary information to fulfill the university standards. The best professors take their teaching seriously and engage students with a full heart of love for the material and the art of mastering the subject at hand. The students receive the information in the banking concept methodology as proposed by Paulo Freire (Pedagogy of the Oppressed, 1973), when the professor inputs information into the your brain. The banking concept suggests the classroom interactions mirror depositing money into a bank account. The information is the currency, a means to an end. The act of depositing money juxtaposes to delivering information. Information and currency are both valuable when used properly. When not used, it is wasted and loses value. Thus, stacking a bunch of information in the memory banks of the students while not allowing them to use that knowledge to gain an advantage in life from the intellectual investments and human capital places students in higher education at a disadvantage. The students need more than a request to regurgitate the information on a test that they learned from lecture. It is important that students experience the art of discovery to obtain knowledge and the power of implementation.

Life is a talent given. Living life well is a skill. We often see the test in school as a final reflection of our abilities, talents, and skills. Without earning a 100% in a class, we imagine we cannot succeed. In life, the numbers game works much more in your favor at 5-20%. You can succeed by making maximizing 1% of your opportunity can be all you need to achieve. With a concentrated amount of knowledge in a focused area of life, you can maximize your production.

We continue to take in information without critically analyzing the information to assess whether this information is necessary for us to build our lane. We often do not have a chance to challenge the information presented, and thus take whatever information is handed down as fact. This perspective is often granted full autonomy in developing the academic perception of students in higher education. Our perception on the banking method of learning creates the value of the information provided and instantly devalues the information omitted. The omission exists because we don't even know the information to consider as a counter narrative to the information conveyed by the teacher. Thus we learn to view life through one lens as opposed to many lenses, which would allow for us to develop our own convictions from history.

    Like scientists, we must construct an investigation to gain an understanding of the full story. It is important to speak to all sides. The world and its perspectives are similar to light. Light travels in a straight line. It is clear and makes everything appear. The light, when it hits a prism, shows many colors. These colors slow down when they contact the prism. They appear in different frequencies, thus shedding a different color light on the world. We are human beings who think on different frequencies. It is fair to assert that we see the world in different colors and frequencies, not pure light. Without coming together, we cannot grasp a full conception of the information presented in a classroom. We each see a specific color. In collective discussion, you will be able to unite your color/frequency with others to see the world's truths in one stream of light. In the moments of dialogue and unity, we can reverse the prism's (structure of society and perspective) effect on perception and see the enlightenment. An education engaging in dialogue, focusing on understanding the whole picture of information past, allows one to appreciate the entirety of the problem solved. Every great theory or discovery solved a contemporary misconception or major challenge. Using deductive reasoning to solve a problem is basic math. It is a problem posed education. It is how you learn in life.

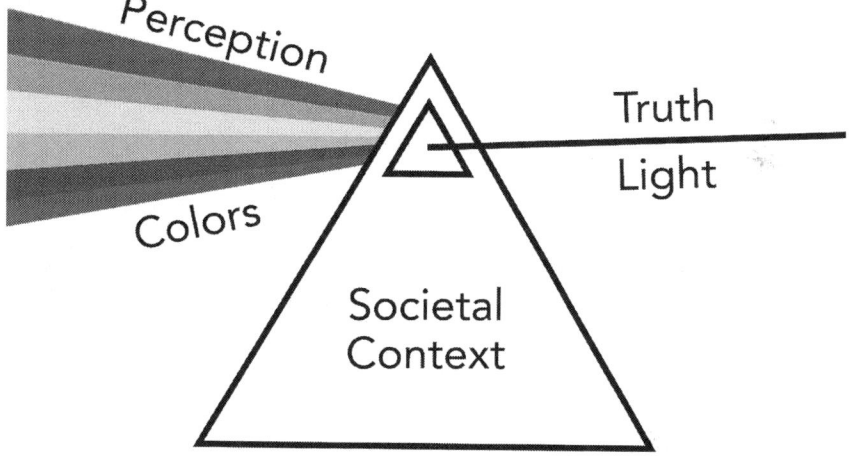

Friere also suggested this educational approach instead of the banking concept. It allows students to analyze a contemporary world's problems using past and present information to solve the current challenges of humanity. It builds knowledge and wisdom, especially with teachers who can manage critical thinking and discussion in their subjects, utilizing interdisciplinary methodologies to make this year's graduating class solve problems currently holding back humanity. The praxis of understanding pedagogies past allows for school to become relative to the development of humanity.

The information we deliver to students should advance their life so as to develop them as tripartite beings. We must love their minds, bodies, and souls. Without embracing the complete entity, we will misunderstand how powerful our communication can be in an educational setting. A purely mental educational system is flawed. The physical and soulful components serve as key aspects to the completion of thoughts and experiences. Picking to use only one component of our three foundations is similar to restricting yourself to one of your five senses. We can hear, taste, smell, touch, and see. Imagine a world you could only see. You could not touch, nor smell a flower. The entire experience of a flower requires touching its soft petals. We must smell its pollenated aroma. We can hear it sway in the wind. To not know the full experience of bees flying in the wind to land on the bud of this flower and taste its sweet nectar is to miss the greatness of life. We can imagine it happening if we just listen to the soundtrack of the bee's wings, but without seeing a bee, we do not know the maker of that sound, leading our imagination astray. The complete understanding of the flower rests in your hands, eyes, nose, and mind. The mental perception is conceived through multiple lenses and senses. **The educational structure should mimic the natural learning habits of the human senses.** With only one sense, the world would be but one dimension. It would be all we know, but also be limiting. **Teaching to the benefit of one's mental, physical, and soulful** power grants the student the best opportunity to thrive instead of merely just getting by.

The ability to teach one to manifest their soul, minds, and bodies into their potential is the basic expression of love. Loving our students is the greatest honor an educator can have. We don't do it for the direct return of money. We love our students because we love the world. We love humanity. We aim for our lives to be a great era in the history of this grand civilization. **We know the minds are the most powerful force on the planet. They control the bodies and souls of humanity.**

Each person, young or old, is humanity's greatest asset. The problems we face hide their answers inside humanity's wisdom. The process to knowledge is twofold. The first step is the ledge. We must take a risk. The ledge is as intellectually challenging as it is physically. We take a risk by jumping off the ledge, which allows us to fall, jump, or fly. This way we see if the risk of jumping was worth it. We gain insight to the requirements of us to fly. There lays the wisdom of how to fly off of this ledge. You go to the next ledge. You jump off the next ledge to see you can't fly to the ledge after that. You fall. The right to soar once does not guarantee the next jump you take will allow you to fly. You fall and see what your wings can really do. You will realize you may need to jump off a higher rock. You climb to the top of a rock. You jump! You get close and touch the ledge with your fingertips. You see your wings are still not strong enough. You get a running start on the ledge, jump to the top of the rock and leap into the sky. You grab the ledge with your left hand. You reach up with your right hand. You extend the right arm to grab nothing. You fall down again. You run yourself toward the rock at full speed. You leap directly from the topside of the rock and leap onto the ledge. Now you have knowledge about the trials and tribulations of taking a leap of faith.

You gained the understanding of the process of completion by first facing incompletion with perseverance. The knowledge we seek rests in the reflection of the experience. Knowledge lives at the top of the ledge, but we gain useful information in the process of attempting the jump over and over again. Knowledge rests in attempting various methods based on prior trials. The errors informed the next trial until you achieve success. The information collected, reflected, and utilized to make a more informed decision is what you know. Now, you can say you gained knowledge.

Knowledge is the key component to the knowledge economy existing today in our global society. The knowledge economy is the current industry of collecting, organizing, disseminating, and controlling knowledge. You can see how universities are at the center of the knowledge economy. They constantly search for patterns in life to discover the best methods of conquering problems. The brightest researchers and minds manifest their advancements at the university. The information they hold, value, and disseminate to the world is regarded as golden purities of intelligence by the academic and American populous. Their advancements will add to the greatest assets of the nation: its rising educational class. It is important that each student within each class understand they are the most prize possession of the United States. Their minds, specifically, hold the keys to success' doors.

Human capital's specific assets are knowledge, passions, abilities, skill, and talent. Human capital makes human beings an economic quantity to be assessed as a valuable resource. The most important resource known to humanity is you. Your assets can be removed or dwindled over time, as a human must maintain practice to keep themselves relative to the current demands of our economic society. Human capital serves as a permanent investment into the human being because each human improvement establishes a new foundation for more growth as a collective race of people. The consistent growth of your human capital allows you to remain a valuable commodity within the present economic structure. The economic structure favors students who have valuable human capital. Those students reward colleges with the greatest economic achievements and advantages, hence the huge preference for STEM (science, technology, engineering, & math) majors. The brightest minds come together to create new knowledge. When someone solves a problem, they are rewarded with a tripartite wealth. Wealth is a mindset, physical act, and soulful balance.

    A full engagement into the studies of the classroom and life promotes the students to benefit themselves with new ideas. Each thought begets another. The mind never stops thinking. It consistently inputs information from the outside world into our subconscious and conscious minds. New exposure allows us to input new thoughts which will create a new perspective. New information sheds new light for us to garner the truth of our life or the information presented. The more new information you input into yourself, the more you know when making the important decisions in your life. To develop human capital, many people only attend higher education. Life does not stop because you entered class. Life is continuous. Learning is continuous. Evolving is continuous. You must embrace all aspects of learning throughout the entire day in order to maximize your human capital potential. It is well understood that higher education may add a million dollars to one's life over their career. I think college adds value to people in a myriad of fashions. The academic learning process teaches you to learn. Learning is a skill. Once you learn to learn, you can truly understand how to learn what you want to benefit yourself without the structure of the university. As you began to critically analyze the world outside of you, you can also critically analyze the world within you.

Millennials believe the Nike slogan more than any other age group present on Earth: "Just do it". We champion ourselves after athletes who wear the slogan proudly. For those of us whose sports lie in the bed of wisdom, we create information. We manifest through applications of our mind in a myriad of ways. We believe we can learn best by actualizing the efforts we wish to see take form in the world. School teaches us about the lessons others learned in life. The university organizes these lessons, which are learned from applying strategy and theory to life's challenges. The greatest minds were not regurgitating information to simply pass a test. The greatest minds of today are not just students of wisdom; they are creators. The greatest people in our history have achieved by having a great impact on people. Universities dominate as the most creative socio-political center for creation that can impact the world. So many millennials are going to college solely to increase their network of creative and intellectual problem solvers. The startup culture is dorm room culture. Drexel University, a pioneer in developing the Close School of Entrepreneurship, has allowed its leadership to operate an incubator for students and alumni to develop their ideas into enterprises. It is the first university to dedicate an entire school to entrepreneurship. It is creating a space for creators to solve the world's problems. The university recognizes the growing economic trends of the last decade and has adapted the higher education format to be a home to research, learning, and actualization. This is truly unique. We have seen universities dabble in the stock market, industrialize athletic programs, and now serving as a Venture Capitalist. The institute serves as a hub for majors to unify their skills into a solid passion, as stated during an Honors Program panel on Millennial Innovation that I organized in 2015. It made me think about the need for interdisciplinary learning within the university. There needs to be a focus on how students can monetize their passions. I realized the university's research usually aimed at understanding a problem in humanity rather than finding self-efficient financial ways to mass-produce the solution. Incubators provide mentorship, funding, and freedom to provide solutions in a problem-producing world, with mass amounts of solutions distributed on a global scale.

Now the university creates a safe space for brainstorming and understanding along with a formal opportunity to actualize. The unemployment rate has decreased, so finding a job in a market that is full of employees only allows one option upon graduation: entrepreneurship. Innovation and determination is the key, a key requiring critical thought. The ability to analyze the world, make an inquiry, and solve it using whatever methods are needed serve as key components to fostering success individually and for humanity.

The previous sentence conveys the true nature of learning. It is inherently a problem-solving practice. Nothing is more valuable than the ability to understand a problem and solve it. Education, in transaction, conveys a multitude of problems and their current solutions. Luckily, once a person understands how they learn, they can learn anything. Higher education knows this and has broken information down into many majors and colleges to study this information. With the wake of the information age, we now can control the content of our learning. Google represents the global consciousness of the world based upon what we search for on the Internet. Before the Internet, information was restricted to physical spaces. Information required you to sit in a library and read. Today we have libraries in virtual spaces. It is mind-blowing. Let's engage the dynamite known as knowledge.

The knowledge on the Internet allowed for information, history, and various perspectives on sciences within STEM and the Humanities to be told in greater detail. We no longer have to believe mass media or mass publications. The challenges of a single story in knowledge creation are no longer present. We have access to small media conveying different truths. These truths place a huge investigative journey of limitless information to hold and understand. Each human mind possesses an infinite amount of knowledge. The knowledge comes from the infinite thinking we do. Our thoughts are constantly analyzing the world around us. Thus, we grow to understand the world better with more information about its inception mentally, spiritually, and physically. By organizing your thoughts, you can learn to truly analyze the infinite knowledge of others. You grasp it and tear it down to the smallest detail to make sure you can conceive each component appropriately before leaping to a conclusion of the data presented. That process of learning yields the greatest thoughts because you can understand the world outward as you gain more understanding of what lies within you.

     To encourage students in the Pennoni Honors College to grasp the concept of looking outward and inward, I founded the Motivators series along with two students. We decided it was important for students to have a safe space to reflect about the impact of education, culture, and society has on their lives. Kyle and Amber were students in my Honors course from Fall 2014, "Creating Culture in America." They appreciated the concept of reflecting in order to problem-solve challenges in society. When we brainstormed about how to motivate students to reflect about our life experiences in the college environment, we thought about how the Internet had so much information that much of it goes unaddressed. Students need to process this information with a guideline of understanding for how powerful their ideas can be. The pursuit of knowledge is inspiring to others. It encourages your peers to follow your example. Additionally, it motivates the community of learners around you to also reflect greatly about the information at hand.

     The overflow of content requires for the information to be organized and presented in a meaningful manner. A manner that promotes a student to R.I.M. shot. It creates the opportunity for new information to travel throughout the mind critically. The reflection allows for an internal discussion with you. As a tripartite being, you must reflect upon the three interpretations you create when engaging information. You feel one thing, think another, and your body reacts to it all. Thoughts can make the hair on your arms stick up. Whether in discussion or reading, reflecting often yields new conceptions physically and mentally that affect our emotional state. Reflecting on the information presented and our reactions to it begins our analysis of life. The R.I.M. shot serves as the center of the Motivators' workshop series Kyle and Amber co-facilitated with me.

Our why encouraged us to create a space of reflection for students to process their experience while being in it? Understand your reason to join an organization, choose a major, and reflect on it while you are experiencing your decision to reassess whether or not you are making tangible progress to your goals. More than anything, we wanted students to find the answer inside of them and push that cause into the world with great force. The first step is for you to understand, conceive, and believe your dream is possible. It's possible to have a dream, to have a cause that lives within you to reflect upon your being. Finding your purpose requires inspiration. Information and other thoughts from other people serve as a great catalyst for the proliferation of inspiration within you. Watching you chase your purpose through reflection, inspires your peers to do the same. You will become a leader. In fact, American culture depends upon your leadership and you achieving your dreams. Culture relies heavily upon the populous being inspired by the creations of people in our community, mentally, physically, and spiritually. When we see the actualization of thought, it encourages you to think and act. The reflections you have from watching others succeed at their dreams are a contagious combustion of inspiration. That inspiration manifests itself in motivation once you allow yourself to take action physically from the internal inspiration. From knowing the journey of reflection is not being conducted alone, great safety is brought to the mind. The mind, often alone, loves to be connected through thought. The comfort of not being alone in thought inspires more thoughts and motivates the body to actualize the mental conceptions. The stimulation of the brain creates physical manifestations. In the simplest way, we think, "Grab that cup" and our hand automatically reaches for the cup, a physical manifestation of the thoughtful desire. An idea is physical once we feel the chill of the thrill in our spine down into our fingers. Our hairs rise as we grow with excitement, writing each image or word onto a blank sheet of paper. The motivation to continue creating yields a circular conviction to make as many R.I.M. shots as possible. In the effort of R.I.M shooting every piece of information we engage, we truly push academics to a level of understanding that is not only helpful to pass class, but also personally evolve yourself as a tripartite human being who has a glorious purpose on this earth.

Know yourself to know your wealth.

03
CO-CURRICULARS

What you commit to outside of the classroom speaks volumes to who you are in a way your academic transcript could never do.

The hidden major at every university is determined by what a student does outside of the classroom. Students will come together in countless ways for a variety of purposes in order to advance individually or community at large. The community gathers beyond the classroom walls. We always want to improve who we are, and our interactions with others greatly advance us. The improvement of the university for being a creative hub of great minds allows for amazing conversations and revelations to occur. In order to engage people, we look to many formal collectives to improve our knowledge of the individual and community. The academics are the most formal space and provide the most important goal of higher education. Nonetheless, classes are not all day. The tuition dollars may be dependent upon the students attending class, but the students do not stop learning and living just because class is over. The learning continues for life. Life lessons are much grander than the classroom transaction of information. Life is an experience. When we learn from an experience, it creates a memory. The memory serves as the greatest reminder of the knowledge we gained. **Thus, the interactions occurring in an education community beyond the classroom serve as a great source of positive education we remember, not just memorize.**

Co-curricular activities are formal engagements students participate in beyond the classroom. To develop a passion, talent, or skill the students possess, she volunteers her time to this consistent activity. The co-curricular activity usually aligns with a student's academic and professional goals. There are plenty of opportunities for you to experience such as: (1) leadership, (2) organizational skills, (3) marketing and promotions, and (4) community building. These are excellent skills to have as a rising contributor to society in any career. These skills can transfer from the college experience into the non-education (real) world, and serve the individual along with their professional community.

Greek life often receives the majority of attention on campus in regards to co-curricular activities. It is definitely not the only opportunity within higher education for students to gain powerful networking skills and develop community building. The students involved in Greek life are often seen as leaders within the community and attract the most attention, for better or for worse. Many fraternities create social and service opportunities for students to engage throughout the campus and local community each school year. The establishment of membership challenges in pledging creates an atmosphere of collectivity for the brothers and sisters of the Greek organizations to establish memories of learning new character traits with each other. You should view pledging as a leadership development course based on the principals of the Greek organization. The members gain a sense of allegiance to each other and the organization in the process. Due to the camaraderie various initiation tasks require, the unity of the pledge class creates a sense of one's collective versus individuality. Not only do the pledges get to know each other, but also the brothers/sisters leading the newcomers learn who their new members are simultaneously. This leadership style creates mentor-mentee relationships. The formal establishment of a big brother allows the more seasoned fraternity members to contribute professional skills regarding the organization. Leadership becomes required for every member of the fraternity as they bring in new members and create activities for non-members to participate in.

The leadership among the pledge class usually allows for corresponding titles and nicknames to be branded upon the individuals involved. The nickname earned becomes an added adjective to the student's persona. The leadership style of the student often emerges in the pledging stage of the fraternity where most nicknames are granted. My nickname while joining my fraternity, Kappa Alpha Psi, was ProaKtive (pronounced "proactive"). The older fraternity members saw me as a buzzing personality who constantly got involved on campus to make a positive impact in every effort I committed to. I did not see it in myself then as an intake candidate, but as I continued my educational (academically and professionally) career, it became one of my most defining characteristics. Dr. Tyrone Howard, a UCLA research expert in male education, states, "you are only as good as the expectations others have of you" (2011). That requires you to become a product of your environment. Your environment influences you, but what you choose to do within your environment determines who you will become. Greek organizations definitely set a tone within individuals as to what objectives on campus are most important. The organizations mold student leadership through a series of traditions designed to enhance your ability to achieve your potential within the school environment. Each Greek organization achieves their leadership development in different ways, but the ability to better you while learning great principles of personal belief attracts like-minded individuals together for unity in action. That is the bond of organizations.

When the unity is organized, students who curate events and meetings, both internally and externally, gain organization skills. Planning, timing, and understanding your peers (market group) become personal and group management skills. These are great assets to further develop your human capital with fraternity and sorority members. As the leaders develop, a hierarchy emerges within the fraternity. The hierarchy, on a formal basis, allows for members within one university to establish themselves as leaders on a local, regional, and national scale. Most fraternities with an (inter) national establishment allow for undergraduate members to hold positions across various geographical divisions. The opportunity to serve in a high-ranking position allows for students to understand the socio-political structure of the organization. The objectives, mission, values, constitutions, and statutes of an organization operating on an international scale place the undergraduate student in a unique space of leadership development. It allows for you, the student, to understand power and influence. Interacting with individuals who have more power and influence gives an individual a unique understanding, thus creating memories of how to interact with the people balancing power and progress within an organization. It is something interesting to learn, but most importantly, it is better remembered.

 I served as a regional undergraduate president, better known as the Junior Vice Polemarch of the Western Province, of Kappa Alpha Psi. It is the third highest-ranking position in the Western Province. I learned formal leadership training in this position with constant opportunities to implement what I learned. National leadership positions within the organization allowed me to travel the country as an undergraduate student. Depending on the specific organization, a travel budget may be accessed for members and leaders. Many a time, the people representing the organization internally and externally expanded their network greatly by traveling to various provinces and supporting fraternity members' initiatives. Establishing a national network within higher education creates many opportunities for a lifetime. Professional preparedness occurs in developing a reputation and image for the national organization. Most students do not travel more than 40 miles beyond their home to attend college. By using a college organization to travel, collegians unite with like-minded individuals who share the organization's mission and ambitions. You can learn to better represent yourself and others as leaders, which allows you to understand the best way to make yourself a marketable leader, prepared for a greater cause while maintaining independence.

Nonetheless, a fraternity or national organization cannot teach you all you need to know. The learning curve in college is much steeper than one organization. It is important to follow your passions and leave your comfort zone. Humans are complex beings with the capability to perform numerous passions simultaneously. For example, I developed a forty-five minute documentary titled, "A Test of Faith: The Impact of Christianity on Black America." I interviewed professors, students, parents, and clergy on how Christianity has affected African Americans in the U.S.A. It allowed me to build skills in film production by lightly playing around with the movie application on my laptop for months. I applied for the undergraduate university newspaper's video department soon thereafter. The leaders of the video department of the Daily Bruin were impressed with these self-taught documentary skills, which gained me membership to the school's newspaper. I felt great. It was so much fun. Now I had access to an array of events covering arts, sports, and hard news.

Acceptance into the video department required training to rise up to the current standard of knowledge for video contributors as well. The entire new class of video contributors received training by a Los Angeles Times video reporter. The university had a great relationship with the LA-based media source's leadership. This was a once-in-a-lifetime experience, the training only enhanced my talents into skills. The opportunity to be exposed to new events, training, and friends allowed me to progress within the co-curricular aspect of college because my cultural knowledge and transferrable skills were enhanced from participating in the Daily Bruin. The training served so many of us well. The leadership even engaged in the training because they enjoyed it too and wanted to keep their skills sharp. I learned to edit, direct, film, and produce media on an entirely new level. I spent many late nights editing film in a non-air-conditioned room, with an out-of-date Macintosh computer, sweating to meet our deadlines. Perseverance skills were definitely enhanced. The ability to stay up late and complete a project is a skill. Many people have challenges finishing what they started. Perseverance skills increase the more we commit to completing tasks and promises. Commitment to persevere not only affects us individually but those around us as well. Our actions inspires others.

Joining the university newspaper required making new friends, too. That is not always the easiest thing to do. The university had over 23,000 undergraduate students at the time. Many times, student organizations united students who never saw each other in class and stemmed from different ethnic and economic backgrounds. Interacting with these unique minds and characters to produce several series of video productions to entertain and inform the entire university populous was no easy task, but I was committed to the passion. Collaborating with my peers from different backgrounds became a challenge as well, but overcoming it with perseverance developed into a great skill of being able to engage all kind of demographics. Being able to adjust to multiple cultures in a room, make new friends, develop the passions of film production, and dedicate myself to accomplish a task within the parameters outlined, developed a great person who can achieve at an accelerated rate for a purpose greater than me.

The challenges did not cease despite my ability to adapt. Learning to be myself within an alien culture was a true challenge. I was not used to being the sole Africana (descendant of the African diaspora) male. Nonetheless, having a passion for film and similar topics unified us. The experience conveyed passion, and our commonalities trumped our cultural divides. In fact, the myriad of cultural lenses allowed my vision within the team to emerge as unique and intriguing since I was the only Africana male. People love new ideas, and I was full of them, because I brought a different socio-economic and cultural lens to the conversation. In addition, I conveyed my ideas in a mainstream fashion so the students at UCLA would understand my perspective. Being able to code switch my American English vernacular into other cultural dialects of the English language continues to be an asset that allows me to travel between different communities. Communication is key. My cultural capital and acquisition of cultural knowledge gave me the opportunity to maximize my potential because I can communicate effectively with people from completely different backgrounds, now.

    The divides at UCLA were numerous, but the most captivating conflict was the difference in academic preparedness. All of the students in attendance were top academic performers in their respective high schools. Nonetheless, the high schools and preparatory academies each held different standards of excellence based on the educational leadership and socio-economic challenges set before them, be it community related or (the lack of) access to resources. Students from more affluent environments had more cultural capital relevant to success within the enterprise of higher education. The affluent students faced fewer academic and socio-economic challenges in school. I recognized this indifference and better understood why the Early Academic Outreach Program (EAOP) established a relationship to visit my high school, Crenshaw High School, every week to properly prepare students to apply to the University of California campuses. Many students coming to UCLA had not been challenged with college level work before in a diverse environment. UCLA is so unique that it operates like its own town within the city of Los Angeles, CA. You wont know if your preparation will be enough for you to thrive at the university, until you take on a couple years on campus.

    For many, attending college is a difficult to transition. It is a difficult application process but getting in is easier than staying in. Inside of Campbell Hall (UCLA), while signing up for tutoring, I began my work-study job with the Vice Provost Initiative of Pre-College Scholars (V.I.P. Scholars). As a product of an UCLA outreach program (EAOP), it made perfect sense to work for an outreach program helping high school students prepare for college enrollment. I would have not made it into the prestige school myself without someone to teach me how to apply to college. Applying to college is a skill, not an innate talent. V.I.P. Scholars held access workshops at high schools throughout Los Angeles and Pasadena County. We worked with students to teach them how to be great applicants for UCLA. Our efforts also made them experts at navigating the K-16 educational industry.

I knew how to navigate the K-16 education industry because I experienced an eclectic mix of public education structures in Queens, NY; Chesapeake, VA; Oakland, CA; and Los Angeles, CA by the age of 13. While attending Crenshaw High from 14 to 17, I nagged every college outreach program that visited the campus. I knew enough information about the college access process in my first collegiate year to help others apply because I obsessed over the college access information from the ages of 14 to 18. By high school graduation, I was an expert on how to get into college. I got into 23 colleges. No, really. I got into 23 colleges! Who ever said Black males from the Crenshaw District don't go to college, obviously doesn't know me. Tell them to go watch Professor Miles on YouTube.

Graduating college is more important than getting into college, so the focus of access to school was just the beginning of my educational career. The procedural steps needed to succeed in higher education are endless, but V.I.P. Scholars allowed for mentoring to serve as the center of communication to relay important skills and character traits mandated for higher education student success. With college students (mentors) serving as the conveyors of knowledge, more high school students listened. The age gap was small. I was 18 leading $9^{th} - 12^{th}$ graders on how to be a successful student. I was just months older than a few of the students but I acted like my mentor who was 23, so I would appear older. My baby face and lack of facial hair made it difficult to fool the high school staff, though. Regardless, I was of age to mentor and I took it seriously. As mentors, we created unity in student culture and academic drive. The information provided a peer-to-peer communication effect. Simultaneously, the interaction with administrators and counselors allowed the mentors to establish a professional reputation.

The college students, serving as mentors for VIPS, developed (1) communication, (2) community organizing, (3) mentoring, (4) speaking, (5) life coaching, (6) listening, (7) loving, (8) professional culture, and (9) interpersonal education skills. (1) Communication skills are the ability to relay information to the required audience in the most appropriate manner for the cultural practices present in the educational community engaged. (2) Community organizing skills focus on the ability of students to gather other students for unity building and human development. Unity building consists of students organizing together in order to develop more knowledge or skills to accomplish a common goal among a cadre of individuals, such as college access. (3) Mentoring requires a more experienced person assisting in the development of a common passion, talent, or skill. Focusing on V.I.P. Scholars, learning to better one's human capital served as the passion. Gaining college access to the UC system as an underserved American youth is the skill we transferred. Through those mediums, we achieved educational advancement. It is difficult to play a game if you do not know the rules. Education is a chessboard. The exception is that everyone (university, department, professor, etc.) has different regulations and strategies, just as each piece on the chessboard has different methods to serving their purpose in the game. Those challenges increase the difficulty of gaining college access. The education industry is decentralized with different institutions responding to students from various backgrounds differently. The University of California (UC) system upholds high academic standard students must adhere to. In fact, most of the students accepted are so self-driven, the UC system doesn't concern itself with helping the students much but rather, making the resources they need to succeed, readily available on campus. I suggest, knowing what you want to do at college before you get there. It makes it easier to understand how to utilize the resources available rather than walking past your destiny every day. Don't worry. I wrote this book to help you achieve that goal, just as I did for many of the students I have mentored and advised in over the last 9 years of my life. If no one else has your back, I do. ☺

    Mentoring requires you to establish a purpose in order to achieve a goal. I can mentor you if I know why you need my help. With a specific set of goals, we can create a relationship focused on progress. General demands and expectations is the wrong way. Mentoring is intentional. Don't leave your life decisions in the hands of chance, but rather in the hands of empowering intentionality. (4) While the students communicate in appropriate cultural fashion, it is necessary for the mentor to speak multiple cultural codes to advance the mentee's opportunity and understanding. Learning to speak in different American dialects becomes incredibly important, because mentors often find themselves immersed in the school community. The job no longer remains a one-on-one discussion with students, but one filled with overcrowded classrooms, impromptu library presentations, college fairs, and serving as an advocate for higher education attainment in hallways and parent meetings. Communicating with different people who respond to various speaking styles enhances the mentors' ability to adjust to the demands of the environment immediately. Be sure to learn to naturally speak different dialects of your first language so you can mentor people in a cultural format that fits them. Mine is English. I can speak the English taught in schools and the English spoken in the street so I can mentor people from a myriad of ethnic, economic, and community backgrounds. I can also write in professional English and in text format. #WordUp

This skill is most important in college and most importantly, in life, because (5) mentoring sessions occur randomly. As a mentor, the friendly approach to developing knowledge allows for the students to become excellent at listening to the students' perspectives. (6) Listening requires hearing what someone said, thinking critically about their words, and responding in a manner that addresses their statements. Being relative is key. At this point, (7) loving becomes a genuine effort to enhance the person's ability to achieve their potential through the combined effort of utilizing the previously defined developments. Educational advancement requires more than the individual effort of loving the individual. Unfortunately, the academic responsibility we feel as students is not completely in our hands. We have much to do in order to achieve a better opportunity for our lives. Remember, your life is not school. School is a part of your life.

(8) We adjust to academic culture in order to achieve our educational goals. We speak with counselors and administrators at the school in order to gain knowledge on our student's academic achievements, behavior, challenges, and advocacy points. (9) Advocacy points consist of trust capital gained between two individuals. The more trust capital you have, the more leverage you possess to advocate on behalf of another person or yourself. Within V.I.P. Scholars, this consisted of mentors needing to gain trust capital with the school's operational leadership and teachers in order to maintain access to the high school. Access to the HS was not simply being physical on campus. It required us to spend our advocacy points with staff, faculty, and parents. We often needed to advocate for students, self, and the program's benefits. Trust capital is a fluctuating measurement of one's faith in others to act in a certain manner, be it positive or negative. Trust capital serves as the most vital component of the co-curricular development of the

students to utilize various passions, talents, and skills to navigate the high school to benefit the college access rates of higher education.

Higher education is not only about the access, but also about the experience within the college community preparing us for the world. Often people say, "the real world is cold" when referring to post-college life. Higher education is preparing you for the real world. It takes a lot of effort for you to maximize the lessons you are learning. Otherwise, the real world will shock you, because you failed to prepare for and inquire about the challenges ahead.

The co-curricular activities you engage in prepare you for your intended career, but if you do not know who you are, what you do in your spare time outside of class will seem useless. Don not leave class and just think you should not get involved. The pressure and stress you engage in a club from holding events and marketing to your peers is are more valuable in your career than any test you take in class.

Secondly, the world is a tumultuous place for many people. Life is hard. I cry a few times a year from the trials I face but I smile everyday from the triumphs. Thus, school is a small component of the real world and will put me through tests that produce tears or smiles. School is a practice ground for real life. The pain and challenges of achieving through the world is an everyday problem that school can help to mitigate. The world continues to spin every day whether you have a good day or a bad day. Whether you past a test in school or not, the school will continue to thrive. Just the same, the issues at hand in our personal development and learning continue forever. We learn a lot from our tears and from our smiles. I learn more from my tears than I do from my smiles but I can learn just as much from each circumstance if I take the time to reflect. Never stop learning from life. Life is class. The more you learn, the more problems you will be equipped to solve. Problem solvers are the leaders of the world and the university. We are all life long learners and problem solvers.

We often create challenges that hold us back

Some students face hardships throughout college, making the real world not a phase to enter, but a place to escape from their problems, while attending college. Attending college is often a positive distraction from the challenges occurring in your family, finances, and personal matters. College can be a safe haven for people coming from challenging environments and broken homes. For the privileged, not facing hardships in life, college creates a huge culture shock. College will challenge you without the comfort of mommy and daddy being able to save you from your hardships. Your parents cannot make you a successful student leader. Only you can. When you enter the real world, you must achieve your goals. Co-curricular activities will show you how to run a business and solve problems better than class. Problem solving requires interacting with people, galvanizing the masses, and executing on the goals set forth.

For example, civic engagement is more attractive to students in higher education wanting to make an impact on the social-political and economic hardships that challenged them before they began post-secondary studies. Co-curricular activities give students a chance to develop specific skills needed to become leaders in their field of interest. You should not do anything for an extended amount of time against your will that is not in line with your ambitions.

During my junior year, I found myself volunteering with the Los Angeles office of United States Senator Diane Feinstein. As a political science major, it completed a dream of mine to work in a political office of a major U.S. Senator. Engaging local organizations, enterprises, and persons to make a national impact fulfilled the concepts I believed were necessary to make a valuable contribution to society. The lesson learned from this office was execution. It did not matter what happened with preparation. Execution held the highest reward in the office, not effort. Effort is great in school but effort is not rewarded in the real world. You can work out all day at the gym but if you don't have the six pack and muscles, what is the point? What mattered in the senator's office, was execution of our goals. The citizens of the California do not want to hear about the Senator trying to make a difference. We want the difference to be made, tangible, and quantifiable. Prove you are a difference maker. No one can do it a lone so even as an intern, I was held accountable for my ability to succeed. Success is doing what you said you were going to do. Senators make promises every election. We must follow through on our commitment to our constituents. It required engagements with constituents to make sure we understood what plan would best serve their needs. The support required a physical presence with a mental understanding. Being prompt was necessary. We were a team relying on each other for a dedicated amount of time every day. We had practice (office work) and we had the game (production or services rendered).

In twelve weeks, I did not see the Senator once. She depended on the chain of command to convey the necessary information to her in Washington, D.C. I read full packets on environmental and medical issues, but was assigned to write a three-page summary, then a one-page memo. The state of California began experiencing more frequent fires over the years so environmental issues became paramount. It makes sense now because California is now in a permanent drought and a dessert. I learned to write succinct 1-page memos from political briefs that averaged 100 pages at first on environmental policies. The corresponding representative would read it and turn it into a one-page statement. I assumed she then delivered it to the proper person in Washington, D.C. Sometimes it was a letter, so I knew which constituent it was going to. I had more to do with the office than I expected as an intern, but it definitely gave me a new perspective on whether or not politics had a future in my life. The experience of volunteering my time for free to the senator allowed me to gain free training in politics, writing, and being a government representative. The best co-curricular activities are the commitments we do for free. What we are willing to do for free, will be an incredible experience to do for income. **What would you do for free for the rest of your life?** Do it for free until you can figure out how to do turn that passion into profit.

I decided I would not enter politics right after college, thanks to that experience. I did not want to be a professional politician. I had a fantasy of officials going into the neighborhoods and interacting with the people to understand what they need. I did that as an intern. The Senator did not do it. She went from meeting to meeting and sent her employees and interns to more meetings than she did. It makes perfect sense to me now but baffled me completely at 19 years old. The fact is that the United States Senators needs to be in the nation's capital to conduct their business. The government is a business and Senators are leaders. The Senator expected us to assist the people within the state while she advocated for the constituents in Washington, D.C. Senators represent the community in the capitol where the policies are made that affect our everyday life.

The state's public affairs come to decision in the state's capital, Sacramento. The California Republic remains strong with its leadership by having them congregate in one city instead of being spread throughout the state. The officials representing us remain in the capital, while the local interns and advocates living in your community interact with you. Now look towards the mayor and council members. They show their faces at many important locations: businesses, events, schools, and more. Nonetheless, they must spend most of their time in an office downtown reading, prepping, and analyzing modern policies and their effects. They too have staff members interacting with different citizens. Staff usually pair with non-profits and community organizations already in existence. Political offices collaborate with those people as their organization and entity. The government operations seemed like another company publicly run with open appeal. I once heard someone say that the United States government, federal and state affairs, is the greatest corporation in the world. After my experience in Feinstein's office, I understood why. I think Apple and Google have them beat in the running for greatest corporation in the world. I love my MacBook and there is nothing that google doesn't know. Lol.

I continued to study Political Science at UCLA with a concentration in international relations after that experience because I learned to value the effect of global decisions more than the value of domestic engagement. I will always live in the United States and be required to understand domestic politics in order to be a valued citizen. The world is much bigger than the United States. 7 billion people in the world but the United States has 350 million in population. Most of the world is not living like American. What is amazing is that we are the only nation with a dream. The American Dream is only for the United States. **What is your dream? How will you use the resources in the United States resources and privilege to achieve your dreams?**

Gain experience from the government, non-profits, and private companies in your community. Introduce yourself and learn what makes them successful. The power of experience is learning more about you.

Politics felt like an overwhelming to-do list. I wanted a "Do Well" list. Instead of looking at a daunting "To Do" list, I prefer to use an encouraging statement. Do Well entices one to be excited to complete a task. It focuses the mind on putting more effort towards a task. The challenge truly lies in understanding what to put on the Do Well list. **What do you do well? What do we want to do well? What will I do well today? Tomorrow? Next year? In five years? Ten? What is the impact that I would be remembered for doing well? Who needs me to do well the most? What efforts can I put forth each day to do well in everything I do?** When I complete this work, I will be amazing. The feeling in my heart will scream "Good job!" Politics has an impact and presence on many different levels through a myriad of positions, engagements, and intentions.

In self-education, my intention is to help people overcome the opportunity gap. The opportunity gap, as I see fit, is the gap between your educational aspirations and your educational goals. The industry of higher education is worth over $1 trillion dollars when endowments, real estate, and assets are calculated to the aggregate. Include athletics, academic research, grants, tuition, property and land ownership, and brand recognition of over 3,400 institutions nationwide, and we see an economic community here for the long haul. Higher education is wealthy but every school and person who attends college is not.

The disparity of Africana men at UCLA stood omnipresent. The experience of walking into a cafeteria and not seeing any Black people shocked me! It was my first day of college. As a South Los Angeles native, I realized UCLA was not built for my success. It was built without the Africana population in mind. We were not considered at all and as I walked around campus, there were reminders of that everywhere. The school focused on bringing in certain racial groups, ethnicities, and students to its campus. I was not preferred, nor was I denied. I saw this as an opportunity to make a difference at UCLA and make Africana people valued at the university. I had to make the difference, no matter what it took. ==You cannot let any disproportionate situation be greater than your will to achieve.== Achievement may not appear the way you imagined. That is okay. Adjust. Do not make an excuse and blame external forces for your inability to achieve. I have learned that complaining about my situation places the power of change in others hands when I must take control of my life. It is the only thing in the world that I can actually control. Control what you can control. In college, you must adjust to your environment. You can change much easier than the 100 year old university and system can. Make the impact you wish to see at the school while constantly improving your personal ability to succeed. Your will power must be incredible. Pass on that knowledge and will power to others so they, too, can excel. Each one teaches one. Your actions are a blue print for those who follow you.

      Upon returning to the V.I.P. Scholars program in my senior year after ending my political tenure with Senator Feinstein, I ran into Dr. Tyrone Howard. Dr. Howard taught classes to the high school students in the V.I.P. Scholars summer initiative about the impact of media and educational engagements for students of color. In fact, his research specializes on Black and Latino men in Los Angeles and Pasadena counties. It was the first time I witnessed a researcher, known for writing and teaching college students, engaging with the people in his research for five weeks straight. He exposed his research to 16-year-old high school students, and challenged them to read Pedagogy of the Oppressed by Paulo Friere, as well as articles by Dr. Patrick Camangian, and Dr. Daniel Solorzano. The students were incredibly interested in these academic interactions, because all of the material focused on their educational experience. It is rare that educational researchers have a chance to consistently impact the people they study directly. All of us are put into the American education industry, but few people are coached on how to maximize one's academic potential within the system.

We often create challenges that hold us back from our goals. We become victims, but with the proper knowledge on how to take advantage of the educational industry, such as this book you are reading now. Students like you can have an advantage in achieving within the higher education environment. The research on education should be handed to the students researchers study for their whole life, so they students can understand the challenges ahead and how to overcome them.

To understand my challenges better, I began working with Dr. Howard's research team, The Black Male Institute (BMI), with my good friend, and now renowned education policy expert, Devon Miner. The team was split into three divisions: elementary and middle school, high school and access, and college and retention. I joined the college and retention group because it was immediately applicable to my experience as a current UCLA senior. After working on access with V.I.P. Scholars, I decided to study the Africana males on campus at UCLA and research their success.

During the time of me investigating the Black male academic journey, I was experiencing it firsthand. I encourage you to conduct research with a professor on your campus who studies something dear to your heart, you! **Research is ME-search.** Search for yourself. Know yourself to know your wealth. Real talk! Life is real but you only understand life from your experience. Everyone you meet is a reflection of you and it is important you understand your wealth by researching the experience of similar people to you.

For the second year in a row, I had a friend of mine, a Black male, sleeping on my couch and housing his belongings at my home. Both students were dropouts/kicked out from the university. Going home wasn't an option, because home would be much further from where they would both want to be: around determined strong minded individuals who are educating themselves, everyday. My food was their food. My things were their things. To study Black male success at UCLA and have friends on my couch juxtaposing the research, I was in a constant battle of introspection. My friends lived on my couch my junior and senior years of college. Junior year I still lived in a dorm. Senior year I lived in an apartment in West LA – Palms community. Nonetheless, I knew that I needed to figure out how to teach these young men how to academically, spiritually, and financially save their own lives. I guess, this is where I began to truly care about setting a great example in my actions to be a good man. I did not have the answers then, but through my success and continuous research, I would soon begin the next phase of my (self) educational journey.

It was the entire spectrum: the Black male professor, the Black male undergraduates, and the Black male dropouts. For two years, I wondered how to help my friends in a tangible way. I did not know the answer then, but I had a feeling BMI was on its way to find the cure to the Black male higher education achievement gap. The achievement gap speaks to the difference between racial groups achieving their college diploma. White males and African American Women have the highest graduation rates. African American men have the lowest. The graduation rates between white males and African American males are growing each year. BMI aimed to discover why this was true and how did some African American males graduate and not others. Where is the gap? How do you we close it?

We gathered information from students' stories. We found and categorized the themes of different students to build qualitative understandings of peoples' statements. The statements often covered family challenges, financial difficulties, and marginalization in the university settings. Race came up many times as a form of oppression due to the negative stereotypes. It was a positive experience at times and a negative one for others. Being a black male at a predominantly Asian American institution required us to be an advocate and constant representative of the Africana culture. It weighed heavily on many African American men upon arrival to the university. Some did not want to represent the entire culture. Others took pride in speaking for the entire culture. For example, I was always asked what sport I played while walking on campus consistently. When people on campus asked me what sport I played, I responded, "Books." I never stopped to continue the conversation. I let the thought marinate and walked away calmly, hoping they would understand most of the African American men on campus, were not athletes but all of us were students. Their stereotype would not change my mood nor intimidate me because I knew who I was. Many of my friends were athletes, so, on the other hand, I was honored to be confused with the pride and joy of school spirit. I had to create a balance of pride about my academic achievements, culture, and school spirit.

    Continuing to focus on my passions beyond my academic performance allowed me to thrive at UCLA as I witnessed these same stereotypical misconceptions placing others into thoughts of self-devaluation. Only through self-education can we maintain the courage needed to know who we are in times of controversy. I encourage you to engage actions that increase your confidence daily. For instance, I joined the choir at UCLA. I had sung in the choir at every level of my education before that, and continuing in undergrad was no exception. The soulful melodies of Christian songs rang vibrations of divine power through my soul. It gave me the confidence to overcome stage fright and anxiety. It encouraged me to perform anywhere and everywhere and to view my life as a grand performance. The world is my stage. The power of singing sets a vibration of comfort into the body, so whether my iPod worked or not, I sang walking down Bruinwalk on campus. I sing, dance, and affirm myself every single day now. I am not guaranteed to hear a positive remark from anyone today, so I take the opportunity every morning to establish who I am before anyone else can influence my mindset, which is a practice I continue to this day.

Creating thoughtful responses for microaggressions and finding my peace in music and knowledge worked wonders for me. It was an excellent time to maximize my talents and have the ability to increase character, passions, talents, and skills. As a renaissance man, I encountered many people from across the various academic units at UCLA. One day, strolling in front of the performing arts building, I remember a student actor emerging from class who noticed me singing and dancing while walking to the public policy school. She said, "The world is your stage, Miles!" I believed her, too. From that day forth, I realized that movies are made after people's lives. The books we read, shows we watch, and theaters we attend serve as replications of the world we are already in. Our imaginations take what has been presented before us and create a new reality. It is up to us to manifest those ideas and make our imagination reality. If we do not like something in the world, it is up to us to change it. If we are not learning what we want in class, it is up to our self-education to teach us. We can learn through experience, what we do not learn in theory. Through co-curricular activities, we gain the skills necessary to actualize our imaginations in ways a classroom cannot manage. It takes a strong desire to achieve outside of the classroom, especially in co-curricular activities and at work-study. School is easy when you are just going to classes and partying. School becomes a life changing experience when you get involved. Our best leaders in society did not just go to work; they got involved in organizations and efforts beyond the 9am -5pm work life. What we do beyond the minimum in life is where we separate ourselves from the ordinary and find our greatness. It is necessary for you to join co-curricular activities throughout life if you truly desire to flourish in the world. The lessons learned and the character built will forever be the catalyst for you to achieve your dreams in higher education and life.

Increase your confidence daily

04
EXTRACURRICULAR ACTIVITIES

We are not judged for what we know, but what we do.

Follow your heart. Your passion can take you through amazing journeys you will treasure forever. In higher education, you have so many opportunities to gain leadership skills that you can use to lead your family, friends, companies, and yourself. Extracurricular activities are so important because you learn to lead yourselves and others. In the previous chapter concerning co-curricular activities, we learned the various skills we gain from engaging in purposeful student organizations, internships, and work-study positions. Co-curricular have a direct professional relationship. Through the various formats of student organizations, internships, and more, we gain exposure to professional development. These skills are necessary to thrive in today's world.

Another form of engagement, highly important to the manifestation of your abilities, are extracurricular activities. These activities differ from co-curricular engagements. Co-curricular activities have a clear alignment with your professional goals. They help to develop professional skills and talents a student can use in traditional corporate American companies, non-profits, and government entities. Extracurricular activities are more focused on the personal satisfaction rather than the professional preparation. Extracurricular activities may develop professional skills, but you will primarily engage in the extracurricular activity to satisfy a passion or interest. Many students can engage in the same activity, but for one student, it might be an extracurricular activity, while for the other, it might be a co-curricular one.

I play trumpet. I am named after Miles Davis, the famous trumpet player who had a 50-year career for consistently elevating the music industry into a different style, every decade. I played in the school band from 5th grade through 12th grade. I earned a few scholarships to play in the band at some Historically Black Colleges and Universities. I decided my interest and passion for music needed to shift, as I wanted to focus on other passionate endeavors. I played in the band at Crenshaw High School mostly because I loved it, and 80% of the seniors in my band received a scholarship offer. What was a co-curricular activity in high school you participated that became an extracurricular in college?

Just as I was a member of the band, membership of an organized activity benefits you for helping you to structure your passion. These involvements contribute greatly to your well-being. For example, plenty of higher education athletes who are not on scholarship continue to pay tuition and dedicate a huge amount of their time to their sport. For the student engaged in college athletics, they often have a high amount of school pride. Their sport and school spirit are linked together in their dedication to their sport. Through the camaraderie developed in sport participation, such as practices and performances, the student creates a reliable source of consistency. Your teammates allow you, as a student, to feel supported. Often, students must recreate a sense of familiarity once they are in college. Creating friendships and a support group are key to your success. College athletes often have a strong career stemming from high school or beyond in a sport. When you attend college, the environment can often be new, especially if you live on campus and/or away from home. The adjustment can be difficult and force you to feel isolated and alone in your collegiate development. In order to make you feel at home, join a sport or competition-based organization that represents the university. Club athletics may also be a good foundation for support and familiarity if you played sports in high school. In an unfamiliar environment, do something you are familiar with to make you feel more at peace with yourself. Your performance academically will improve if you provide a structure to your life that you enjoy. The demands of competition-focused clubs will require great time management and commitment to a schedule that best helps you achieve in competition. People with a competitive edge achieve more in life because they have an internal drive pushing them to succeed. Academic performance is greatly dependent on the comfort and confidence you have as a student to persevere semester after semester. Managing a student course schedule, along with an extracurricular activity you have prior knowledge and experience in, creates the comfort you need to succeed in higher education.

Not everyone wants to attend college and repeat the activities they engaged in before. "New school, new me", say many new students when they arrive on campus for the first time. It is that mentality that made my trumpet decorative and educational advocacy became my new passion. For most students, college organizations serve as great openings to new passions and interests they could not engage in before. College is a great opportunity to reinvent yourself. Shower yourself with new passions and interests. An extracurricular activity for many students in college is stress relief from the institutional challenges inside and outside of the classroom. It is important for students to have outlets in order to manage their stress. Extracurricular activities provide great stress relief due to the volunteer nature of participating. It is not required and you are only engaged because you love it. They are stress free environments or a source of positive stress.

You can be your best and still make mistakes.

Many times, the course requirements and collegiate environment push you to feel peer pressured into academic excellence. In recent years, the University of Pennsylvania witnessed an increase in student suicides due to an unspoken traumatic effect in the socio-academic experience. Socio-academic is defined as the social and academic components of the university experience. For students who do express themselves on campus, performing art serves as a great exhale from the battlefields of academia. It is importance we continue to believe in ourselves during hard times and create a comfortable balance that promotes a healthy self-reflection and perception of who we are. We cannot loose value in ourselves because college is hard. Life could always be worse but being alive is the best way to make change. One form of performing art is poetry. I have written many poems in order to deal with the stress of life and the challenges I must overcome. Not only does poetry serve as an outlet for me, it also reconfirms notions others have, who may not be brave enough to recite their perspectives publicly. The ability to create community through poetry serves many of us well. A poem I often recite to students who find it difficult to manage school and the racialized socio-political injustices of the United States is titled "Foolish."

<u>Foolish</u>

To be young, gifted, and Black
We make it out the hood hoping for equality but we don't see that
My ancestors survived, the mental attack
Coupled with the demands of the Atlantic, we crossed that
So, with the urge to live, we sat in ships
Only to be bred by haters for a nation's profits
I forgave you and don't hate you
Racist ladies and gents, in fact I even love you
Because this country is my home
This country is my heart
But the killing of my brothers, been here from the start
You beat us to death, and then you hung us from trees
This is the price that comes with the land of the free
So this Black on Black murder remains a norm and

Killing men inside this nation takes a myriad of forms
So, as Dunn shoots kids over loud music
Zimmerman beats and shoots whomever he chooses

(Sing painfully)
But I'm talking foolishly, about life
It's never really, going to be so wise, (mm hmm)
2x

My degree is not bullet proof
So if a man sees my skin, belittles my kin
He can stand still and shoot
They victim blame as if my skin is a threat
Or I'm in your debt, so America stands on the grounds of techs
So the nine is divine. Especially when it shines
A fiery light of death, in claim of a defense crime
No value for Black men, shoot, its confirmation
The power of a man to invoke intimidation. False Intimidation
As the manipulation of legal rights and norms set unequal limitations
But Uncle Sam won't help a colorblind nation
Moving towards notions of acceptance of assimilation
Operations on the hearts of eagles
More cinematic than Regal
Expecting young feeble minds to agree
But no longer will we find comfort in conformity
Accepting false generosity for America's slave property

(Sing painfully)
But I'm talking foolishly, about life
It's never really, going to be so wise, (mm hmm)
2x

All grown up and no longer looking for mules
A generation of CEOs loaded ready to duel

So let the shots of freedom rain down on me
And she and he, as we create the new we
This commodity, you can't trade it
You actually freaking trained it
A picture is what I'm painting
White campus and colored dots
White campus I'm jumping spots
The pressure to excel, forces gravity on top
And we stay up later
In hopes of making the same paper
And to the hood, we're never considered a traitor
So I wake up every day with a prayer
Meek told me that there were layers
And to these blood suckers I'm Buffy the Inequality Slayer
That's anybody who believes that we can achieve
Without this corporate mercy
Or service level diversity
As we run the world, run up to boys and girls
And hug them with all our might
Instead of shooting up out of fright
For our differences make us unique
From our resilience levels to our varying physiques
We been climbing way too long not to reach the freaking peak
So when we meet, just greet, and don't ever shoot me!

(Sing painfully)
But I'm talking foolishly, about life
It's never really, going to be so wise, (mm hmm)
2x

As a student, racial issues were mostly focused on misconceptions people had of various cultures. Extracurricular activities often have a particular focus and serve as a great space for various ethnic cultures to unite in honor of the competitive culture. As a Black male, overcoming stereotypes is a constant challenge on the university campus. Many times, people of different cultures only have media and entertainment from mainstream sources as references to the character and habits of African Americans. As a staff and faculty member, I found myself constantly sitting in silence during the televised killings of my fellow African American citizens. I feel as if my demographic is being hunted. I constantly find myself as the only African American present in many university settings. When expressing my concern for my safety, I meet the eyes and ears of misunderstanding. I spoke up about my feelings, but the best response I received to my concerns was, "Oh, I'm sorry." I soon learned my cultural experience, the hunted feeling and public killings, were an experience only I would know in the majority of my socio-academic spaces, not only as a student, but also as staff and faculty. It became my responsibility to serve as a shoulder to lean on for those coming behind me, to be a resource of mentorship and safe spaces for African Americans and marginalized populations. I served as a faculty advisor for a south Asian sorority and an African American fraternity in order to help these marginalized student leaders feel supported on campus.

    I decided I needed to write poetry in order to express myself and take control of my experience. My emotional response to institutional racism became captured in my poetry. It taught me to master my feelings and realize racism is a deadly disease stemming from ignorance and hatred. The jealousy of racial identities has killed man and African Americans and misunderstood demographics are often the target of violence. It is an injustice, but when life gets hard and I see the killings of a fellow American citizen on national television or social media, it is important I stay focused on my goals because I do not know who will be next, but someone will. I must live today as if it is my last. I must make strides in my profession and become successful in order to add to the cultural legacy of my people. Focus is not created easily but is easily taken. Distractions in life and society will be constant.

Injustice has been a constant in human civilizations. It will continue forever but you must not become complacent in life because you are scared to live and scared to die. You must stay focused on your goals while you have an opportunity to achieve. Tomorrow is promised to no one, regardless of ethnic background. Everyone dies. We each have a purpose to live out. In times of turmoil and hatred, perseverance to capture and create opportunity lives each day. We must live with them. You must live greatly in honor of your fallen brothers and sisters who suffered from a culture of violence. The children, men, and women who fight in wars for our freedom, died so you can achieve the American dream. Those killed in hate crimes trust that you will live your dreams since they cannot. We humans are one people and as a piece of us dies, another piece of humanity must live even more than we did before. We embrace the challenge and face it, but we must continue to overcome any distraction. Express yourself. **Use extracurricular activities to find ways to express your love.**

Dance is another performing art you can use to express your love. Many people love to dance. In fact, you can find many college parties and local late night locations having open floor space for people to dance. Many party dancers need encouragement from alcohol to dance. Some people rely upon alcohol to achieve their dancing confidence. I encourage people to dance whenever they can and become comfortable with their dancing style. I encourage people to dance walking down the street. It is an invigorating sensation to free oneself through dance with or without music. It may not have the same appeal as a dark room, loud music, booming bass, and a red cup, but it will keep you healthy. Dancing relieves stress, as well as lowers cholesterol and blood pressure. To dance while walking is to create a happy mentality along with those physical health benefits.

For people who dance often, we can call it an extracurricular, a hobby if you will. The extracurricular activity does not need formal guidelines like a co-curricular. It requires consistency more so than competition or guidelines. People join dance teams but have no intention of becoming professional dancers, while some take it more seriously, like a co-curricular activity or professional practice. Regardless of intention, the unity from dancing in a collective allows a student to create camaraderie with others. The peace they find in their soul from dancing satisfies their sense of belonging. The intensity increases, and they can manage themselves in a productive manner. Togetherness is a huge source of safety for students. Being accepted by others and receiving praise for your passions serves as one of the greatest validations you can have. The focus on your passion may even isolate you from the ordinary population. The truth is that none of us are ordinary unless we let our passions die. The ordinary does not pursue happiness through multiple means. The ordinary person chooses to ignore their heart's desires because they just want to survive in life instead of thrive. They accept whatever life is offered to them in their neighborhood. The ordinary looks for acceptance first, passion second. The ordinary allow for others to dominate their self-approval. The ordinary can become reliant upon the social permission of others to progress after their dream. Oftentimes, the ordinary addiction can lead to self-destruction. The passion must come first. The acceptance from self comes soon thereafter. The confirmation of our actions from others is never required, even when appreciated. You never need confirmation from others in order to choose yourself. It is nice to have, but not a need.

In pushing the ordinary desire as a primary goal, we can lose ourselves and fall to the whim of external validation. External validation speaks to the need we, human beings, have to be approved by our peers and strangers. It is common in every person but controls many. We have an innate desire to seek the gratitude of others. The gratitude of others confirms our ambitions and our actions. External validation is not necessary. External validation will drive you crazy if you let it dominate your life. People will love and hate you regardless of what you do so at least let people hate/love the real you. Become you.

The human spirit's desire is the strongest force on the planet. The human spirit's desire, combined with physical action and mental determination, knows no bounds. The whim of approval lives within all of us. The source of approval needs redirection. Instead of needing the approval of others as a sign of direction, we need to have others respond to our behaviors. Remember, you are only as good as the expectations others have of you. Set their expectations with your actions and soon your own standards of life will dominate the external validation you think you need. People will respond to the standards we set before them. This allows others to know what to expect from you. Control the perception others have of you. You must convey in your actions why you should be respected. If your peer sees you dancing all the time, they will expect you dance, often. Be proud to dance or stop dancing. Pride will take time to develop, but embrace it more and more every day. There is no limit to the freedom your unique extracurricular activity may bring you. If they see you reciting poetry consistently, peers will expect you to write and recite poetic literature consistently. They will approve your acts, based upon the actions we present to them. This is the reason first impressions matter so much. How we meet people is how we see people.

The power of social media allows us to serve as our own public relations agents. Post the best version of yourself. Live the best version of yourself. You will be expected to be your best at all times. You can be your best and still make mistakes. That is okay. Keep being your best. You should expect the best from yourself more than anyone else. Your personal standards in life should always be higher than everyone else's. Take control of yourself and you will have greater control over your perception. After consistent media and in-person interactions, your peers will begin to recognize you for your passions and best self. You are seen as what you do most. What you do everyday is who you are. You are what you publicize about yourself the most: specifically, the passions we intentionally expose. Extracurricular activities give you the opportunity to expose that which you enjoy most, even if you only do it for college. But if it truly your passion, why stop, ever?

As a human being, you are addicted to knowledge.

05
SOCIAL

Learning from others and uniting to have a great time with others, is a huge part of the college and human experience.

The social components of creating a positive self-education are infinite. Co-curricular, Extracurricular, and Social engagements are equal in the creation of a positive self-education. While attending school, you should realize that you learn outside of class in these three spaces. Learn to manage your time during your college experience by determining the true value of your interests. In higher education, on campuses across the nation, we refer to our consumers as students. It is incredibly important you remember you are acquiring knowledge in exchange for monetary capital. Thus, you are buying the teaching, knowledge, and experience. The knowledge is the product and the teaching is the service. As a person, school is a part of who you are. It may be what you do most but it is not all that you are. School should not be your entire day. It should be a part of your day. It can be the most of the day. It can be the least of the day. You will learn all day from your experiences whether you go to school or not. Your ability to RIM shot consistently will keep you ahead in social settings.

As a human being, you are addicted to knowledge. As curious creatures getting our hands into everything we can, we have to reflect about the lessons we learn daily. We watch television programs and read tweets, posts, blogs, and media articles from a variety of formats such as Forbes, the LA Times, Buzz Feed, and Facebook daily. Spend time with yourself daily to center yourself. You need to reflect on whom you are just as you reflect about the thoughts others provide you. With media platforms dominating our social time, higher education squeezes plenty of people into a singular space. The students remain on campus and begin to live where they study and engage other people on a consistent basis.

Food is located throughout any campus worth attending. In the eateries on campus, students have a huge chance to interact with peers or people watch. Schools like UCLA with large student centers create a unique space where students can catch up over food at a round table while eating pizza. Food is love. When you eat food, it is a ritual in human interaction. Do not eat alone for eating an entire experience that is best when embraced with others.

In higher education, many students do not eat a healthy and balanced diet. The better you eat, the better your mood will be. We can even get "hangry" if we wait too long. That is a combination of being hungry and angry because you have not eaten in a long period of time. When you do not eat for an extended period of time, your biological balance is thrown off and it affects your mind, body, and soul.

As you consume your nourishment for your body, you have a great chance to connect with your friends through personal stories over food. Listen to the stories of your friends' lives as you eat. Nothing brings people together like food. The casual conversation of experiences with family, loved ones, or dates can all reach the forefront of the dialogue.

I think the phrase "Let's get coffee" was created at a college in the United States. Coffee allows for a quick chat. The simple socialization can be anywhere from 30 minutes to 4 hours. In college, some people begin to rely incredibly on coffee to stay up later and increase their metabolism. It has some health benefits but in excess or with daily use can be dangerous over time.

Nonetheless, like beer, it is a common social connection many people use to catch up and network. It is a friendly engagement. It has more purpose and possibility than we often contemplate. The challenge of learning all of the information you need to know can be daunting. Many a time, we increase this anxiety by avoiding the important test coming up soon. Then, at last, the night before the test is here. Studying began in the morning but as the review continued, it became clear that there was much more information to be retained than predicted. A trip to grab coffee with a friend allows conversation to occur over the same stress before the test. The coffee trip becomes a medium for camaraderie in the struggle to overcome the challenging examination.

It is most advantageous to create study groups and have someone bring coffee. Camaraderie works best over delicious consumptions. Two forms of study groups exist. One focuses on creating a group of people to assist each other in the same class to collaborate on their preparation for the test. Your study group should set goals, expectations, and responsibilities that include the entire group. When studying for the same class, the information disseminated to everyone is the same. If I were meant to have your vision, I would have your eyes. **What do you see in the world that other people usually don't catch on to?** You do not value the exact same information as your peers in the classroom, so uniting to study throughout the entire academic term multiplies the information acquired in class. Two people can watch the same movie and deduce two completely different messages from it. Creating the collective of knowledge makes sense, and it has been proven in history that the greatest minds were team orientated. Assign leaders for different chapters or concepts so each person becomes a specialist in a certain category of the course material. Everyone must summarize and teach their responsibility by (1) preparing organized notes, (2) committing to set meetings times, (3) learning simple concepts, and (4) efficiently communicating. If you can teach someone something, it means you actually understand the material. Remember, everyone is a teacher. Regurgitation does not equal understanding or the ability to apply knowledge. One must be able to critically understand and, from memory, apply the knowledge in the test-required format.

The discussion surrounding material and critically engaging the information through dialogue, reflection, and debate will positively impact your intellectual capabilities. As a collective, you will have memories of the information and each other. Your college memories will be tied to the bonds of friendship and creating memories. In a fun learning environment, we are more likely to remember information. The camaraderie will be a major component of academic success due to the collective effort put forth to master the material in a fun, exciting, and joyful experience. Creating those memories of unity and development serve each one of you well. Everyone comes individually prepared and contributes greatly to the group. When people have memories of overcoming challenges together, people remain friends for extended periods of time.

Let's attack this final together. Group study does not replace individual study. It is in addition to it. The study group should mirror the NBA's Golden State Warriors 2014-2015 championship run. Everyone must contribute and be prepared to help and learn. It is mandatory not just one person visit the professors office hours, but all students. The professor has a lot answers and each student may ask different questions from the professor. We all have different perspectives and understanding that create multiple thought processes within the group that we can all benefit from. The creator of the course has all of the knowledge. Without acknowledging the creator of the course in your process to master the material the course creator established, you place yourself at a disadvantage to excel in the creator's designed course. The best advantage is to have your study group members go to office hours and come together to unite the information gathered. Each of you may ask different questions. Therefore, everyone brings new light to the darkness of midterm season.

In life, we do the same thing. We all research differently. We each ask different questions. In addition, we continue to learn from our life experiences differently. Thus, our perspectives on life are different. We make different decisions. I went to a party in college with my friends. Half of us went into the party and danced all night. We did not stop. We kept dancing whether we liked the song or not. The other half of my friends held the wall up with their backs. They crowded the wall to serve as decorations because they did not like the wallpaper at the establishment. They did not have a great time at the party. Those of us who danced at the party all night, we had a blast. Our decisions were different. Our experiences were different. Our goals were the same. Let's have fun at this party. Social gathering, inclusion, and engagement say a lot about your approach in life. When we reflected on our experiences from the party, what we saw as the necessary decisions for a good time were different. Only in uniting together to bring the different experiences in the party did we truly understand that we can have a great time at the party in different ways. Some of my friends on the wall did have a great time. They had a successful night because of how they defined fun for themselves. The next time we went to a party, we knew we would have fun in different ways. My friends and I did not have to approach the parties in college the same way. We just needed to make sure everyone had their preferred type of fun. In a study group, when everyone focuses on their strengths, some people will be more active in the study group than others. Some people will be quieter. Having a good balance of people who speak and those who are quiet is important because everyone brings a different perspective. Talking more does not imply more intelligence. Talking less does not always mean you did not study at all before coming to the study group. Different people bring different styles of fun and studying too the group dynamic.

The second manner in which we see students gather together is more so like a social gathering of focused energy rather than sharing notes for the same test. Students may not always study for the same class, but group studying can benefit many people who look to study together. A swan may fly up to 75 more miles in a group than it can fly alone. As human beings, we are built of atoms. Atoms move so fast collectively that our human bodies appear to be solid and hold form. We hold many items within our body that are constructed of atoms vibrating. Thoughts, like atoms, have a powerful hold on humanity through vibrations. Thought signals travel like radio waves. When thoughts are sent from the mind, other people can feel the vibrational energy waves.

If you have ever felt someone staring at you, you understand my logic. We feel eyes burning into our souls when someone is starring at us. We feel them thinking about us because their thoughts and concentration have collected together like radio waves to our bodies. The vibrational energy waves move with a force that feels like matter. The atoms of thoughts know no bounds and do not hold form like the physical atoms. The mental energy affects the world differently. Thus, the unified vibrational energy waves of multiple minds can make one thought more powerful because there are multiple antennas, minds, sending out the same message. Just as the swan can fly longer lengths with others, so can the human mind achieve more when a unified vibrational energy wave is created.

Only in togetherness can we create stronger waves. Physically being together maximizes the power of the vibrational waves, although it is not necessary. Over Facetime or a phone call you can feel the energy of another person. Find a quiet library filled with students during midterms or finals. Feel the energy when you walk in. There lies the greatest example of the united vibrational energy waves. Students across the many colleges will be focused on achieving high marks. They thirst for academic achievement. They drive their attention to acquiring the necessary knowledge required to succeed academically. When midterms and finals arrive, the unified vibrational energy waves of collegiate institutions galvanize to push forth the mental capabilities of each student as everyone begins to study for exams. It is then that we see the collected mental focus set a tone or feeling to the campus. Each student believes they can study for hours on end and find themselves spending countless hours in the library. Many a time, a collected group of students in a library who do not even know each other create energy from the mental waves of dedication to excel at the task before them. This is an asset and skill much needed to accomplish ones dreams. It is a ritual skill, not a daily practice.

Unify your thought waves with others in formal and casual manners. We eat every day. I dare you to not eat alone. I dare you to socialize and eat with others while sharing ideas. Discuss favorite foods and preferred experiences. Debate the presidential campaign. Dive into other's minds, especially others who think differently than you. **Juxtapose the experience of American economic classes. Discuss the intersection of race, class, and gender today. Ask someone to define love. Can you define love? Are there various types of love? How does love differ in your family, romantic, and platonic relationships? Yet in one relationship, we make ask for all three to be present. So what's the limit on love? Is love the answer? What exactly is the problem?**

I think self-love is the most important love. As a person developing in modern society, the love in the world has as many different faces as people on the planet. With over seven billion people on earth, we often cannot interact with the majority of people. Appreciate those around you, in your study group and your family. We look to a myriad of media platforms to understand the world we live in. The world you live in is around you. You were introduced into the world, not the other way around. The world we want to know lives inside of us, but we have to bring the world we wish to see into reality. You have a purpose, and by bringing out the most loving version of you, people will love to engage your vibrational waves. Being a loving person will make you a social leader. Your self-love will be an example of self-love others will wish to emulate.

Love thought waves affect our intelligence and serve as subconscious reminders of our ability to overcome prejudices. In college, the diverse population will love differently than you, but in order to create a loving and studious environment, you must reach beyond your comfort zone and create a study group that will master the material. The more diverse people in the study group, the more diverse the understanding of the material. Like-minded study groups will create blind spots in the knowledge. Expand the backgrounds, ethnicities, economic classes, and experiences of the student study group and you will expand your understanding of the material, thus creating the best possible academic advantages from social interactions. Living on campus in the dormitories allows the best unity because students in close proximity to each other allow for easy collaborations.

Ease the social gatherings of study groups in the beginning by discussing coffee chat topics such as those provided in the bolded questions above. When engaging media in modern society, we often discuss what we see. The media intake for the average U.S. citizen increased dramatically with technology and the Internet, which allow for more engagement of our selective biases. The increased quantity of resources to accumulate information allows human beings to introduce new thoughts. We cannot believe everything we engage. Through collective discussion and reflection, we can grow to understand others and develop our own beliefs. The two sides of the coin show heads as a means to convey notions in person. Tails conveys information via media. Both provide a different sense of expression. They influence each other.

When statements are said in media from major public figures, we are much more impressionable to regard that opinion as true. Nonetheless, social media has allowed greater access to many public figures of all kinds. It has also allowed for people who did not have public notoriety before to gain popularity. Thus, the world is smaller. As our personal universes grow, our worlds shrink. We have more access to the same information we always took in. We have not diversified the many avenues of access the Internet has afforded us.

We now have daily access to our friends and multiple avenues of engaging people. I can see a picture album on Facebook, then scroll into the best picture that is also posted on Instagram. I can go to my Twitter feed and see she tweeted the picture and a few comments on how amazing that moment of her life truly was. Then I can see the whole backstory of how the moment really happened, thanks to SnapChat. Everyone becomes a public relations agent for themselves due to social media. We have complete control over our public image. Each image we post and produce sends vibrational waves into the universe.

The opportunity to create a specific image to present to the world is an exciting opportunity everyone now owns. It requires one to become what they promote. People will see you for the images you present in social media. The people who you interact with in person will confirm your identity by commenting on social media. Being honest and truthful is the best route to controlling one's media output. Control requires understanding of your goal and how you want to present yourself, with a public resume of information, private, public, intimate, and more.

The Internet is forever. So is your spiritual journey. No one has proof of it lasting forever. Give everything you got to be the person you want to be socially. I am sure it will require you to rethink your co-curricular and extracurricular activities, or maybe your lack of them. The glory of who we are and all we are to become can be expressed in our social media. Control your perception. Social media conveys to the world that we want to be seen as. It is who we are to become as well because we are sending our vibrational waves with each post. We create vibrational waves because people begin to think of us as we are represented online, whether they like the picture or not. Follow me on Instagram and Twitter: @ProfessorMiles_. You can see I scream education and motivation. That is who I am. I love to learn and I love to motivate others while teaching them what I learned. I wrote this book with the same intent: to educate and motivate you to achieve your dreams within higher education. Use higher education as a practice facility for what you wish to do in the real world. If you positively impact enough people, your effort now will feed directly into your future.

I began teaching at Drexel University at 24 years of age. Since then, I have convinced myself. It took me until I turned 26 to feel completely comfortable in most social settings. I'm a geek.

When we accomplish our dreams, that journey takes everything we have and more to achieve. Often the journey to be a success makes us uncomfortable. Discomfort creates new neural pathways in our brains that serve as foundations for how we will decide to act when we face this discomfort next time. This is vital, not only to successfully overcome our fear of opportunity, but also for when we engage with people socially in an educational setting. When we speak to people who have different experiences in life, we learn a new perspective in the world. The perspective of the world through someone else's eyes can only be told by story. The story of his or her eyes lives in attentive listening. Your attentive listening demands understanding, asking questions, and affirmations. When you listen and make an effort to understand others' stories, you create a strong bond spiritually and mentally. It allows you to increase your unified vibrational energy waves. The conversations we have with people serve as information being inputted into our minds. Our minds are the greatest computers in the world, consistently processing information whether we want them to our not. Our subconscious will forever remember our interactions, but only through conscious engagement with positive intentions do we create social setting in parties and study groups that give us a chance to have positive vibrational energy connections.

All throughout high school, I wanted to join a fraternity. It was my idea of having an ultimate brotherhood of friends I could collaborate with. I went to one fraternity that had a great presence on campus. I spoke with the brothers and had lunch with them. I thought they were cool. Attending UCLA with them, we had a good connection about being a male student on campus. But when I embraced the brothers of Kappa Alpha Psi Fraternity, Inc., I grew incredibly excited because the vibrational connection matched. Thus, I knew what fraternity was right for me. The vibrational connection conveyed an incredibly important tone for my decision to pursue membership.

VIBRATIONS are not just for the mental but also for the physical. Food satisfies the physical and opens the harmony of the mental. Our mind, body, and soul are interconnected. The satisfaction of the tripartite being requires a constant check in with all three parts. Just as much as we eat physically in a day, we should eat mentally and spiritually. The social engagement of eating serves as a great bonding moment. Eating is a human ritual of satisfaction. The eating ritual opens the mind and soul to many conversations and perspectives.

When we accomplish our dreams, that journey takes everything we have and more to achieve.

I love movies because they are as close as we can get to seeing through the eyes of someone else. They are a compilation of sights, but nonetheless great experiences. Cinema, documentaries, and television tell interesting tales. Sitcoms and reality television shows usually depict DESIRES of many. They set the tone and expectations of the children. The ability to dream comes from our imagination. Our imagination is heavily influenced with what we engage our senses with. All of that enters our subconscious and influences our thought patterns, which establish neural pathways. Everything a human has created, no matter how vile or tremendous, once grew from a seed, planted in the soil of imagination: the building you are in, the chair you sit in, the pen you write with in the margins of this book, the money used as a means to garner resources, and the creation of FEAR (false evidence appearing real).

Fear destroys many minds, bodies, and souls from purposeful lives. Fear creates conflict and restriction within the imagination. The subconscious does not know the difference between imagination and reality. The conscious deciphers the information. We hear it and decide whether to believe the words someone says immediately based on our prior experiences. We can imagine where certain people may lead us to in life. Even when we use our consciousness to make a decision, our subconscious will retain the information as fact. As you grow up, you may hear people say, "You look like your parent(s)." You may even say to yourself, "I do not want to act like my parents". Then it happens. You're having a normal day and say a phrase just like your parent(s) would. You hear it as you are saying it. You can hear them in your voice while you are saying it. You can't believe it. You can't stop yourself. Just by seeing something happen repeatedly, you were able to repeat it naturally. It is a part of you. Whatever you see is a part of you. That is what you can imagine. The media intake we consume, whether engaged or not, becomes a part of who we are. It enters your subconscious. A wise woman once told me during my undergraduate studies at UCLA: "Out of sight, out of mind." What we cannot see, we often do not believe in, whether or not it is God, air, love, someone's experience, etc.

    Behind your eyes is a mind full of sights we have never seen. Therefore, it is an endless universe of information forever collecting in our subconscious. I dare you to spend some time listening to other people's stories for a day each month. We don't even know how valuable our memories and subconscious information truly is until we communicate them to others or write them down in a journal. Treasure that which cannot be seen anywhere else such as the memories of our lives. Your perspective is valuable. Your expression of your experiences is truly valuable. Protect your voice, thoughts, and contemplations, all the while allowing your thoughts the OPPORTUNITY to embrace challenge and validity. Travel to new sights led by others eyes. The stories of others' experiences can provide our imagination with a new view of the world, which holds the power to change our thought pattern forever. The more meaningful questions you ask someone, the better your conversation will be. Don't be scared to dive deep into someone's soul. Move past the surface-level conversation where everyone says, "I had a good weekend. How was yours? The food was excellent. The party was nice. I really enjoyed myself." Low and behold, these statements are generic and hold little value beyond the surface of vibrational connections. It is good small talk but every now and then we need a larger conversation.

Listening to deep notions will give great insight to us. Ask others, "What inspires you to work in this occupation? Was your weekend much better than expected? What three positives moments best sum up your weekend?" We are often scared to get attached to people. We are scared to get to know someone. We play into politically safe zones of engagement, hoping to not offend someone more so than we wish to inspire someone. We see negatives in others constantly and become blind to our own faults. In deep conversation, many a time, the mirror is placed in front of us and we realize that the negativity we face in the world lives within our individual VIBRATIONS. Many a time, the flaws we see in others are flaws we ourselves have. The compliments we give to others often highlight our own best features. We meet reflections of ourselves. Every person you meet is your soul mate. The percentage of soulful compatibility may differ, but your engagement is no accident. I encourage you to treasure LISTENING as full back stage access to the library of the universe. You will never know the way your soul mates see the world unless they tell you. We can never know what you think unless you write your book, make that album, write that poem, or speak your future into existence. When you gain access to other people's infinite source of knowledge from behind the human eye, the gateway to the soul, you grow wiser by understanding and learning from the journey of others.

The reason you love music is because it expresses a perspective you appreciate. The collection of the instruments and vocals comprises a vibration you value. The content may be redundant, but the expression is not. Music expresses your desires, fantasies, and truths. Somehow, musicians express notions and emotions you have felt for years but say it better in one line than we ever could. It is an expression of emotion new to our minds and hearts. When you socialize, music makes you feel more comfortable because its vibrations become your vibrations. It creates comfort and a vibrational tone for the social gathering. Any emotion has a twin living in musical vibration. They serve as waves of communication entering your subconscious. We love music because of the way we feel when we hear it. I remember the young ladies in my school days screaming, "Oh, that is my song, guurl!" when the right tune hit the speakers. Whether we were in the car, a party, a classroom, or at home, my lady friends' reaction to their favorite song remained the same. The music's autosuggestion to the subconscious mind is powerful. Reactions to songs show the power of vibration in many settings. It can give us focus and concentration while playing video games, exercising, and more. The most powerful person at a party is the disc jockey (DJ). The DJ determines the unified vibrational energy waves for the party. We identify with the music and adjust to it. The need to feel free is addicting. The music can take us out of our negative thoughts or drive us deeper into our pain than ever before. This dive into freedom can release emotions you are too cautious to release in other moments. The music allows you to say what is truly on your mind. The music is a propellant of unified vibrational energy waves communicating and directing our souls. The freedom is led by a tripartite component. The mind, body, or soul leads the way. Some music makes us think. Some music makes us feel. Some music makes us embrace our animal nature.

The sexual tension from our animal nature took lead toward the end of every party I attended in college. Something the DJ did at 1am changed the whole tone of the party. Late nights in crowded apartments packed with sweating bodies, the musk of the Thursday night college affair.

The buildup of sexual tension begins before the first dance of each person in the room. The men are there. The women are there. The music is playing. A few good jams come on. The songs everyone knows begin to play. We sing the songs and join the DJ-led unified vibrational waves. The unity is created, and with a great

DJ playing the best songs at the best times, you can dance all night.

The often short-lived romance of college nights requires positive intentions. It demands the freedom of intentional decisions. It is important both parties agree upon sex, preferably in a sober mindset. I encourage you to have safe sex by wearing condoms and have honest conversations about your STI status, **romantic commitments, and goal(s) for every sexual/romantic encounter.**

When someone is under the influence, they are just that: influenced. It is important we do not take advantage of other's poor-influenced minds. Influence in addition to peer pressure can lead to regretful decisions for both parties involved. No matter what external forces may exist, your decisions are your responsibility. You must take full responsibility of yourself and make sure you do not put your trust in the wrong hands or become the wrong hands. It is incredibly important you have friends to check in with throughout a party so you can keep track of each other's safety, not only in romantic situations at late night parties, but in all of life's moments. They do not make the final decisions for us, but having council when you face peer pressure situations can assist us in making the right decisions. In some cases, we may stand alone, and our moral compass will speak to the right thing to do or not do. As we enter the social scene of college, our focus cannot go astray. It is great to have fun, but it is not the primary reason we are here. Fun must be incorporated into all aspects of our lives and not be perceived as only partying or engaging in socially risky behavior. Make yourself enjoy every minute of every day in life. We have to create a joyous life that holds more power and virtue than a red cup and jungle juice.

Fun must be incorporated into all aspects of our lives

Ideal Partner

<u>Mentally</u>	<u>Spiritually</u>	<u>Physically</u>
MIND	SOUL	BODY
_____	_____	_____
_____	_____	_____
_____	_____	_____
_____	_____	_____
_____	_____	_____
_____	_____	_____
_____	_____	_____
_____	_____	_____

06
PROFESSIONAL

Your best professional track is going to be your best passion.

Your job is what you do, but it is not who you are. Your job pays you money to work. You have a passion that gives you fulfillment. That feeds your soul in a way your job cannot. Your job is not who you are, it is what you do. You cannot stop becoming who you are. Life is not a destination but a journey of becoming. Your true work is your life's passion. It is what you must do at all times. It is what you yearn for in the morning and the wee hours of the night. Your passion project is who you are. Understand God has placed a great power of passion within you. The power is a gift to solve a problem here on Earth because we are given the task of recreating heaven on Earth. In order to bring peace to this world, we must find our passion and pursue it. Our profession should align with our passion. Many a time, people find themselves engaged in a job on a daily basis that does not fulfill them. It is not meant to. You are meant to do much more. Do not expect one job to give you complete fulfillment when you have the ability to do so many things that cannot fit into a job description.

I served as a Program Coordinator (PC) in the Honors Program at Drexel University from 9am to 5pm. It allows me to serve the interdisciplinary studies of the university's Alumni, graduate students, and undergraduate populous. With a wide range of university affairs and academic administration, I developed a job to perform at Drexel every business day. It is a large component of who I am, but it is not all that I am. It is my job, which I enjoy. I have a passion of creating and leading safe spaces for people to learn how to develop their own passion projects. My work at Drexel fed into a part of my passion but did not encompass it completely.

Write and state, *"I am a human on Earth. Every human is my family. In order to provide for my family I must create my passion. I must become my passion. My passion will solve a great problem on this earth only I can lead. I am a purpose in physical form creating a passionate pursuit. I am a gift of God using my gift from God, passion. I will use my gift to solve a problem of _____, in this world. I am valuable. My passion is solving this problem for humanity. My passion is _____."*

Saying this reminds you that you are worth much more than bills, debt, and just getting by. You can do anything else any other human being has done. You may have to be the first person to do something that has not been done before. Another human was once the first. Another human took a similar leap of faith. You will not be the first king, queen, business owner, doctor, father, leader, or artist ever. Despite the fear, you have to take that passionate leap of faith. Create the environment. Not only be interviewed by potential employers but also interview them. Take control of your life. In your profession, you will produce. You best work is your passion. In order to become your passion, you must put forth a strong level of commitment.

Practice makes perfect. When preparing to do something, practice it. It makes you better. Perfection is not a destination. Perfection is a pursuit. As an action, perfection requires a habitual dedication. We are all committed to something. If you do not work out everyday, you are committed to not working out. If you show up to a job you do not like everyday, you are committed to that job, regardless of what you say. Talking is easy. Walking is brave. We all have a strong interest in something. What we spend most of our time doing shows where our dedicated commitments stand. Each day, you execute your greatest habits. In order to become habitually educated in the endeavors of your choice, you have to practice becoming your best daily. You don't get in life what you want; you get in life what you are. You have to become who you wish to be in order to achieve the goals you have for yourself. For many students attending higher education, the purpose of attendance is to earn a professional career and refine our passions. Therefore, we begin our practice of perfection by pursuing the career through knowledge acquisition. From specific majors to internships, we can learn our desired trades.

The first step I encourage everyone to take is to find a role model. It is important we have role models to emulate their greatness. You already have some role models. (1) The guardians who raised you serve as the first examples of our lives. We adopt their mannerisms and their attitude toward life. (2) Second would be the musicians, authors, and entertainers we constantly read about and engage through various media. Choosing a role model requires much greater analysis. **What impact do you desire to make on the world? Who works on this impact already, and how can you find out about their life experiences? What specific characteristics in this person do you idolize? How did they build those characteristics? What characteristics do you share with this person?**

Understand the details of what makes a person great. It is important to know how these professionals conduct themselves in order to emulate their best characteristics. Choose three role models who exert great characteristics. They do not all have to be in the same career field. You want to emulate their best characteristics. My first role model is Malcolm X. I idolize Malcolm X because of his tenacity towards learning. With little help, he found a focus in prison to begin reading and understanding as much information as possible to analyze his current situation in life. He analyzed the socio-political context of the American prison system, economics, and racial barriers, then preceded to embrace all the rights he earned as a citizen of the United States to eradicate oppression. His bravery to learn and spread knowledge is unmatched by any other. In his autobiography, documentaries, and movies about him, he is committed to his ideals. He has an idea of what justice, equity, and fair treatment are. He did not see his ideas in reality. He dedicated himself to his ideals and making them come true by any means necessary. For many people, he spoke that equality into existence. Not only did he hold himself to those ideals, he held his audience, followers, fellow men, police officers, and federal, state, and local governments to a high standard of truth and dignity. Everyone was responsible for the prosperity that needed to be created in order to make Malcolm X's vision of equality a reality. Everyone was to blame for the creation of oppression Malcolm X experienced in mid-20th century United States. All races had to contribute to the solution in order for fair treatment to be established. Malcolm X proved to me that truth is a great virtue. More importantly, truth is a commitment to self, family, and the community. Malcolm X was a global traveler and speaker who never wavered from his word or the values he held true. He communicated fully to his ideals strongly around the globe and thus lived as a man representing truth and justice.

His spoken truths remain prevalent in modern-day United States socio-political debates concerning equality and fair treatment. He dedicated a promise of faithful actions toward his wife, Betty Shabazz. He promised to never cheat nor love any other woman the way he loved her. He promised to dedicate himself to the vows of their marriage and to be an honest man, fit for raising children, and leading a family. When Malcolm X spoke to himself in the mirror, he saw the man that he promised the world, his family, and himself to be. He became the man he needed to be for himself, his family, and his society. He did not wade in water hoping to be rescued. Instead he rescued himself. Malcolm X dedicated himself to his beliefs, which set him free internally of external oppression. He did not shy away from his passion. He used his words, passions, and actions in order to create a more prosperous world. The comfort Malcolm X found in the mirror is what I admire most about him. My eyes, when glazed with morning's dew, should too be opened to see the image of the man I promise myself to be. By any means necessary I should live my truth. By any means necessary I should live my passion. My any means necessary I should not let anyone prevent me from being my best me. Not even myself. This truth should be told to the world through my voice, and with his guidance, I must learn all that I can, all that I need to know, to make my truth blossom like a redwood tree in northern California.

My second role model is Denzel Washington. He portrayed Malcolm X in a movie directed by Spike Lee in 1989, the year I was born. I remember going to watch Washington's movies with my family like it was a major world event every time we attended our local Magic Johnson's Theater. The endless compliments my community gave Denzel Washington came only second to President Barack Obama when he began serving in the White House. Washington is known for being tenacious with acting and film production as a whole. His relentless approach to getting the scene done correctly and in a manner of great efficiency can be perceived as off-putting to those who do not have the same fervor. I see him as someone pursuing greatness in every second through his roles. He acts very similar in mindset throughout his various movie characters. Each one has a relentless dedication to an idea, that "no one can stop me", in the movie. His type cast is the "unconquerable man." In many cases, the relentless attitude towards accomplishing the character's goals is so serious that the plots usually end with a killing to provide emphasis on the importance of Washington's character's idea. His movies always challenge me to wonder, **what am I ready to die for? What calling is so great to me that I would prepare for it without any promise of it being actualized?** The movie that best conveys this notion, starring Washington, is The Great Debaters. Denzel Washington directed the film and starred in it as Professor Tolsen. One of his greatest moments in the film revolves around the Berber legend Antaeus. Professor Tolsen conveys to his students, during an intense time of turmoil in the 1935 Texas Jim Crow legality, to never quit when oppression opposes you. The possibility of achievement is too great to not control your dedication to your idea. Tolsen encouraged his students to be like Antaeus when facing defeat.

Antaeus is a Berber giant-warrior, known for being a descendant from Mother Earth. Every time he was thrown to the ground in battle, Antaeus would grow stronger. His strength came from his mother's love. Defeat made him stronger. The love of his mother and the power to learn from failure taught him great strength, resilience, and the ability to conquer his opponents. He stood up in every fight stronger than he was when first thrown to the ground. To the Antaeus student, your degree weighs more than your peers'. For many students, the stress of college stems way beyond classroom assignments. For the past decade, as a student, mentor, coordinator, advisor, and professor, I witnessed countless geniuses manage much more than a college curriculum. For many of you, the struggle of college comes as a need. Your family does not come from wealth. You view college as a requirement to advance in society and earn the salary necessary to take care of your loved ones. Your families need the Antaeus in you to achieve in school in order to gain access to careers with financial opportunity that will create generational wealth. At Drexel University, these students are marginalized but have a great presence, for they are inner city youth, international students, and middle-class Americans. My interactions with Antaeus students put me in a predicament of restriction. I often speak to students about how to gain internships and manage a student-worker lifestyle. Similar to the student-athlete who must maintain her commitments to stay enrolled in school, the student-worker must do the same. The Antaeus students pay their own way through school or sign up for thousands of dollars in loans. The academic financial gap rests on their hands to manage a work-study position(s), scholarship commitments, and work off campus if need be. For these students, their degrees are more valuable because they put more sweat equity into their studies. They experience much more adversity and only rise up to be stronger, as Antaeus did with every fight in his life.

    The consistent threat of being expelled from school, not for grades, but for financial insecurity, forces these students to go above and beyond the ordinary call of duty throughout higher education. They must perform extraordinary acts on a daily basis to achieve the "normal college duties". Ordinary students can party and study much more in college, for the ordinary worries about nothing else but the minimum requirements to achieve in higher education. The ordinary student's initiative to work while in school serves as a valuable co-curricular activity. For the Antaeus student, their employment is a must. It serves as a requirement to achieve in higher education, unlike an ordinary student who perceives employment as an extraneous act. These students, descendants of Antaeus, are stronger than their peers. They are thrown to the ground many more times and overcome these challenges time and time again. They have survived their worst days. Alive and strong, I salute you, Antaeus student, for you are my heroes and heroines. You are the untold Berber myth rising up to achievement, with degrees of great weight, and stories of resilience, unlike anything else I have ever seen. Be great! You already are.

    My third role model is Paulo Freire. He wrote the greatest education book I ever read in undergraduate school. I encountered the book twice. Both times were through the V.I.P. Scholars program. As a mentor in the program, the students I worked with were 15 to 17 years old. The young scholars came from communities were the college-going culture was not as strong as most students who attended UCLA. In order to properly prepare the students for the college experience, it was important we convey to the students the necessary benchmarks, skills, and academic strategies best suited for a UCLA student. In order to be successful at UCLA, we knew the high school students needed as much preparation as possible to succeed. Students who enter UCLA get lost in the massive 43,000-student campus. To prevent poor college retention, we had to increase student access and preparedness. During the summer component of V.I.P. Scholars, we enrolled the students into an education course taught by Dr. Tyrone Howard of UCLA Graduate School of Education and Information Studies (GSE & IS).

Transitioning from K-12 public high school to a tuition-based higher education institution provides many challenges for many people. In order to make the transition and retention process smoother, we believed the students should understand education from the popularized and hidden curriculum perspective. Higher education is an avenue for many to transition from one economic class to another. It serves as a gateway to financial stability, societal uplift, and progression over all. The hidden curriculum speaks to the notion that the barriers that exist in the United States on a legal, societal, and systematic oppressive manner are mirrored on college campuses. In fact, many research universities focus their investments on the creation and dissemination of knowledge. Professors gain employment due to their ability to accrue funding for their research interests, not teaching students to command the knowledge at hand. Higher education is a self-taught practice. Self-education is the greatest autodidactic practice. The assignments are organized, but the responsibility of accomplishing them is completely upon the students'. It was necessary for the all professors to have two hours a week designated as office hours so students could inquire after more instruction on mastering knowledge. The focus on research is so important that professors often lose the ability to care for others to learn due to the requirements of their profession. The pressure from university leadership demands professors to accrue more funding for research than to genuinely teach students. Students who are truly taught can teach others what they. It was important for the V.I.P. Scholars to know how to teach themselves and understand where students stand in the education profession. From being free recipients of public education to being consumers of knowledge in higher education, we have to know what we are paying to learn. Higher Education is a profession for the faculty and staff. The students are receiving the product of knowledge and the service of teaching. The focus for those delivering the service is on the creation of the product. Thus, to be a great college student, one must understand the schools' goals for every community member, student, staff, and faculty.

As stated before, Paulo Friere is well known for the Banking Concept. The students are consumers in higher education. Students are often being banked in lecture. The students receive information like deposits into the brain. The brain is a bank of information. The students are not using that information to formulate knowledge. Therefore, the students are being told their value and their abilities in banking education instead of discovering themselves. The regurgitation technique of United States education makes for an efficient escalation of students proceeding through an education that does not seek to greatly develop the individual human identity. In fact, educational communities have often been reduced to cultural centers focused on behavior control of students. If we control the minds of the students and aim to control their belief in their abilities by what we do and do not convey, they students will become what we wish for them. What we say in verbal and nonverbal communication is eternally entered in their brains. Everything matters, because our subconscious can collect everything. The students studying Pedagogy of the Oppressed in the V.I.P. Scholars Program became more prepared to understand the cultural training of behavior and value in their K-12 experience. Additionally, they understood the opportunity available to them in higher education, but also the challenges of being a consumer in college.

I learned from Paulo Freire that it is important to work with education on all levels, be politically active, and understand that education is a huge component of society. Additionally, education is more kind-hearted than many corporate industries and is still part of a capitalist enterprise. Therefore, it too must be analyzed and propelled into prosperity for the global community's benefit.

Paulo Freire wrote Pedagogy of the Oppressed criticizing Brazilian education as a microcosm for colonized nations who have earned their independence from European dominance. Secondly, it speaks to education as an industry of cultural acquiesces and group think. It serves as corporate conformity for the directed advancement of the minds. School does not teach us all we need to know, but it does instruct us for what we should appreciate based on the information the state finds valuable. School communicates that what society says matters. All lives matter, yet history shows school play an integral part in the devaluing of many people within our country. Thus, we are taught all lives do not include all people. African Americans are mentioned four times in USA history. First as slaves. Second is Crispus Attucks. Third with Martin Luther King, Jr. Lastly, Barack Obama. If American education is the standard of what is most important to learn, African Americans only have value 4 times in 400 years. We all know that is not true. The African American population fought in every war, built billion dollar businesses, and has created more musical genres than any other nation group in the United States. Therefore, Black Lives matter. What we learn in school is what society says matters. And who matters. And when they matter. And why they matter. Anyone omitted from history, in an educational context, does not matter. School was never meant to teach us everything. We must control education with introspection and autodidactic practices. When entering professional spaces, critically think about the value others experience in history and everyday society. The best way to become a great professional is to understand the various experiences people have in school and society. Treat people equally and listen to their experience in life. Most people do not do that. Most people do not listen. Most people do not read history beyond the classroom. Understand how others feel invisible or forgotten in USA history and you will become a great professional because you will know more about the people you work with and have a greater ability to treat them appropriately. Every business, every industry, every professional space is a person-to-person dominated environment. You will be more successful because you understand people.

    Education is a universal avenue to understanding the universe. Universities are institutions that study the universe. We have different majors because of the various perspectives people have on analyzing the universe. Humans have a mental, physical, and spiritual unification that serves as a microcosm of the entire universe. Our pupils look like black holes. Our eye colors look like nebulas. Our body, when our limbs are stretched out, has five points like a child's drawing of a star. Our skin's prints have similar patterns to those we see on leaves. Our brain waves' electrical currents move throughout the mind in similar fashion to lightning moving across clouds. The reason people continuously demand for you to look within yourself to find your place in the external world stems from the notion of as above, so below. Whatever we find above us in the universe, we replicate in the human body.

    Therefore, the professions we often hope to find in the world live as a passion hidden inside of us. As we continue to find ourselves, we must dedicate ourselves to working in professions that build upon on internal passions. We must know that the strengths and weaknesses we see in others also live in us. At our occupation, we spend 10 to 14 hours of our day working for the organization. We must work during the day with one of our passions. The people we work with must share our passions and pride. Consider the people we spend our time with in the profession because we are going to spend more time with them than our own families and friends. Their vibrational waves will impact your vibrations and your mindset. The mindset your coworkers will verbally express through their body language will affect you for body language is 93% of all communication. This concept rings true within families, friends, and organizations. Who you spend time with will make you who you are.

In fact, the word corporation has a root word "corp." Corp is an English descendant of the Latin term corpus, meaning body. A corporation symbolizes the formation of a body. The body, comprised of collected individuals, usually gathers under one mindset, just as the various limbs and parts of our body physically live under one mind. A corporation establishes for the employees, consumers, and leaders to all come together under one mindset. Schools are no different. We see the existence of standards, group teacher trainings, qualifying examinations, etc. For the university, there is no unifying examination. In fact, the standards vary for every college on what the requirements are to teach. For the greater majority, a doctorate of philosophy (PhD) is needed to teach. That usually guarantees the ability of someone being able to conduct research and communicate the power of an organized data analysis, written by them or conducted by another, to an audience in an academic manner. Nonetheless, we know from life that the smartest person in the room is not always the best person for a job. What school does not teach you, you must teach yourself.

When students begin looking for a profession, many of them have built up skills that are valuable in academia but not in the traditional corporate world. In fact, they have built skills not valuable to a professor or staff person on a collegiate campus. I am completely unaware of any profession that requires you to take a test every week in a similar way to high school or college. Your profession and life will tests you everyday. You must produce results in order to stay relevant at work. The demand to perform at a high level is required to provide for your family and achieve your dreams. Life is not a paper test. Knowing something and proving you can do it are two different things. Innovation is praised but execution is worshipped in the real world. Employers complain that college does not prepare people to be effective in their professions is accurate. It is not designed to. Few institutions are. The only reasonable skill to expect from someone who only attends school and does not engage in co-curricular or extracurricular activities is for them to have the ability to learn, read, and take paper tests. School requires proof of understanding or regurgitation. School rarely tests the ability to think creatively, be innovative, lead, or problem solve. The current market of occupations continually asks for work experience in order to acquire entry-level employment. Employers hire proven problem solvers. Employers seek the work experience to make sure someone can immediately contribute to the industry and the position. Employers should value a student's co-curricular and extracurricular activities as experience. Every student should list those activities as a professional benefit on their resume. Thus, students can begin to increase their professional marketability.

 Every corporation does its best to mimic the human body on a grand scale. It is important you see yourself as a business. The corporations are mimicking you and your abilities within a specific industry, product, or service. Do not forget: every man-made creation stems from another person's imagination. If you can believe it, you can achieve it. Therefore, when you take a job, a contract of exchange is decided. Your imagination, passion, talents, and skills will now be serving the mindset of another in order to accomplish the unified vibrational energy wave of the creator(s) of the company. Your abilities could serve to establish a business on your behalf. Too. They are not mutually exclusive. The skills you are hired for at a company you can contract out as a private consultant on your on behalf. Henceforth, I encourage you to become the

Chief Executive Officer (CEO) of your life while you become the highly qualified employee of another CEO.

You can learn from others. With an infinite source of knowledge beyond the eyes of every person, those professionals who thrive in an industry you wish to develop in can propel your success. Not only as a resource of information, but as a person who can advocate for your ability to utilize skills and knowledge appropriately. When meeting a professional, impress the individual. Every moment matters, so be mindful of your interactions in your life. Decide what to do with your body language, for it is 93% of all communication. The handshake is incredibly important. The firmness of a handshake speaks volumes. The power of a handshake also speaks volumes. Regardless, what the professional is looking for matters the most in an interview. By conducting research, one can find out what they need to convey to the employer in order to present their best self, based on what the employer is looking for. In regard to handshakes, a firm handshake has the two crevices between the thumb and index finger meeting. The firm handshake grips the other hand so as to not take control but establish a positive and slightly powerful presence. The firm handshake does not hurt, but it is far from loose. A loose handshake communicates weakness to another person. It conveys that the person does not take the engagement seriously and the meeting of the minds is a simple formality.

    The power of the handshake must also be decided on. If the handshake allows one person to turn the other person's hands beyond the 180-degree angle, the person with their hand on top now has self-proclaimed dominance over the other. In opposition, the underhand may feel intimidated or disrespected by the dominant hand.

A mentor serves as a great resource

The Ideal Handshake

    The feeling of oppression will encourage one to shy away or stand their ground from the dominant hand. My suggestion for the best handshake is to meet, crevice to crevice, in the middle of the index and thumb fingers. Next is to remain at a 180-degree angle and establishing eye contact. With eyes being the gateway to the soul, it is important we recognize each component of the tripartite being. Looking someone in the eye creates equality of value. It tells someone, "I am equal to you. I am strong. I am here. I am present. Acknowledge my God given life." Looking someone in the eye acknowledges soul. Shaking the hand appropriately acknowledges the body. Saying hello acknowledges the mind. Although western corporate culture is a secular environment, the lack of acknowledgement of the soul does not erase the soul's presence.

Luckily, the soul responds to our energy, not our words. Our soul is our feelings. The soul lives between the mental and physical expression of our emotions. The soul thrives in between the mental recognition of happiness and the physical expression of it. Therefore, we have to acknowledge the soul by having positive energy in our handshakes. The positive energy permeates from us when we use it to maximize our presence and presentation.

The traditional corporate businesses (Banking institutions and government) prefer a well-groomed individual who resembles the wealthy white Protestant property-owning heterosexual man. In 2015, we see more people being accepted into the "professional" environment and labeled as diverse. Secondly, the era of the entrepreneur and small business owner is currently growing at a fascinating rate. With more people who modernly accept people carrying themselves in multiple fashions, whether born diverse or not, the acceptance rate of performance and merit has outshone the corporate branding that has dominated employment opportunities. When seeking professional development as a higher education consumer (student), one should research the culture of a company's perspective on attire, religion(s), sexuality, ethnicities, class, and gender makeup to understand the company's actions holistically. Every company is legally required to state it is an equal opportunity employer, but the statistical actions and remarks of current employees will speak to the experience of employment far better than a distant news source's article.

When entering employment at the company, we want the money. Monetary capital serves as a good encouragement to work. The most important capital to acquire is human capital. Gaining the knowledge, skills, and abilities to advance serves one for a very long time, if not a lifetime. Monetary capital came about as a trade result, thanks to a human's imagination. Yep, someone just made money up to simplify trading their stuff. We often spend money to secure other actualizations of another human being's imagination. We spend money to buy stuff someone else made up in their head. Outside of earth itself, we are usually using money to buy something someone made up. Funny, ain't it? **What will your imagination create for the world to value? What can you create that people will buy?**

Money is a means to an end. Monetary capital is infinite. It is just our belief in numbers on a screen. Numbers never end so money will never end. What can be lost or spent can also be accumulated, money wise. Therefore, it often does not serve as the motivator in producing our imagination's best creations over the long run. The use of it to experience or acquire creates a passion. The passion you have to acquire knowledge or a skill greatly benefits your human capital. Critically analyze why the professional experience you aim for can truly make you more valuable. A job is free school. A job will pay you to learn how to add value to the company. Not only, will it boost your resume, but you will learn to problem solve and build skills. Learn and profit at the same time. Engage in employment for self-development. A genuine passion for growth and development of human capital is a great way to grow personally. Once you create an avenue of professional development, be persistent to achieve with consistent action. Most importantly, be passionate.

Once professional development occurs within the professional space, a mentor serves as the greatest resource. A mentor can provide constructive criticism to help you go to the next level. Your mentor(s) should know the industry best, give personal appeal, be candid, and have your best interest at heart. Mentorship is major key. I will speak more to the development of mentorship later in this book. I dedicated an entire chapter to it because mentorship has been my greatest service.

When working a summer internship, co-operational learning experience, or your first professional job, the most important concept of time allocation and management to conceive is the Covenant Hand. Look at your hand. Pick a hand. Any hand will do. The left or right hand will be perfect. Stare at it for thirty seconds. What do you see? Lines and designs of the hands that mark your unique handprint may be all you recognize. Your unique ability to make a handprint no one else can replicate serves as an extension of your *soul print* or *energy mark*. Your soul print is how you make people feel. It is the mark you leave on their minds and soul. When someone misses you, they are longing for your soul print more than anything. Therefore, it is incredibly important to understand yourself. Understand your presence in others. Make others smile. Make others feel inspired. Make others feel as if they want to have you around because your energy leaves a positive soul print. Employers have interviews in order to get a feel for who you are. The employers want to see if your energy and mindset matches theirs. They want to see if you vibe with them. To make sure your soul print permeates a genuine aurora, you have to discover yourself.

Act Now!

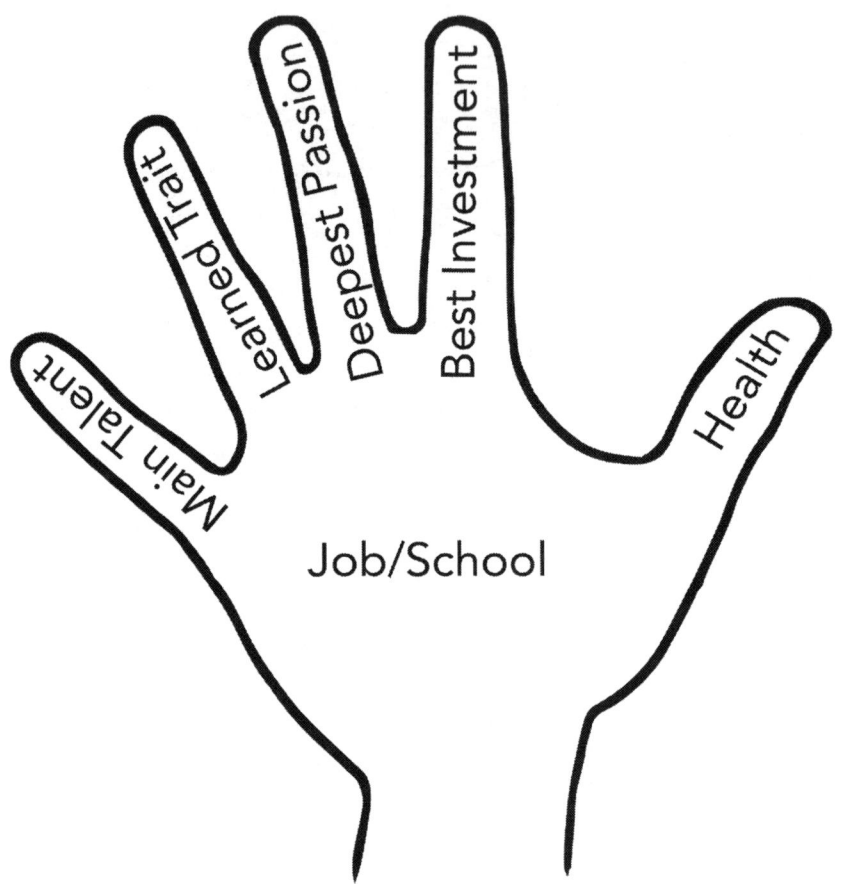

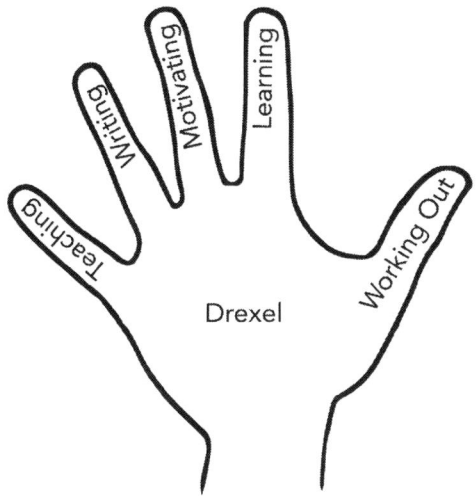

Know your passions, talents, skills, and knowledge (PTSK). When the PTSK combines with a genuine burning desire, the world will appreciate you with great esteem. If you use your PTSK within the professional world, you will be using the best of you. Your job should only be the palm of your hand. It will be what you spend most of your time doing. It alone cannot grasp fully the person who you are becoming. Everyday you are becoming. Therefore, we must understand that the palm of our hand, the largest component, essential in many ways, is only powerful in combination with the fingers. Thus, our life, our ambitions in particular, when compared to our hand, have to be organized in a similar importance. The main job is the palm. For students, school, classes, and your part- and/or full-time job would enter the palm. The palm makes you unique and is usually what most people know you for. The school or job we attend is the answer most people desire to know when they ask you, "What do you do? What school do you go to?"

My palm is Drexel University. Inside my palm rests many lines that define its uniqueness. The unique qualities of my Drexel University experience are the various capacities I facilitate within educational administration. I create programmatic events, complete administrative duties, organize Alumni engagements, lead the graduation review committee for the Honors Program, develop retention pedagogy and praxis, mentor geniuses, retain students on academic probation, serve as a marketing and brand ambassador to parents and interested/incoming students, construct specific entrepreneurial curriculums, co-manage national service trips, foster positive engagements within residential life, and co-chair an advising diversity committee. I am a full-time educator, and my palm is complete with a wide understanding of the entire list of services I am prepared to offer every day to advance the mission of Drexel University. My time, my day, my palm.

After establishing the palm, the hand grows a thumb. The thumb is important because it is what comes most naturally to us. It is opposable and allows us to gain a great grip on life. The thumbprint of our lives is what comes most naturally to us. The thumb in evolutionary history serves as the finger that allows us to build tools. The thumbprint in your life permits you to build a tool in your life. The thumb tool is a tangible talent you can harvest. Most likely, it will be the God-given talent most people will see in you or the image of yourself you project the most. The most natural tool I have is teaching. I can teach anyone. I have a great talent to speak well, conveying my thoughts in a creative and understandable manner. I am a motivational speaker for colleges across the nation and often travel to tell my life story and provide tangible steps as to how others can succeed in their life. The thumb is significantly smaller than my palm but it sticks out, even from the other fingers, and stands as a unique symbol of who I am. At Drexel

University and throughout the world, I am referred to as Professor Miles. The students began calling me Professor Miles in and outside of the class once I started teaching my own classes at the age of 24 in the fall of 2013. I teach Honors Seminars focusing on the overlapping concepts of education, culture, and society in order to teach young adults how to maximize their opportunities in life, like college and building a career.

    My entire life, I have taught friends how to maximize their opportunities. All my life I have gone to school and it was all I knew for a long time. I used to only know the student perspective, but with the knowledge I gained from attending the University of Pennsylvania to earn my graduate degree in higher education and my palm full of experience, I know I can help students across the world excel in the industry of higher education. I was not the smartest person in school. I was always the hardest working student. In graduate school, my professor told me, my test scores were not impressive, my writing was not up to par, and my reading comprehension was not on the same level as my classmates. I was encouraged to rethink my attendance at Penn. Basically, "drop out Miles". I refused. I bought coffee for smarter students to teach me how to write and read better. I soon learned, I needed help to succeed. It made sense. I had tutors at Crenshaw High because I did not catch on to concepts as fast as the other kids in the Gifted Magnet. I had tutors at UCLA because I could not achieve to the same academic level as my peers. I repeated some classes three times. I never had anyone tell me to think drop out. It was the fuel to my fire. My desire to become a university professor was ignited in order to show my haters that I could achieve my dream. The pain to gain my dream and graduate pushed me further than positive interactions. I began wearing suits to class and sit in the front row. I drank endless amounts of coffee and studied all night just to pull off B's but it worked. My drive allowed me to become the youngest professor at Drexel while I was teaching there.

To become a great professional, students must become greater learners, listeners, and people. My openness to learn and listen to my students allows me the opportunity to advance my educational understanding. I become a better person each day because of it. You have an infinite source of knowledge behind your eyes. The black holes, pupils, living in their eye sockets, gravitate to the acquisition of information. I need this knowledge in order to be the greatest educator for my students. When we get to class, Professor Miles shows up with research, well-read knowledge, and personal stories of educational challenges and triumphs. My thumbprint makes me unique. My thumbprint capitalizes on the human capital I have acquired from my experiences on campuses throughout the United States. I speak my truth. #Thumbprint

My index finger points out a learned trait. My natural ability is teaching, but my best learned trait is writing. The index finger serves as the most useful skill I have developed. The difference between a talent and a skill is the work ethic. The talent is a God-given ability. It is a raw force of nature. The skill has to be developed and learned. I can speak well naturally as a talent and I developed it into teaching because I am the son of a math teacher. In order to take my teaching skills to the next level, I had to analyze the best traits of the best professors. In the world of academia, no one cares if you are a great teacher. The ability to learn and listen from others and communicate that knowledge in a classroom only serves as a valuable ability in primary and secondary school. In higher education, the value of a professor lives in literature. I attended a conference and witnessed one of the most decorated professors speak in a monotone voice that put me to sleep. As a faculty member, he received accolades from everyone for the writing he produced on his research but not his teaching skills. It proved his ability to convey his concepts on knowledge. Therefore, I had to develop my writing skills. In graduate school, I wrote my first paper for this professor, and received an 8 out of 40. The percentage of this score stands at 20%. Every school in the world claims this is an F grade. Therefore I needed to develop this learned trait of writing.

I was 22 years old in a graduate school with an average student age of 28. I was six years younger than the average student. I had no full time work experience, unlike many of the people enrolled. They were way more experienced than I was as professionals and students. The professor criticizing my writing was very busy so he offered no constructive criticism. He just told me to get better. In fact, he encouraged me to reconsider my enrollment in graduate school if I could not improve. I had another professor who also graded my first paper for her class. She was known for establishing her own review process of major universities' and states' abilities to educate college students. As a pioneer, I valued her classes more than I valued those of any other professor. I went to her office hours and asked her, "How do I write for graduate school?" The best advice she gave me was to say exactly what I meant. Do not make sentences longer than I need to. Lastly, don't summarize, but use the information I read to tell my own story. From that point forward, writing became a skill, my index finger.

Next to the index finger rests the middle finger. The middle finger, in the comparison of life to the hand, allows us to grab a great deal of abilities in combination with the thumb, index, and palm. The middle finger serves as our soulful attraction. It resonates in the manifestation of our best or deepest passion. The middle finger becomes a centerpiece of our Covenant Hand. For example, my deepest passion is motivating others to succeed. I love the ability to inspire people to find and keep their best self. In August of 2015, I began to produce and star in a weekly YouTube webisode titled, "Word Up Wednesday by Professor Miles" (https://www.youtube.com/channel/UCRu05vUen7jRr06NkyrxeFg). It is my weekly motivational for self-education that I created to empower you to excel in college and your career. The centerpiece of my efforts in the palm, index, and thumb all motivate others to achieve when I use them collectively.

    The hand continues to grab hold onto your life with the ring finger. It is most known for marriage, and I encourage you to marry the best person for you. People in monogamous relationships can focus better. In regards to the individual, the ring finger is designed for your best investment. The best investment you can make in yourself represents a bond of excellence and persistence. For me, learning is the greatest investment made and continues to benefit my growth. Learning only improves my knowledge and understanding. Everything I learn informs my daily decisions. In fact, we cannot stop learning. It never ceases. Learning happens all day. The power to choose what I want to learn is a great responsibility. The mind never stops working, so you learn from every experience. The subconscious mind does not know the difference between information collected from reading, experiencing, watching, or listening. While watching television, our mind is being programmed. Television shows, no matter the length, are referred to as television programs. It is programming your mind.

    ==We must think of our mind as the greatest computer on earth. We must program it ourselves with the information we wish to have.== Many of us are incredibly intelligent at knowing things that do not advance our lives. Your mind will learn from whatever you interact with. I create positive and intellectual engagements for myself to maximize great thoughts. That requires learning from my role models, elders, children, students, staff, faculty, entrepreneurs, doctors, and books. I learn from reflecting on my experiences with the latter information forces. After reflecting, I put that information into action. Books are the best form of information, but they do not take away from the power of conversation. Discussion will spark the human psyche to develop new concepts and perspectives of information. Acquiring information is not the best part of learning, but it is the foundational step that cannot be overlooked.

When we apply information to our lives, it becomes knowledge. We understand how the purpose of information within the physical world gives us the know-how of its applicability. The world is about mental acquisition for physical application (actualization). Information is just the facts. Knowledge is the use of those facts. Passing tests in school proves your ability to remember those facts. Using information to understand and impact the world is what we need you to do most. No one sees the world the way you do. No one can impact the world the way you can. Before you can change the world, you have to change yourself. Learn internally in order to actualize externally.

The pinky is your health. The pinky is your physical well-being. The pinky is there, sometimes small but very useful. The pinky is health, for it is often the last thing we think about in college. I attended UCLA. It is always spring or fall at UCLA. We had to be beach-ready all year long. Health became a huge component of my life. I work out every day. Some days, I work out harder than others. Every day I discipline myself to commit to a better and healthier me. The better my health is, the more at peace my mind is. Your mind is stronger when you are healthy. Healthy living is putting the best foods, energy, and liquids into your body. As a tripartite being, you must never forget to take care of the temple where your greatness lives.

Once you have a great grasp on your world with your five fingers and a palm, you can mold that hand into anything you wish. You can make a fist or a hand sign. The hand is the greatest collection of individual fingers. It is amazing what togetherness can achieve. The hand is unique, yet simultaneously an easy component to be forgotten. The hand represents actualization. Once you have mastered the fingers of your life, the only action left is action itself. The hand represents the future product of our abilities. It is our result of the unification of passion, talent, skill, trade, and benefit.

I teamed up with the Path to Greatness organization to create a college preparatory course designed to help underserved and middle-class families from Philadelphia with the intangibles of college success before they enroll in one. I take what I learned in the many realms of my career at Drexel University, University of Pennsylvania, and UCLA to create my own course-teaching students to manifest their dreams with their own hands. **Take the time to draw your hand. Tell me what you see! How can you get a grip on your life?**

Activity:
Draw your hand and determine for yourself, how you handle life.
(Blank hand for reader to fill in)

The hand represents actualization.

127

07
NETWORKING

Make Friends. Appreciate Mentors.

The key to networking is to make friends. Friends will go ten times further for you than your associates will, especially when it comes to accomplishing your goals. Never forget, your dream is yours and no one else's. Your friends don't owe you anything. You owe yourself everything. They should help you within reason of their abilities just for being your friend. An associate or acquaintance is defined as a person who enjoys your company but does not need you nor invest in you directly. Oftentimes, you all have overlapping commitments. Having people you all interact with in common, attending the same school, or engaging in a similar activity over a period of time makes up your acquaintances. We can assert from these engagements that an acquaintance has been established through a medium where you all can associate with each other and unite over a common interest. A friend commits to you. They invest in your benefit. The friend does not need any reason to interact except for your presence. From this support, they understand who you are and look for ways to assist in your manifestations. The friend has much more reliability because they remain beyond the medium of interest. They are interested in you and your well-being. In networking, we often treat people like business requirements. This approach, although direct, does not have genuine appeal. It often results in gaining someone's contact information but does not persist. The initial emails may go back and forth between acquaintances but, eventually, the contacting will cease. Someone will not reply and allow the conversation to die for it holds no true value. A friend will reply because they care for your feelings and your message holds value for them. A friendship is a two-way street, so it is incredibly important for you to befriend them as well. The genuine appeal and interest in someone will come through when you network. Therefore, your email shows you have done your research to have an engaging conversation.

Small talk should be a big part of the conversation; do not drag on about little things. The weather is on your smartphone application; so don't talk about it forever. The popular media is only interesting for a couple of days, so don't talk about it. Talk about the topic of the event. Meaningless jargon does not impress even though it occupies time. It reinforces mediocrity. People are addicted to learning. No one can stop learning. It is best to embrace our mental capabilities in networking. Discuss the industry and a recent advancement. Discuss personal exhibitions of developing in the industry or the last book we read. One's genuine interests are important.

Small talk is necessary. You must be able to engage people of all intellectual levels. It is incredibly necessary for people to feel comfortable. Be able to talk about the weather, sports, and current events. From there you can be sure to develop into a deeper conversation. The vibe you have and create with others matters most in developing your network. Body language is more important that your verbal statements.

We must become the friend we wish to have in order to establish a vibrational energy wave that leaves a wonderful and insightful soul print on our new friends. People will aim to emulate your friendship example. It is easier to find what you are passionate about and speak to people who live within that sphere so your connections are genuine. Be authentic and people who reflect who you are will be attracted to you. You attract who you are. Not what you want to be. When first entering a new industry this may be difficult for the undedicated. For those who value the benefits of this industry, they will have read books and articles, reviewed interviews from the leaders, and develop countless thoughts to discuss with others. As most of us are usually the go-getters in the network development, persistence is key. Contacting someone every day may be a bit much, but once a week is reasonable for non-responses that have not been clearly outlined as undesirable communication. Continue to correspond with these individuals. If they have secretaries or employees they lead, be just as courteous to those people as you would be to the friend you are networking with. That energy of respect yields unexpected benefits and positively contributes to your reputation. Our interactions with all people contribute to the perspective people have of us. The SOULPRINT we establish in the universe serves as an example of the energy we wish to receive. Our SOULPRINT attracts others to us who value our energy.

In order to achieve our desired goal of having a solid network, we must understand the value of our conversation. In addition, the person who outreaches to establish a friendship becomes the leader in the relationship. When communicating the desire to acquire someone else's time and energy, the person who reaches out must establish the time, location, and purpose of the conversation. This communicates to the recipient a clear intention of the engagements. Thus, it becomes the recipient's decision to agree, disagree, or not reply. All of these situations can be stressful. Every person breathes and uses the bathroom the same way. He or she is human, just like you. As your anxiety increases, remember that this person you are networking with is not the key to your success. You are. Your success is inevitable.

In order to acquire my first source of employment after graduation from the University of Pennsylvania, I needed to expand my network. In order to obtain a job, I did not believe the typical job application online process would work in my favor. I applied to 55 jobs during the months of May, June, and July in order to offer my services in exchange for a salary. I emailed directors, deans, and leaders across higher education institutions and non-profit organizations. After three months without responses or interview requests, I decided to take action. Sitting in my room on 40th and Market Street in University City, Philadelphia, I knew I had two options. Option one: go home to California and listen to my long-winded parents give me countless tips on how to get a job and continue to pester me on my need to gain employment. Option two: earn a job in Philadelphia, NYC, or Washington D.C. by using a 1970's search approach. In the pre-Internet era, collections of papers were put together. These old grey pieces of paper were placed together with important information of the day. Thus the collection of papers was titled newspapers. People would search through the newspaper to look at job listings to see about employment opportunities. Luckily, we have the Internet, and I performed the same search through sites such as higheredjobs.com and the job listing of specific institutions I respected. People would call the number listed on the job listing to inquire about the possibility. I began to call offices and speak with people. Completely unsure what to say, I used the Internet to Google and research the individuals before I called them.

When I did not sign in to LinkedIn, I could Google someone's name and see their profile without them knowing. Additionally, I could read articles and informative sites via my search engine results to learn about the personality and character of the individual I intended to speak with. It began my preparation for job interviews well because I was gaining insight most people would not know. Most people did not call. I began calling the employers to speak with them about their experience and asked questions about the company culture. Only two questions of the five I asked would be generally applicable to the organization, institution, or university.

As a result, their personal appeal and engagement increased because I was fascinated about the person more so than the company as a whole. People are best equipped to speak about themselves more than anything else. Self-reflection is rare in the United States, and most people wait for others to inquire about their day. In fact, many people complain often in order to increase inquiry. It conveys a poor relationship with the self. Through providing an avenue of reflection and self-appreciation, the person on the other end of the phone conversation would gain a more positive energy because I asked the right questions. For example, "What do you accomplish in a day?" Always respond positively with a notion about being excited to do similar tasks and how you have experience doing them.

Unfortunately, none of my phone inquiries led to employment. After a week, I decided to travel further back in time to the career searching strategy of the 1950's. Men dressed in a full suit printed their resume, practiced introductions, performed elevator pitches, and visited the offices of potential employers unannounced. I had an old torn-up fraternity canvas material briefcase holding twenty copies of my resume. I put on a blue pinstripe suit I have been wearing since I was 15 years old. It was small but, over the years, with the recession of the baggy clothes era and the emergence of the slim fitted clothes, the suit remained fashionably relevant. Philadelphia served as hipster central, so old-fashioned attire combined with a modern flare worked perfectly. God is good. The pinstripes screamed old-school Scarface, so I lightened it up with a white button-down shirt and a red tie to convey my leadership. Blue represented the people. The suit was navy blue with white pinstripes, so I looked like a dedicated corporate Yankee traveling around Philadelphia speaking with educational leaders about to the possibility of work.

After a week of failed attempts, I discovered a program coordinator position open at Drexel University in the Honors Program. Job 62. I wanted to give up at this point, but the job description actually fit everything I wanted to do. I worked in higher education access for five years prior to the summer of 2012; I thought it was time to make sure I could not only get my students *into* college, but also *through* college. I had friends and former students of mine live on my couch during my time at UCLA. I had no tricks to education except my welcoming personality and a dedication to understanding people's stories. When students' real-life problems drove them toward drug abuse, alcoholism, poverty, homelessness, depression, and more, I was there to help their personal and human development. When the challenges extended beyond the classroom, co-curricular, or extracurricular engagements, I often found myself helping others achieve triumphs I had recently learned to overcome.

    After four years of being a mentor in V.I.P. Scholars at UCLA, I became the Mentor Coordinator for the Christian Association at Penn; I learned to assist students as they faced these tribulations time and time again. In addition to being a shoulder to lean on, overcoming these barriers years earlier in undergraduate school with my friends allowed me to sympathize with the current undergraduates from Penn serving as mentors in the Dana How Scholars program. My retention skills served social purposes and safe spaces for my friends dropping out and needing consultation. At Penn, I created the space formally for the Dana How mentors. The Honors Program at Drexel attracted me to serve students from international and domestic spaces. It required me to make programming similar to the curriculum I developed for the Dana How Scholars Mentoring Program that I had coordinated from within the Christian Association. The overlap and room for growth existed. Once I began traveling in person to potential places of employment, I had to gain more depth of information and knowledge about the organization. Therefore, I could not apply to 55 jobs and visit 55 offices. I had to be more selective towards potential places of employment in order to concentrate my energy. Before I visited Drexel, I took a full day to research, memorize, and organize notes on the program. I had to know more information than the people who worked in the Honors Program. I wanted to show them with my casual conversation that I appreciated their work.

      When I arrived on that hot July day, the director spotted me and told me to enter his office. I thanked the administrative assistant for greeting me nicely and used his name every time I talked to him. Next, I had a chance to talk to the leader. He told me he created the position and wrote out the program coordinator description. I was already sweating from the heat, but now the director had turned up the heat. We discussed our school experiences. The director and I had a lot in common, and that worked to my favor. We were fraternity brothers and graduates of the same master's program. For twenty of the thirty minutes, we discussed those experiences as well as some interesting educational concepts. For the last ten minutes, we specifically spoke about the position. He informed me the position application was closing soon and that my in-person rhetoric should be reflected in my cover letter. Additionally, he stated the importance of speaking the Drexel language as it was different than Penn's. Penn taught me many pedagogical concepts regarding higher education, but there is no class on job applications, interviews, and engagements. UCLA may have had a class like that, but finding anything at UCLA is like finding a needle in a haystack.

      The ability to excel in this process across the nation usually comes from cultural capital attainment and a powerful network. With a busy schedule for him to maintain, he dismissed me. I thanked the director and also thanked the administrative assistant as well. I left confident, informed, and prepared. I spent the rest of the day perfecting my resume, cover letter, and application. I had a trusted friend of mine review my resume and cover letter. That night, I submitted my application materials. The next morning, I sent an email to the director to thank him for the conversation. Nonetheless, being creative and unorthodox in my employment approach allowed me to stand out as a candidate. My early meeting with the director of the Honors Program served as a free interview for him to know who I am. When my application was read, I am sure he could see my face and hear my voice in the tone of the cover letter. That in and of itself propelled me to the forefront of the application process. There is no better source than the creator. I talked to the man who designed the position I applied for and curtailed myself to be marketed as the perfect candidate for the job. I know my in-person interactions spoke volumes beyond my written representation. I used my best talents and skills to my advantage in order to impress the leadership and improve my written materials.

On September 4, 2012, I entered professional training at Drexel University and began my educational career on a full-time basis. The networking structure of basic communication did not work in my case. Emails and phone calls prepared me to have a strong in-person conversation.

Four years later, I can say I am ecstatic to be at Drexel, and have grown a lot as both a man and an educator. The potential for me to make an impact and assist student retention has been met and exceeded. It took one year after starting to begin teaching college courses, and 18 months to chair a university-wide committee affecting the academic advisors guiding 13,000 undergraduate students. I once heard of a limit, but they are always behind me, so the strength of its sound is faint. I broke through limits like lightning from an angry night sky.

My network cannot be left behind. It is a representation of who I am. It holds the power to propel me forward into my dreams. My network can increase my net worth and my self-worth if constructed properly. We cannot pick the family we are born into. We have the power to pick our friends. Pick friends as if you were given the chance to decide your family. One day you will. Marriage and conception stem from a love of phenomenal decision-making skills to carefully create your network. The network must be catered to like a very nice garden of flowers.

A friendship is a two way street.

Flowers Bloom
By Miles Goodloe

Flowers bloom and I be

Proof of the seed before me
I stem from the ground beneath me

The soil serves as foundation for me
So I thrive like my roots did before me

Pollen from bee's wings save me
So I spread my seed in the wind bee

The petals of my network protect me
Each one adding to my beauty

Blood stained with the river of life, see
I am not first of the concrete rose in this city

Ancestors paved the road before me
Every year but we bloom just to be

A symbol that you cannot destroy me
Because the cycle of love, loves me

Flowers bloom and I be...

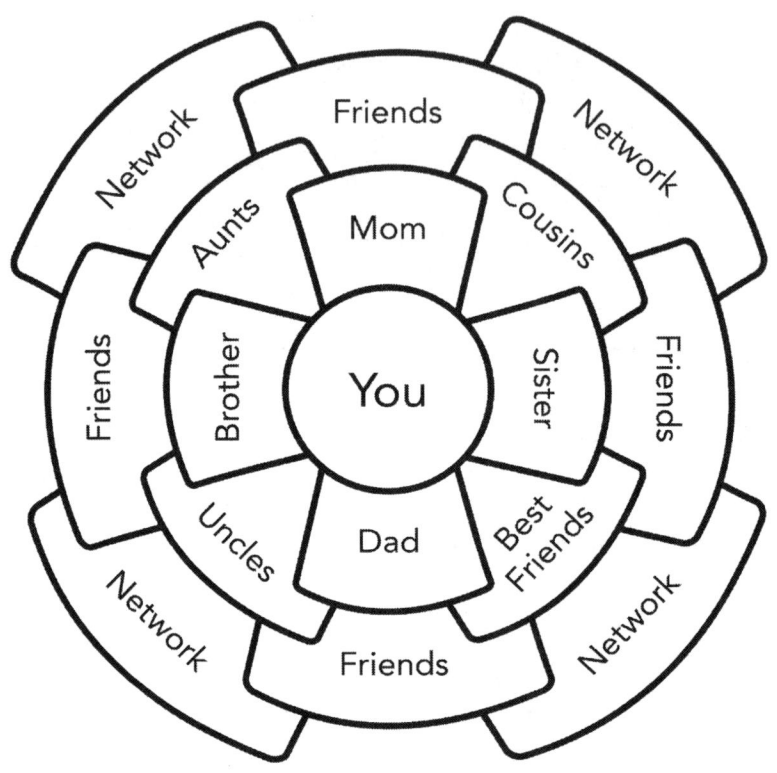

The Network Flower

In building the garden for your flower, it is important to understand each petal in your network. Each friend and professional contact you have is a petal. At the same time, each petal that is yours is its own bud. Therefore, you are a petal to other buds while simultaneously being your own bud. Thus we must be our best person at all times. Not only will it push us past the self-imposed glass ceiling of limitations from stagnation, it will also allow you to assist other people to blossom. As you pollenate the world, the garden of network flowers begins to grow. The greater you are, the more tremendous you become. Everyone has a part to play. Society is the water to our roots, soil, and life. The more tainted our society, the greater strength we need to blossom. We cannot pick our circumstances in regards to where we first live and to whom we are born. We pick how we respond to life's circumstances. We have to make the best ourselves. Then, and only then, can we be strong enough to emerge victorious internally and externally.

We persist and become greater by using our crown chakra. I've heard and read many interpretations of the crown chakra. Debate on the actual use and purpose is very long, but there is some general consensus. After much effort to build understanding, I decided the crown chakra is the agreement between mind and soul to move the body into excellence. It's the perfect peace of mind. Thus, actualization of the crown chakra's beliefs represents our best foot forward. It makes our pollen a positive impact on the world. We will spread our ideas and energy just by thinking and breathing. Being our best self allows for us to truly attract who we are and wish to be. In addition, we can become better. When we give our best, we push the limits of our best a bit higher each day. Soon, our best reaches new heights of achievement. Our best knows no limits. Chase infinite growth! You must blossom, so show your best self and the whole world will follow. Those who respect and honor your best will be your brightest and healthiest petals. They will shine bright as their own buds next to you because you have managed to unite your mind and soul. Your vibrational energy wave will bring you the people you need to better than yourself.

Self-understanding creates a clearer understanding for others. The further we constructively dive into our minds, bodies, and souls, the better we can exhibit our true selves in the world. Understanding our true selves provides clarity in which people we choose to associate with. We allow ourselves comfort within our tripartite being, thus engaging in a cultural exchange. The exchange begins as a geographical experience. We enjoy the physical similarities and can discuss the physical differences between cultures on a domestic and international scale. It then turns into a physical exchange of body language and behavioral comparisons. In America, it is politically correct and popular in mainstream culture to smile and appear friendly. We have a strong fear of the unknown in the United States. We also do not value experiences that have no monetary cost. Consequently, we love to give our most sentimental possessions away and keep that which we have paid for. The physical is important, but we often confuse it with the material. Therefore we smile when we are afraid or intimidated in our culture. It is our favorite preservation move when we have an awkward moment by locking eyes with some stranger or friend. We also smile to express great joy and happiness. The French believe only the latter is worth smiling. They believe the prior reasons for smiling confuse an individual and are not genuine. The smile is precious and should be earned, not given away to strangers who know not the power or privilege of the teeth we share. In Paris, my smiles were not returned, but the cultural capital is invaluable. Not only did I learn this in France, I witnessed the love for wine and cheese while sitting under the Eiffel tower. The cultural exchange of networking continues as the flower petals blossom. Understand the different exchanges. The different level of cultural exchange extends into the mindset. The mindset of someone to achieve his or her dreams no matter what it takes is a great networking technique. People love to support the passionate and inspired. This person does not play the victim. This person is the victor. This person overcomes the odds even when the light at the end of the tunnel is faint. This person believes in themselves due to the unity they have within. The comfort we hold inside of us is projected into the world through our vibrational energy waves. This person lives inside of you. This person is different than you. You must care enough to dive inside your mind, body, and soul in order to understand. To understand yourself, read more books and actualize your imagination. Information changes the way we see the world. Knowledge changes the way we act in the world. Act soon and act often, young scholar!

You are a flower. Your petals are your networks. Your pollen is your impact on the world.

The Network Flower

08 RELATIONSHIPS

Love is an Ocean

I was watching the Green Lantern. The movie focused on the battle between fear and good faith. The good faith was colored green. The fear was represented by yellow. The fear persisted throughout the universe. The good faith republic leaders tried to harness the power of fear. They trusted one of the council leaders to lead the charge, but soon, fear consumed him, and he had to be defeated with good faith. Once again, fear managed to dominate a council leader's mindset and emerged as a threat to the good faith in the universe. It is important that we understand that fear exists and that it will always need to be combated with good faith.

==Fear is always there because life is hard.== We are always faced with a problem, just left a problem, or headed toward another problem. That's scary. The fear of change usually intimidates people a lot. Change is the only constant. Get used to life not being the same. Master change. If you can become more adaptable to problems in life, you can learn to be a master of life.

==The power of an idea is unstoppable.== Fear ideas stay in our minds and stand out much more because they are unnatural to our constant life of good faith. We expect life to be a joyous experience. Positives are normal, but the abnormality of fear and pain stand out as different. Therefore, the abnormal interaction with fear takes over our minds and permeates into our actions. From fear, humanity creates negativity. Unfortunately, the math of life states a negative can only be counteracted with another negative and then we have a positive. For example, when we fear the actions of someone, we attack. In expecting a negative interaction, we produce a negative interaction in order to create a short-term positive sense of security. We perpetuate the negativity in expectation of the fear and make it a focus. We are what we think. When we fear, we attack, we distance ourselves, and we grow to be negative. Only when we trust others and ourselves do we eliminate fear. FEAR is false evidence appearing real. Thus, we create fear in our minds. Simultaneously, we can create trust in our minds to combat fear. When we can trust someone to act in a certain manner, be it negative or positive constructions, we are more at ease. It is important to trust ourselves so we understand what trust is in others. Trust trumps fear to permit love to reign supreme. Love is represented by crimson, for crimson is the color of blood. The blood flows through us, translating information and carrying nutrients to make sure our body thrives. Love lives in you. The same body filled with crimson holds our brain, which needs our blood in order to operate. Love lives in your mind. The brain holds our thoughts and ideas, the strongest and most powerful possessions of anyone in humanity. The idea sets the tone of who we are to become, especially once we have molded that idea into our spirits. Your spirit creates a great vibration of energy others can feel, love, and desire.

    There is no spiritual experience more important than the romantic relationship. It occupies everyone's mind. It is a consuming road that holds many truths. Romantic relationships are like stars. The sun is very heavy, yet it is still a bright light. A star is a great ball of fire that burns but serves as our source of energy and life. We aim for glory in life and always imagine ourselves sharing it with our loved ones. We cannot pick our family until we pick our spouse. From there, we begin to unite our vibrational energy waves with another. We live as two whole beings uniting in romantic love. I characterize romance as the persistent stimulation of another human being in which we wish to establish a tripartite empire with. The empire will exist at its greatest moment in time as a result of united efforts. It will create a bloodline for all to witness as representations of our greatest selves. The empire built on romance sets the tone for the values of the family. The romantic relationship is the most important relationship because it takes our time, energy, and thoughts. It serves as the foundation of family. The purpose of romance is to know love's deepest treasure.

Love is an ocean. It is the water of our life and planetary salvation. Love has many depths, and for us to understand love's ocean, we must become amphibians, whales, and water-based creatures. As a killer whale in the ocean, I view myself as a massive mammal lover. I can dive to the bottom of the ocean and swim on the ocean floor. I protect misdirected lovers from the sharks swimming about love's ocean with the intent to restrict the depths of which we swim. As I engage fellow lovers in the ocean, I search for my mate, the one for whom I wish to swim forever, exploring the vast waters with an open mind and love filling the crimson tide of my passion. To educate ourselves on love, we take the biggest risk. It also can produce the biggest reward. Life is very similar. The greatest love to know holds similar values to the greatest achievements, for romantic love is a great achievement. It takes courage to dive to the bottom of love's ocean and not take a breath. The greatest moments in life take your breath away. It is because you must rid yourself of our old ways. You become anew to see the world in a different place once you let love consume your being. Every night, you lay our head down, not knowing if we will rise. Love requires us to enter the unknown. Falling in love is drowning in love's ocean, unaware if you will turn into a fish that can survive there. The risk is worth it, but caution is necessary. The ocean is vast and has many different creatures to swim with. The decision of whom we choose to swim with is yours. That part of love remains in your control. Unfortunately, we do not know the tides and rides we will experience as a result of the ocean's currents.

I suggest to students not to make an effort to fall in love while in school. You will not be the same person when you finish school if you challenge yourself. If you develop and look to advance your own life on a consistent basis, falling in love will be difficult to manage along the way. **You must first swim alone and fall in love with yourself. Secondly, love's fish for you must be able to ride the tides with you. It is the unity created to overcome the waves which allows love to flourish.** Nonetheless, each creature in love's ocean has a different rhythm to which they swim. Each creature does not overcome waves and tides in similar fashions. Thus we can dive into a romantic relationship and be in love with the wrong creature. Therefore, our journey and our experience in love can only be drowning. It is a sad experience of love's ocean. Everyone defines love differently. The personal account of love, dear to my heart, states love is protecting, providing, and supporting your lover to the best of your ability. Each person has a unique gift to bring to the world and a journey only he or she can embark upon. Thus we must support them in their moments of life and provide clarity and opportunity if we can, protecting him or her from unnecessary anguish and despair.

This love is not unique to romance, and can be extended into plutonic relationships. The friendships we hold must also be filled with love. The definition of love is still to support, provide, and protect. With plutonic friends, we have to dive into love's ocean with a different pair of goggles. You are not looking for a lover to build a two-person duo. You are looking for a small team of friends. The imperative nature of this understanding is crucial. Some friends come and go. You do not need to spread your friendship time beyond fifteen people. You can spread yourself too thin to have a positive impact with all of these people by engaging too many people. You want high quality friendships more than 100 friends. That speaks to having an impact on your friends and also the ability of your friends to have an impact on you.

In 2015, the Los Angeles Lakers wanted to draft LaMarcus Aldridge (LA). LA spoke with the Lakers and was disappointed because they pitched him the city and the prestige of the Lakers organization. He looked at the current team roster and asked, "How do we win?" The Lakers' answer did not matter. The roster spoke for itself. The greatest moment in the season prior to the summer negotiations came from Nick Young celebrating a missed shot. The new rookies in the NBA were seen mimicking his missed shot just months after the draft. Losing was the most recent memory. My band director, Mr. Carter, used to always say, "You're only as good as your last performance."

People want to win. Even the lazy people who do not put effort towards winning still want to win. In order to win, we have to protect our friends in need by being our best. To prove that, we must protect ourselves at all cost and let that serve as an example to others, indicating to them that we can also protect you the same way. In order to love our friends, we must provide them a safe space to be themselves. This is similar to a basketball team having practice. It is safe to mess up in practice. We can receive intense criticism and have combative issues in practice. In the game, we show up and show out as an unit. The time spent with friends in private creates the amazing bond people will notice when you all attend school events and classes together. At the same time, practice serves as a safe space to provide criticism and the opportunity to mess up. You must support your friends in their triumphs as they overcome the challenges of practicing life. You have to support their growth. Offer advice and build a plan of success with your friends, with values you all can agree upon.

Friendship is about quality team growth in order to win in life. No team in the NBA lead by a single person wins the championship. The playoffs are made for team competition. Even the great Michael Jordan was stopped 8 years in a row attempting to win a championship by himself. Only with a proper team of people committed to the same cause with a great level of dedication and skill can triumph. The San Antonio Spurs only play team ball. Thus their leader is not always their best player or filled with arrogance; the basketball team must work together. No single individual wants to win the game for the team but every team member is ready to do so if need be. Therefore I imagine their coaches demand one intense practice every day to push the individual conceptions of what the team's best is, requiring every member of the team to advance his individual best. There's an old saying: what you do in practice you will do in the game. Many people want to be great in the game but don't want to be great in practice. Practice makes perfect. Perfect is a pursuit. Therefore the constant willpower to better yourself serves as a driving force your friends will appreciate. We come together, as friends, in a unified vibrational energy wave to demand excellence from everyone in the friend circle. Life is a game worth playing. We don't really have practice in life. Practice in life is every day. The everyday effort we put into life becomes practice for the next day. Someone is always paying attention to you, whether or not you notice. Therefore we should do what we truly value every day. The time we spend with friends communicates how much we value them. Having to choose between your friends and your aspirations should never be an issue, because your efforts towards your goals will attract the people who truly support you. The support may vary physically, mentally, and spiritually. You friends may have certain purposes in your life to teach you a lesson or be a blessing.

  As CEO of myself, I must decide the members of my executive board of Professor Miles. In your life, decide who stays and who will leave. Your friends are the first row of petals on your flower after your immediate family. This is your garden. This is your team. This is your corporation! Profit from these people or perish by them. The platonic relationship holds many options for growth, stagnation, and recession. The only direction worth traveling is onward and upward.

In your life, decide who stays and who will leave.

(You may need to fill this out again for the friends you pick in your life.)

The Network Flower

    Developing yourself to move onward and upward takes a community of individuals dedicated to the goal of being successful. We are only as good as the expectations others have in us, so it is important we set the tone of engagement for everyone we interact with. Our people must understand our dreams in order to help us. You have to establish these dreams and set forth a clear path that your friends understand so your friends know how to help you grow. Unfortunately, everyone cannot help. Unfortunately, everyone's help is not needed to succeed. The road to hell is paved with good intentions because the results of many people's action can be a hindrance. Your friends may genuinely want to help you. You must understand what is good for you and what is not good for you. You are the CEO of yourself and you must make executive decisions each and every day.

When receiving advice, we must look to our trusted teammates, but not the world. It takes no effort for someone to develop an opinion. It takes experience and knowledge for someone to develop useful advice. Know the difference from an opinion versus an experience versus expert advice. An opinion is a though with no support. An experience is usually someone who says, "I did that once and it was horrible." An expert has done it for years and has proven results they can show and tell you about. Listen to the expert. Respect the experience. And let the opinion float throughout the universe on it own. **Don't pay attention to opinions.** It is up to you to decide which advice to engage and which to ignore. Later in the book, I will discuss the great resources known as teachers, mentors, and parents. They are great counselors for making decisions, but they, too, have limits. For many of us who have goals grander than the achievements of our parents, we have to understand where our parents' advice must be placed when making decisions. Parents have our best interests at heart based upon their life experience. If you want to be just like your dad, do exactly what he did. If you want to achieve something your parents have not achieved, listen to why they were not ability to achieve it. We can love people and not use their advice. Then speak with an expert who knows how to do it. Only experienced people who have gone through what I am asking about should give me advice. I would not ask a football player to tell me how to be a great golfer. Understand the limits of people's knowledge.

I can write this book about self-education being greater than higher education because I have served as the undergraduate students, grad student, advisor, and professor at the university within four years. Most people are still an undergraduate in that time frame. My experience and a proven educator who has trained hundreds of students across the nation to apply, attend, and graduate from college grants me the insight needed to instruct you on how you can best take advantage of the opportunities Even with a gun to your head, what you do is your decision. That is an extreme decision but it communicates the power of the mind. No one, not even God can control, but you can. It is your life. You only live once. You might as well have a great time while you live it. Therefore, understand that your parents have your best interest at heart based on the experiences they have had in their own life and interactions with you. Their expectations of you do not have to become your reality.

 Your parents created you from a sexual experience, hopefully full of love. Everyone does not have a great fairy tale of how we came into this earth. Since you got here through sex, like the rest of us, it is important we talk about sexual relationships in college. The hook up culture is real but sex is what we make it to be. The sex many people enjoy in college serves a physical and emotional need. It often does not carry the weight of a spiritual intention to reproduce the greatest species on the planet. The sanctity of sexual intercourse has lost much of its passion due to the hyper-sexualization of women available on a larger scale than ever before due to the increase of media and online human interaction such as porn, music videos, commercials, etc. Sex sells and in a capitalist society, everything is for sale. Though previously the negative patriarchy, binary gender domination, and sexualization were limited in both reception and production, there has been an exponential increase to the engagement of sexual conduct in recent decades. Many people still fight against sexual assault and rape culture present on the college campus for students in undergraduate, graduate, and doctoral studies. Unfortunately, most aggressors are men and have familiarity with their victim. Sex while influenced also blurs many lines that lead to miscommunication, criminal activity, and regret. The safest sexual encounter is a sober one. In fact, sober sex enhances performance for both members involved. In regards to sexual encounters, it is absolutely necessary to gain consent from every person you sexually engage. If there is any doubt to the permission of the sex, stop! Sex is a great experience under consent. When forced, it leaves mental, emotional, and physical scars. Rape cannot be forgotten. Wounds can heal but scars last a lifetime.

On the other hand, great sex as a positive interaction can be a long-lasting memory. A sexual connection is best when the tripartite beings use all of their components to engage. Mental and spiritual connections create the most positive experiences. It takes getting to know someone and having the ability to empower your partner. From empowerment and intriguing the mind, the sex can reach new heights of physical satisfaction. Although casual sex within the hook up culture promotes unattached intercourse, the soul is too strong to experience a loveless experience for long. Many people are not mature enough to have a deep and powerful sexual experience. Most students will graduate from higher education never having a mental, physical, and spiritual experience that feels like heaven because of the hyper-sexualization college culture contains. A disproportionate amount of women will not even experience an orgasm. Male satisfaction is more common; sex may lose its value and become a disconnected habit for young men since reaching a climax is physically easier than a spiritual peak. Additionally, many women are not satisfied in sexual encounters physically or spiritually, which can effect their decisions romantically as they mature.

Nonetheless, the science of physical sex does not diminish. The penis has an alkaline pH (potential for hydrogen) balance. The vagina has an acidic pH balance. When sexual interaction occurs, chemistry is involved for the change in pH of the sexual organs during sex. In fact, the experience changes the pH slightly after every sexual encounter, which alters the "natural fragrance" of your sexual organs. When people reference "chemistry" between certain lovers or people, the chemistry is real. Secondly, the alteration to the pH balance cannot be reversed no matter how many times we clean ourselves. Therefore, you carry the imprint of all your partners' pH and their life partners' pH imprint on/in our sexual organs for the remainder of our lives. Sexual education classes may have skipped this in grade school and there is no mandate to understand sex from a positive interaction or scientific perspective besides the usual safe sex, pregnancy, and "don't rape" pedagogy. You have to find a sexual balance you are comfortable with when romantically engaged with your partner. Thus, the sexual encounters we have may be regular or far in between or non-existent. Regardless of your sexual activity, you are a walking transcript of sexual encounters based on your pH balance. Manage your pH and be sure to have the right chemical balance for you. Check with you doctor every three to six months for sexually transmitted infections. Check with your mind, body, and soul daily to make sure your sexual encounters are a great decision, not an emotional one that makes sense for the moment. Men and women, you do not have to have sex if you do not want to. You are not obligated by any means to engage in sexual activity per the request of an individual. Since most sexual encounters do not involve strangers, our friends serve as our greatest allies and enemies. It scary, I know! Control what you can: yourself. Other than that, be sure to take care of your soul by not offering your precious temple to unworthy suitors. Retain your self-value by engaging in a sexual practice that excites and benefits your wellbeing. Everything matters. Everything counts. Thus, every sexual encounter can be practice for a positive and purposeful sexual experience that leads to a covenant of the mind, body, and soul in romance. The unification of self in combination with another yields the greatest returns on sex. The entire tripartite human being needs to consent to every sexual engagement. Every sexual experience is different, even with the same person. Consent is needed every time, even with the same person. Reassess your experience every time. You do not owe anyone anything. You have your life and they have theirs. **Every time you have sex, ask yourself, "what's right about this decision?" Will this person add value and pleasure to my life consistently, beyond the physical pleasure?**

Our connections to people matter a lot. Asking ourselves what is right about this engagement only propels us forward. We have multiple formats to engage people today. Via email, we can now send letters in seconds to friends and family. It allows instant receipt and response from people. Snail mail takes days but is more personal. Email is more efficient. It is on our phones and can serve the development of prospering relationships really well. In the professional chapter, we discussed email communications. In establishing a worthwhile network, we know to pursue our professional relationships like a friendship with a direct purpose or goal attached. Professional relationship building can take the strength needed by pulling some teeth. Friendship is definitely a two-way street. The individuals are equal. In life, we earn professional and social hierarchies that create a norm of engagement that often times make it difficult to genuinely develop a proper friendship. In communicating with only friendship in mind, this relationship is a two-way street. Every dollar of gas spent to push the friendship forward should be matched in similar fashion or another. If your friend does not have a car, putting up gas money and taking turns while driving on a road trip serve the same cause. That's friendship. The friendship is the basketball team. Everyone may not have equal value to the team, but everyone has equal opportunity to contribute to the friendship within their role. Not everyone can be the franchise player, the best player, or the point guard. Thus everyone must complete their part in order to achieve the championship level of friendship. In college, I served as the leader sometimes, while other times my friends were leaders. Your role in different relationships can change. Depending on the friendship, professional relationship, or romance, you may not need to be the leader the entire time. Know your role and execute very well.

    I loved college so much I became a professor and have always had a strong relationship with my alma maters UCLA and Penn. As a good speaker and known advocate for educational opportunity, my friends could rely upon me to always have a study plan together or have great connections to gain access to classrooms at night so we could study to the best of our ability throughout the entire school year. One of my good friends aimed to be King Turn Up, the best social butterfly on campus. He led party after party. Another one of my friends was great at bringing people together across divisions no matter what by using his humor. He was the greatest mediator on campus. When we needed help in someone else's specialty, we looked to gain the aid of the others. We led our best roles and as a group of friends, we followed the others lead with faith that they were the best. We all did everything and often stepped into each other's realms. When we did so, we knew who was the captain of the team for that engagement and did not question their leadership. The lack of questioning came after we built up trust for each other. To demonstrate how trust is built, we must understand the circle of trust.

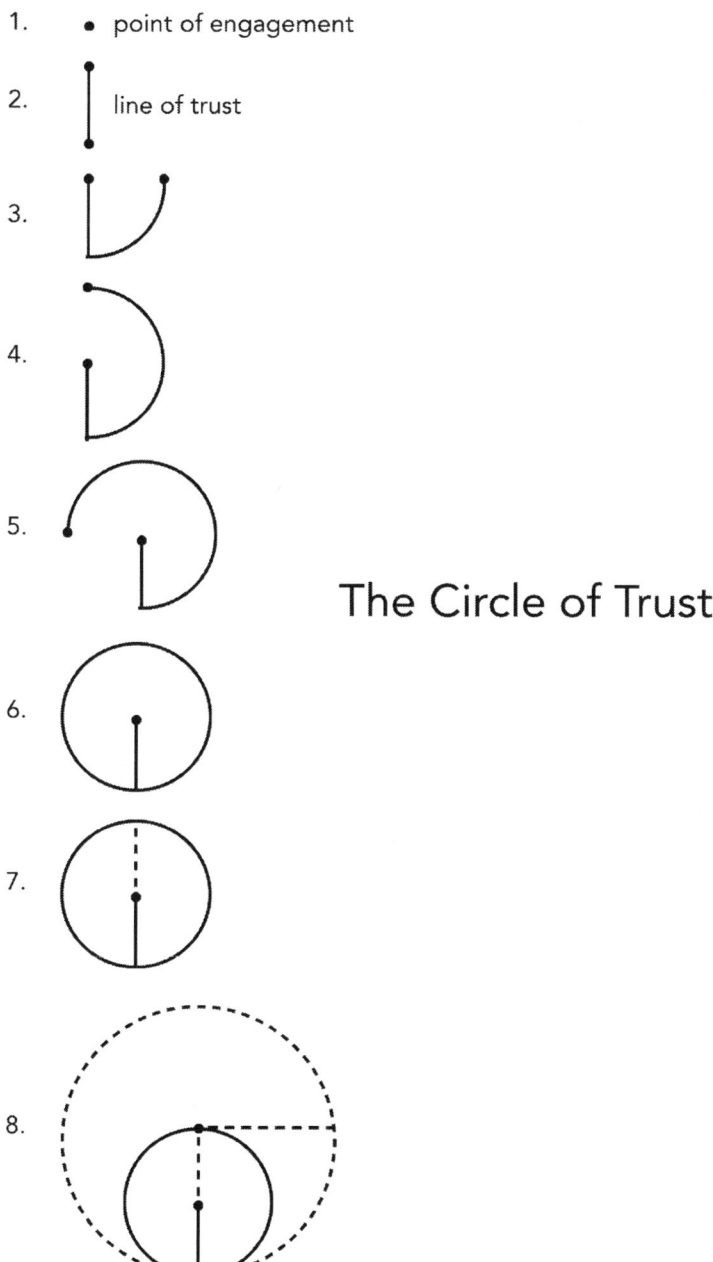

The Circle of Trust

The circle of trust starts with a black dot, the point of engagement. The point of engagement is the first interaction we have with someone. The feeling of trust we have with someone determines the length of the line of trust. The line of trust will swing in a circular motion, serving as a diameter of the circle of trust in formation. Once enough engagements have been made, the circle of trust will develop. The development of the trust increases based on the positive engagements one has with another individual. With the circle of trust developing based on the quality of engagements more so than the quantity, the circle of trust can become complete with 360 degrees. The circle of trust is like a cypher that moves like a rolling stone. Therefore, continued trust and development continue after the first cypher finishes.

    We see multiple cyphers of trust developed, each one bigger than the last cypher as the diameter of trust extends with the positive engagements. The speed of trust differs with each person interacting with another person. We all trust someone based on personal values accrued from interactions with people prior, expectations, desire, and need. Some people will tell you their entire life within moments of meeting, while others will hold the secrets of their life until they reach their deathbed. Thus, multiple cyphers can grow over time, but it is important to know that trust is an atom. It is in constant movement. As an atom, trust is involved in the creation of everything humans are involved with. Whether romantic, professional, or personal, all relationships are in constant movement. Trust is either growing or not growing while the relationship develops. When the movement stops, no matter how much trust has been established, the circle of trust will be incomplete.

    The last cypher must be complete in order to begin the next cypher. Without the continuing growth of a relationship between individuals, the trust is diminished and leaves the cypher open like an unattended wound. Understand that trust reflects the interactions we have. You may trust one person with your life and trust another to only benefit them. We understand selfish intentions. As we learn to understand students, staff, and faculty on campus, we grow a greater understanding of how to trust, when to trust, and who to trust with our time, decisions, and academic success. The cypher is always moving. The circle of trust has no limits, and requires a careful understanding of what the use of this trust will be. The potential of trust rests among the stars. The incomplete circle of trust lives in agony.

Individuals are equal.

09
DIVERSITY

No two people experience the world the same.

Engaging diversity is not easy. When we hear the term, we all know what it means. Most people have a limited understanding of what diversity means. For many schools, diversity speaks to a wide variety of people from different means and creeds attending class on campus. The largest representation of diversity on campus rests in the varying majors people enroll in to achieve their academic aspirations. There are so many subjects one can study and, oftentimes, the university, dedicated to the study and understanding of the universe, creates in-depth intellectual subjects that students can engage in as minors or certificate programs as well. The university can become diverse by simply offering multiple majors of study to engage for the duration of a student's academic career. Some choices are Science (Biology, Chemistry, Kinesiology, Micro- Biology, Health Administration, etc.), Technology (Informatics, Media Production, Robotics, Video Game Programming, Game Design, Web Development, etc.), Engineering (Chemical, Material, Aeronautical, Biomedical, etc.), Art (Social Sciences, Philosophy, Religion, Humanities, English, Political Science, Calligraphy, Sociology, Education, etc.), Mathematics (Statistics, Applied Mathematics, Computer, Business Applications, Teaching, etc). The acronym for these prior general majors is STEAM: Science, Technology, Engineering, Arts, and Math. The STEAM majors serve as the most important fields of study. Together, a complete STEAM education equips a student to be able to understand the philosophy and pedagogy of the universe we live in through multiple avenues of perspectives. We experience each component of STEAM on an everyday basis. Therefore, it is incredibly important to have a breadth of the entire STEAM education. In a university, researchers have dedicated years, if not decades, to exploring the depth of these studies to understand a specific aspect of the Earth and the universe it thrives in. In a capitalistic economic system, we have learned that a capital advantage, one's ability to manufacture a specific product or service, serves as the best avenue to the acquisition of monetary capital. Thus the university promotes students to keep thine eye single. By focusing on a specific major within one of the acronyms, one can bet their abilities into a specific industry and maximize their opportunity within that space. As a student, the advantage of having overlapping concepts and pedagogy will allow an easier understanding of the information at hand. Therefore, we construct majors throughout the university for students to focus on, creating an opportunity for each student to maximize their knowledge acquisition of the major of study to the best of their ability.

  Many students transition into the workforce under a specific focus of study directly related to the industry of choice. They aim to earn the best opportunity to apply learned pedagogies into a profit-rendering praxis, thus creating an individual capital gain within the industry of choice. The majors offered at the university do not limit the diversity of industries entered by graduates. The entire application of knowledge studied by the person rests as the student's responsibility to execute their vision. Thus, one's major does not have to define what they will do for employment. How students apply the knowledge they purchased at the university is up to them. What you will do with your developed passions, talents, and skills is your choice. Universities love to discuss the diverse interest, majors, and careers students engage in to promote their brand of knowledge acquisition and dissemination. Advantageous universities create relationships with companies to create a pipeline of employment. For the University of Pennsylvania, many corporations engaged in finance come to the school to discuss Wall Street opportunities with students from all majors. These corporations, such as Boston Consulting Group, Goldman-Sachs, and Bain, create internships for all students across the United States to apply but market themselves to the University of Pennsylvania. Regardless of the institution one attends, many of the people working these finance positions come from Ivy League institutions. The undergraduate culture of the Ivy League institutions creates a learning environment that benefits these financial institutions. Therefore, we see an intentional pipeline of recruiting created between the schools and the corporations. The corporations' leaders are often alumni of the schools they recruit from. We would all pick our alma maters to develop professional talent if we had billions of dollars in our corporations, assuming we had good experiences while in school.

    Thus, the school we attend and the omnipresent culture become incredibly important to our development as professionals and people. The diversity of financial and professional opportunities varies for each college. To better understand the university opportunity, one should look at the statistics of employment for students once they graduate. I noticed at Penn, many of the students did not major in finance, but still looked to take advantage of the opportunity to work in the industry because it served as the best post-undergraduate professional experience they found on campus. Many a time, we do not seek to create advantages beyond those delivered to us.

    Luckily, in the millennial generation, we look to capitalize on opportunity by becoming entrepreneurs. **It may appear to be a huge wave now because of the Internet, but being an entrepreneur in a capitalist nation has been the greatest advantage since the inception of the United States.** The systems and operational cost of creating and sustaining a business have enormously dwindled. The U.S. benefits the entrepreneur more than any other corporation. The U.S, as a government corporation, prefers to assist those who benefit the overall economy. Our economy is the largest in the world. In capitalism, we find a way to profit off people, ideas, and creations. To create a company in the U.S., just a home-based business with the intent to make a profit for at least four hours a week, we can then look to use the four hours of Internet, electricity, and other utilities used to benefit the business as deductibles on our taxes. Thus, having an intent of profit, whether achieved or not, can reduce your overall taxable income. The development of technology has progressed career opportunities. Ideas at universities that would have been considered great research topics or college organizations now have the opportunity to be a corporation. The need to be approved by the university in order to start your business is not needed. The great resources available on campus can now serve the student entrepreneur.

The campus network may be the greatest resource available. In fact, the campus network can serve as the first market to test the product or service by the students on campus. Research knowledge, usually only maximized by professors, can assist students to better understand the world's problems. The best business solves a problem. Websites such as jstor.org serve as digital libraries of academic journals, books, and primary sources that have research-supported answers to problems. Faculty on campus serves as professional researchers. They are primarily hired to create research. Unfortunately, much of the research created by faculty remains in the reserves of the journal and publications they submit to. We find answers and don't implement them. Thus, individuals must pay each journal to access the information published. Jstor.org creates amazing collections of this private research. The research is private because it requires funds in order to access it and remains managed by individual corporations and not federal- or state-regulated officials. The research continually analyzes much of the world's greatest problems. Published research aims to understand and disseminate conceptions on the world and how it is progressing, regressing, and changing. **It is through the creation of research that professors find their foundational knowledge to be taught in courses.** This research informs many leaders but, truth be told, the research is hardly engaged by anyone, including the researchers themselves. Many write the research and then never read their work again. Before the researchers know it, they continue on to create their next research article or project. The circle keeps spinning and so does time. Researchers often meet each other at conferences and then decide, based on their interactions or insightful presentations, whose literary works will surface as pertinent in their courses.

    The personal and professional network of the researcher informs the decision he or she makes to create a course. Thus, what you know serves as a result of whom you know. The diversity of resources used to inform students in universities across the nation is a result of professional relationships formed. Some may see this as sinister but, in fact, every industry operates as a result of professional networks developed from personal relationships. When analyzing corporations' and universities' diverse populations, or lack thereof, the representation of people often serves as a macrocosm of the personal relationships its leadership finds valuable.

    In regards to racial diversity, the proportions of races present in the student population often reflect the personal network of the student leaders, staff, faculty, administrators, and executives in place. I refer to the previous list of university members as the leadership of higher education. The leadership sets the tone for the students interested in the university. Most presidents of universities in the U.S.A. are wealthy, property owning, white men. Race is a sensitive topic in higher education and the U.S.A. It makes everyone feel uncomfortable because race only serves as separation and stratification in this nation and on a global scale. Race, a social construction of the depiction of various skin types, finds its foundation in the melanin count in people's skin. Melanin is a natural occurrence in humans and serves as a result of geographical location. Melanin also serves a natural system of extracting Vitamin D from the ultraviolet rays of the sun. The more melanin one has, the more vitamins and energy one can extract from the sunrays. The sunrays can turn violent when over exposure occurs regardless of one's melanin count. Everyone can get sunburned. The social construction of race has made it so some races get burned in society at a higher rate than others. Race as a social construction became a huge factor in the creation of the U.S.A. and higher education.

      Once continental divisions were crossed between humans due to the expansion of trade and naval exploration, conceptions and beliefs tied to melanin counts were contrived. Geographical cultural traditions and practices began being stereotyped and misconceived; negative attributions and fears were soon attached to melanin counts. The impact of European imperialism on the world created a global stratification to which no nation is immune, including the United States. The mistreatment of the poor and religiously restricted in Europe turned the many people into a race for resources to establish their own freedom. Unfortunately, it took many genocides and the enslavement of racial groups in order to create the new nations around the world under British rule. The sun never sat on the British Empire. Society's racial sunburn eclipsed the freedom of many Africans, Indians, Native Americans, Latinos, and Australians. Race in the United States served as a socio-economic classification system. One's race determined their economic status. After the Native Americans died at the hands of disease and the European's advanced weaponry, their genocide proved them to be poor slaves. The European settlers in American then looked to enslave the poor of their homeland to indentured servitude. Unfortunately, only ones' clothes served as an indicator of indentured service among whites. Runaway indentured servants became a norm for those managing plantations. Thus, Africans, who held the best immune system and a much greater melanin count, were captured, bought, and stolen from Africa for labor. Colonialist enslaved millions across the world.

In fact, free/cheap labor serves as one of the greatest economic advantages of the strongest economic nations from this time to the present. For the United States, outsourcing manufacturing to underserved nations and renting prisoners from privately-owned prisons allows a much greater profit margin for many industries in 2016. In understanding that capital is not only monetary but also human, universities have a human capital profit margin to create in higher education. Just as slaves, human beings, were an economic class and value, so are students today in higher education. Obviously, it is much better to be a student than a slave but the economic implications of human value in our modern economy are huge. The percent of African-Americans in undergraduate schools across the nation does not equal the percent of African-Americans in the nation. In fact, the number of African-American men in prison today outnumbers the amount of African male slaves in the United States circa 1850. African-Americans are disproportionately represented in today's prison system. Luckily, the number of African-American men in college outnumbers African-American men in prison in 2016.

The word lynching came from his last name.

The war on poverty, the wars on crime, and the war on drugs, these government action items disproportionality attack non-white ethnic groups of the low socio-economic class, thus extending the efforts seen fit by Willie Lynch, a ruthless slave owner from the West Indies (Caribbean). The word lynching came from his last name. His message to the oppressors and systematic enforcers of the racial enforcement of the United States economic hierarchy let the Africans keep their bodies but take their minds. It is my belief that all people intended to be low-class or slaves are at risk of Willie Lynch's convictions. This includes the uneducated, women,

Native Americans, poor Europeans, and enslaved Africans. For the universities were constructed to educate the wealthy English males descendants of the colonial era. Universities have opened their doors to almost everyone who can afford it in modern society. Nonetheless, I believe there is more work to be done to grant equal access to underserved populations, such as the aforementioned groups. America relies upon all of us to make it a more inclusive multi-cultural nation. The American dream lives on because of those who began legacies we uphold today. The founders of anything set the tone. The creators of universities made it with strong intent. As long as these institutions exist, they will thrive upon the legacy established by it's founders. For better and for worse.

    Everyone not fitting the wealthy, property owning, white male stereotype is an amended student. Just as women and non-white males were later considered in the U.S. Constitution, so we were added later to the population intended for attendance at universities. The advancement of the university to accept students of all backgrounds and economic statuses does not remove the experience of those persons. In fact, many of these people are idolized in a singular experience often used to show other students from similar communities an avenue of success. The university will tokenize one person as proof of their ability to be diverse, a success predicated on the achievements of their unique abilities despite the countless challenges placed before them in an education system founded in oppression. The strength and resiliency needed to be an amended student requires them to be Antaeus students to succeed. You are a diverse being. Your gender. Your sexuality. Your race. Your ethnicity. Your nationality. Your experiences. Your economic situation. You are not just one experience. It would be a shame to tell your life story from one perspective. With all this diversity inside of you, imagine the various ways we can positively impact the diversity of a university serving 30,000 students.

In modern higher education, the goal for the country is to lead the world's top twenty nations in degree attainment by 2020 as declared by President Barack Obama. From an increase in intellectual capacity and human capital, we can look forward to a continuing economic boom for universities and the Sallie Mae/Navient loan service. Top higher education research universities desire to make a profit of human and monetary capital. In order to achieve this goal, the low socio-economic class must be educated, prepared, and retained. Retention stands as a much greater problem than financial affordability. A student needs policies in place to feel safe and accepted on campus. The students need to be welcomed and continuously mentored throughout their entire university experience. Through many racial, national, and ethnic experiences, students experience microaggresions and prejudice. Additionally, the aggressions experienced also extend into financial disparities. People within an economic class, regardless of education attainment, rarely exit and transcend the economic class status of their parents. The people who raise you set your expectations and develop the human capital you have. Without you knowing how to expand your knowledge and its applicability in a profit-bearing manner while in school, the chance for you to transition from a low socio-economic experience to the middle or high class is low. Your professional network may not have increased with your grades. When students from affluent communities interact with students not financially well off, the misunderstanding of the Antaeus work ethic is often devalued. It takes so much more to be average coming from a low-income home. The community environment, mental toughness, and ability to stay focused on schoolwork are a host of skills in of itself. Thus, alienation tends to occur from either or both parties, for students wish to be accepted for who they are. Fortunately, people attract who they are, not who they want to be. The safe space for many students is homogenous social groups consisting of similar racial heritage, gender choice, and socio-economic status. People like to engage people who are like themselves, especially in social environments. People love to be comfortable.

Additionally, students experience marginalization and cultural dissonance. The distance in educational harmony comes from a varying understanding of culture and experience. Rarely do people accept the bad with good when listening to the recounts of someone's experience. Higher education community members consistently forget the infinite knowledge we each hold behind our eyes. The world is not only seen differently through everyone's eyes. The world is experienced differently, resulting in a variance of interactions. Upon arriving to college, many people, all races included, come from homogenous environments, homogenous in the context that everyone has an agreed-upon understanding of interaction and behavior. At a university, the majority of people will come from many walks of life and hold a different approach to the world. Thus, miscommunications on how a positive interaction or what a positive interaction is can stagger across people coming from different communities. **Define love**. It will be different for you than it will be for your friends. **Define a positive day. What happens in a day full of positivity, from your perspective?** The definition of each word and experience in life varies. We cannot take the different opinions of positivity, love, and acceptance as a denigration of our value as human beings. Merriam-Webster may be the most popular person to define words, but he is not the only human being who can write a dictionary. Self-definition serves as a grand component of who we are. The ability to define our experiences creates our individual humanity. As we travel through the realm of higher education, creating spaces to speak our peace, learn, and develop as humans in a multicultural world, we will improve our ability to be the best human we can be. Therefore willful understanding of various cultures serves as the best integration method to exchange cultural capital.

Gender dynamics within a university serves many challenges as well to overcome. Universities in their original construction held no intent to educate women. Although women create life and often raise children, thus making them the first teachers EVERYONE has, the nation did not care to improve their minds, reinforcing the notion of the mind being our greatest asset. Ignorance is only bliss because what we do not know can kill us spiritually, mentally, and physically. In reference to the Willie Lynch letter, the taking of the mind did not only apply to the slaves, but also to the women citizens. During the inception of the United States, only white, property-owning males "earned" citizenship. The schools only educated men until the brave Oberlin College, a liberal arts school in Ohio, graduated the first woman to earn a bachelor's degree in 1841. Oberlin was founded by abolitionists and also admitted African-American students. It was an incredible leap of faith to be a leader in this endeavor during a time that did not acknowledge either of these populations as humans with full citizenry or agency in life. Today, the aftermath of oppression against women continues. Women make up the majority of college campuses, but the preferential treatment to acknowledge and uplift the male still dominates the mentality of schools. Schools reflect the society, which thrives for schools to establish the culture of the nation to which we refer throughout our lives. School serves as the foundation of cultural assimilation and understanding. Gender binaries continue to develop but also dwindle. Most importantly, women are still few in presence as the leadership of higher education, thus making it more difficult for the campus cultures to reflect an advancing and progressive nature. Women make up a large part of the advising and counseling services on campus, but only a small portion of the administrative and executive roles.

You are not just one experience.

Women are the creators of life. Women lead families, homes, businesses, and nations. The low presence of women in leadership does not stem from a lack of desire, but the overall negative patriarchy demeaning women in body language, verbal abuse, and discrimination. The pay gap for women performing the same jobs as men across all industries proves women are devalued in society. Somehow, being the primary source of creation and the development of humanity became an underappreciated position. Women are worth much more than their weight in gold. In fact, they are the most priceless entities on the planet. Look at the huge disparity in Mother's Day card sales versus Father's Day card sales. The difference is great. In addition, women tend to be smarter human beings. The mental maturity of women occurs faster due to the acknowledgement they make at young ages of their ability to create life. Also, the countless men sexualizing girls and young ladies in public and private spaces increases the need for women to think more maturely about their decisions and interactions at a young age. Thus, in school, women are more likely to perform better, because society requires women to critically think consistently in order to overcome and outwit countless sexual advances, predators, and the non-gendered restricted negative people.

In order to stay positive, people create many outlets. These spaces to speak one's mind and build happiness vary. For some, religious practices serve as a great avenue of security. The diversity of spiritual concepts can expand many conversations. I remember constructing my first documentary, A Test of Faith: The Impact of Christianity on Black America. At the time, I felt the need to understand Christianity from a historical perspective and its present-day impact. The campus received a huge influx of Disciples of Christ through the Christian movement entitled Passion for Christ Movement (P4CM). P4CM lead many trips to churches and were consistently found on campus giving ministry to students. Many students not involved in the movement became greatly insecure in their actions during or after conversations with the P4CM members. Being the passionate brother I am, I decided to make my documentary to highlight the significance of Christianity, as we knew it. I interviewed the campus community, clergy, history professors, P4CM campus leaders and participants, Muslims, agnostics, parents, and more to gain a clear perspective on positive impacts of the Bible and Christianity. Through my fraternity, of which I was the 19-year old Vice Polemarch (vice president) at the time, I premiered my 45-minute documentary. The classroom soon filled with students, P4CM members from on and off campus, UCLA staff, graduate students, parents, Christians, Muslims, and more. People stood up in the back when seats became scarce. The room was packed. The heat began to rise as the conversation critically analyzed the perspectives across the spectrum of religion on campus. The acceptance of religion varied in what acceptance and practice of Christianity meant. The purpose and value varied. No two people thought alike. The conversation did not aim to have a conclusion, but to provide perspective and give a fair voice to people from completely different backgrounds in religious activity. Spiritual concepts on how we should conduct ourselves as human beings continue to be tumultuous endeavors as religious beliefs erupt in grace and graves on a global scale. The diversity of thought within and across religion makes managing spiritual practices very difficult on university spaces. Nonetheless, it is vital to allow these students to peacefully unify and practice the best components of their religious practices. Regardless, the difference in conception can stretch too far to not have a meaningful and intentional conversation about the various religions on campus. Diverse religious perspectives exist all across the world. The United States and your college are no different. We must learn to understand various perspectives. Having a conversation about our life choices makes everyone a better team player contributing to society.

The perspectives on religion vary within denomination, even across generational lines. We arrive at different conclusions within religion. Colleges grant degrees to students but not all students enter college in the same way. Not all students on campus arrive straight from high school. Transfers can vary by age. Students attend college at any age. When World War II concluded, the G.I. Bill allowed financial assistance to veterans willing to attend higher education. With military men ranging in age, some began school in the low twenties. The 18-22 year old age range expanded. Today, we can see students of all ages attending school. Diversity at a school can include the variance of age of the students. The generational differences in thought for students expand the length of the equator. Not only is it a very wide range, it is also an imaginary line. Thus the difference in thought can restrict people from growing. The decades past and today teach different lessons. Simultaneously, many lessons of life are taught again just the same. Lastly, similar lessons are taught to people in different ways. We have to open our minds to seeing the world in different ways. One way to unify our perception is to understand we are all the same age. The information available in the world is the same for all of us. We all live today. The same information with the same 24 hours makes us the same age. Some people experienced the history; others read it or watched a documentary on it. Regardless of the information's avenue of transport, the information available is the same. Thus, we have to respect the ability of everyone to learn and convey pertinent information to our lives regardless of his age.

We all learn differently as well. Oftentimes we discuss learning through one of the five senses, but that notion is very elementary. Although life provides many complexities, and bringing our conceptions into a singularity makes life easier in some ways, learning is not singular. Learning occurs through all five senses. Each sense provides a different form of intelligence. The thought process of truly learning in diverse manners is not easy. In order to maximize our learning, we have to understand the complexity of thinking. Thinking serves as the source of conception, perception, and critical analysis. In order to embrace the Circle of Thought, we must understand how thinking is best processed. Thinking best occurs as a two-part action of input and output. We input information through all of our five senses: eyesight, touch, smell, hearing, and taste. For eyesight, we can watch films, see people talk, take in lectures slides and notes, and read in a multitude of formats. Touch permits us to have memories of feeling and doing something. We can tie ourselves to a certain pen grip for specific classes. Touch also engages the action of beings hands-on to learn the sciences and technology many a time. Smell serves as a fragrance or stench we may never forget, like the potential lover who passes us on Locust Walk. We spend countless hours inside of the classroom listening to professors and peers discussing course material.

Learning occurs through all five senses

The Circle of Thought

Taste is a sense that may be specific to culinary majors unless we attach a mental significance to a certain gum flavor to a specific subject we are studying. In advising probation students, I often convey maximizing the human senses by using them to attach subjects to a specific interaction of the sense. For example, to study for biology, I encourage students to chew cinnamon-flavored gum. Every time the student takes a test in biology, chew the cinnamon-flavored gum to activate the learning sense. The biology information grasped while chewing this will become readily available as the mind attached, over the entire semester, the motion of chewing gum, the smell of cinnamon, and the taste of cinnamon to the biology information, thus creating a trigger of intelligence. It becomes muscle memory for intellects.

Additionally, the output of information can also be tied to this practice. In fact, school does not test anyone on their ability to input information. The expression of knowledge is valued. To prove an understanding and application of the information at hand, the colleges and universities challenge students to output. Including the practice of outputting information proves more beneficial for testing, especially when students practice outputting information in the same format as the test requires. The three most beneficial outputting abilities include speaking, writing, and creating. Speaking has a dual input and output component. As we use our mouths to convey information aloud, we practice outputting the information we understand. The method of stating and speaking serves as one of the most powerful components of communication. In speaking while studying with self, we listen simultaneously, thus every word spoken is heard twice (two ears). Therefore, we now create a Circle of Thought because we speak input and output at the same time. Writing has a similar duality. Writing tests our ability to convey information in a concrete manner. We output information via writing and can see what we write. Thus, the Circle of Thought becomes complete due to the simultaneous inputting of the outputted information. The double engagement of the material improves our ability to remember the information.

The touch of the pen is important as well. **In cases regarding writing for memory gain, the color and texture of the pen creates a**

muscle memory. For example, when studying Middle Eastern political theory, write with a blue erasable pen. The consistency of the blue erasable pen will create an attachment in sight to the blue ink being associated with that subject matter. The feel of the pen maximizes the sense of touch to associate the pen's structure to the information at hand. Most political science courses rest their application of knowledge on constructing in-class final essays, so practicing the expression of Middle Eastern political theory throughout the semester with the same pen promotes a comfort of information acquisition and release, thus creating a successful routine to develop one's ability to master the higher education institution's course requirements.

The last format of outputting information is creation. The ability of one to make the information into knowledge by innovating their ideas allows memories to form as opposed to remembering information. Creation serves as a learn-from-failure experiment, which is similar to how we grasp life lessons. Being told by our parents to not touch the stove as a child only applies listening. Having a conversation about why we should not touch the stove when it is on creates a complete Circle of Thought. Fortunately, human curiosity knows no bounds. When parents apply fear as a method of restriction, humans grow more attracted to the known caution. We engage the sense of touch and see what the fuss is all about with the heated stove. At last! The burning of the hand strikes pain into our brain. From that moment on, we know and understand why touching the stove is not a good idea and deserves caution when being engaged. It creates a memory with the feeling of pain and heat. The memory of creating an experience with multiple senses engaged serves as the greatest Circle of Thought. Learning by doing greatly outweighs learning through singular senses.

In fact, the mind is so attached to the physical that the double interaction of the two creates an actualization process.

Whatever the mind can conceive, the body can achieve. The mind sets the tone for the physical limitations and accomplishments. For a very long time, the popular belief was that it was impossible for a human being to run the four-minute mile. Many have tried and failed. They could not make it through the challenge. Roger Bannister broke the barrier of the four-minute mile. People could not believe it. Since then, thousands of people have accomplished the four-minute mile. All because Roger Bannister believed it was possible and now the rest of the world does, too. Human beings have not advanced that much within the last century physically, but mentally we have made incredible improvements. The growth of possibility is infinite. Students must believe in themselves to be able to master the material at hand and know mastery will yield an A grade. The greatness you seek is within. Knowing how to diversify your interactions with other students, staff, and faculty will create your greatness. Diversifying the learning tools and sensory attachments will create your greatness. Diversifying the intellectual experience inside and outside of the classroom by inputting and outputting information you master, will turn your information into knowledge applicable to your life. That is the key to creating your greatness. Greatness is not an achievement. Greatness is a daily routine. Greatness comes from always being willing to learn new perspectives and ideas that can maximize your ability to innovate in a modern world of technology. Diversity of thought, learning, and people requires a progressive perspective. CEO of Pixar and Disney Animations Ed Catmul stated, "Art classes are not about learning to draw, but learning to see" (Creativity, Inc., 2014). We have perceptions based upon our values and soulful yearnings. We often do not see the symmetry of life but see the preconceived notions. We notice what we want instead of what is really happening thus limiting our ability to input properly. This results in an output or outcry of misinformation. Perception is reality. Your life is art in motion. It is important you take full control of your life and what you want it to be in every aspect.

Greatness is a daily routine.

10
TEACHING

You are a Teacher! Every day you teach others who you are.

The teacher-to-student relationship is sacred. It holds a valuable bond of information exchange and cultivation. The teacher, who is established as a wise individual, must educate the student. The student, too, has wisdom to convey, and the teacher must create an environment in which the student's knowledge can be conveyed safely. No one is all-knowing, so the exchange of information must take place. **Everyone, including teachers, have much to learn and contribute to the classroom.** Everyone holds an infinite source of knowledge behind his or her eyes, so everyone has the capability to be a teacher. Our brain cannot stop thinking, and we are constantly internalizing everything our senses are interacting with, especially when we mentally focus on the information being absorbed. Many of us concentrate on television and entertainment to such a great extent that we know more information about fictional and celebrated characters than we know ourselves. We all understand that external information is intriguing. Yet we gain value for the information we reflect on alone and with others, for reflection sheds light on our contemplations of the notions conveyed, be it fiction or reality. We contribute value by viewing this information. Whatever we pay attention to the most teaches us what we know the most. By scrolling through our timelines on social media, we learn whatever information we internalize. The greater consistency of the information and knowledge, the more we conceive. Although our conscious may not acknowledge all of the information, remember that our subconscious is an infinite sponge that knows no bounds to how much it can consume. The subconscious informs our initial (re)actions. Additionally, the subconscious sets the vibrational energy wave we send out to the world in order to attract others to us. Our subconscious is filled with every interaction, feelings, and thought we have ever experienced. You environment influences your subconscious mind. Thus, your environment can determine your pattern of action. The community of birth we are assigned to determines our initial energy wave. The community's headquarters for each person is their home. The home creates perspective. The perspective of opportunity, ability, and actuality is bred in the home. Thus, learning begins in the home. ==The learned behavior and thought process of the home creates the ideas we formulate for how we process the problems of life and the solutions we accept or create.==

    The creation of thought stems from other thoughts. No thought is original. All thoughts, just like all people, have a legacy of evolution. From one mind to another, we see that the inception of an idea can always find roots in the expression of another idea. Considering the intellectual complexity of human communication, we must understand that an idea does not need words to live. Actions speak louder than words. Martin Luther King, Jr. once said, "In the end, we will remember not the words of our enemies, but the silence of our friends." Body language and the tone of one's speech comprise 90% of our conveyances. What we do not say also strongly influences our mind. The home is dominated by the parent/guardian. **Thus, our parents/guardians serve as our first teachers. They teach us love, social skills, right and wrong, etc.** The conscious mind becomes what it interacts with on a consistent basis. The morals of humanity have much overlap across many nations, but the habits of culture vary greatly. What is right and wrong is not discussed often, but the process of how to accept, deliver, and perpetuate those rights and wrongs reach many debates.

Parents teach children conceptions of how to process the problems of the world. The formulas in life we use are taught to us from our parents. Parents provide a thoughtful foundation for what is valued in society, home, life, and liberty. I watched a lecture by Joy DeGruy, PhD. She is an internationally recognized social worker, clinical psychologist, author, and researcher focusing her efforts on understanding the experience of pain and anguish within American society, past to present. She spoke about the differences in parenting. The parents' experience becomes the child's reality. Parents will enforce the best notions of success, safety, and security known to them upon the child(ren) to best prepare the offspring for the world the parent has come to know. She speaks on an experience in a bank. She enters and sees two mothers, each with their young child. Mother #1 permits her child to run around the bank. The child learns to have freedom and exploration. The bank serves as the child's playground to roam and wander. Mother #2 sees her child running around and calls to the child, punishing him by stating he must remain attached to her. The child learns to not venture out and explore. This creates a mental attachment to the mother and a fear of exploration based on the intensity of the mother's resistance to allow child #2 to wander in the same fashion as child #1. Both children understand the parents' learned behavior and respond accordingly to their guardian teacher. The two children also perceive the restrictions and abilities of each other. This interaction informs the children of the freedom to act upon whatever notion each had to decide to roam the bank as a child's adventure.

Your environment can determine your pattern of action.

One summer in elementary school, I asked my father if I could ride my bike down to Crenshaw Boulevard, the main street in our community. Fast cars, gang members, police, pedophiles, and drug dealers often roamed the boulevard, making it dangerous for a young American child. Crossing the street would put me into a world of danger. I visited my dad in the summer, so the dangers of Crenshaw were unknown to me at the time that I asked. No one ever addressed the dangers because, as a family, we drove down Crenshaw Blvd consistently. I asked my dad, not knowing the dangers of the boulevard, if I could ride my bike down to Crenshaw and back. He said "no" very quickly. In my culture, parents were not big on explaining themselves. The reasoning behind their decisions often remained unknown. I asked why and he responded, "Because I said so, Miles," a typical response from parents in my community. They often enforced their authority and despised any questions implying their word was not enough. The statement served as another learned trait of dealing with authority in corporate America and military settings: the order from above serves as reasoning enough to act without question. My dad and I were separated for some time after my parents divorce, so at that time, I was 9 years old and rebuilding our relationship.

    My previous guardians, my grandparents, were very talkative, and explained much about life because they learned from raising three children that not explaining your thoughts to children is a detriment more than a benefit. Every decision came with an explanation. I usually received an explanation and was often encouraged to ask questions about decisions made affecting my life. My prior guardians proclaimed Martin Luther King, Jr. was well known for asking many questions, his greatest one being "Why?" I decided at 7 years old that questions were the answers to everything I did not know. In comparison to adults, I could tell all that I knew could never be enough. Thus, my stepmom, having information my father was not telling me, held more answers than I did. Now, the bike trip soon turned into an investigation into the mystery of Crenshaw Boulevard, a street I traveled to with my family but on my lonesome, at 9 years old, on my bike, was not an option. I am not often persuaded by such a general and bland response. Thus, with my bike trip now cancelled, I decided to learn more about Crenshaw Boulevard. "Why can't I ride my bike to Crenshaw?" I asked.

He looked at me with stress. The anxiety of having to answer a child must have bothered my father greatly. I stood there, scared of his response. We were rebuilding our relationship, so I was unsure as to what her reaction would be if I pursued my investigation seriously. The tenacity in his facial expression then slowly oozed out of his nostrils with a strong exhale. He looked at me. He placed the television on mute, signaling the seriousness of the answer to come. He swiveled in the black leather computer chair towards my direction. His incoming response required direct attention and complete body language involvement. "Why are you so focused on riding your bike to Crenshaw Boulevard, Miles?"

"I think it will be fun. Plus it's a big hill on the way down to Crenshaw," I said, calmly holding back my excitement.

"The hill is mighty. It will be difficult to ride back up, don't you think?" he said.

"I can do it. I promise I can do it," I reinforced enthusiastically.

"I think the trip to Crenshaw is too dangerous for you," he said.

"I won't fall off the bike. I swear."

"You may not fall, but I am afraid."

"Afraid of what?" I questioned curiously.

"I am not afraid of you or your decisions, Miles. Do you know why I tell you to be safe every time you leave the house?"

"Because you want me to make the right decisions and not put myself in danger."

"I tell you to be safe not because of my fear for your decisions. You have proved to me that you think about yourself and your actions carefully. I applaud you for that. I tell you to be safe because of what other people may do. You can control yourself, but no one can control another person. Going to Crenshaw Boulevard and back may seem like an innocent bike ride for you. For the gang bangers and dangerous people along the way, I am afraid of their decisions."

"Oh, wow! I did not think about other people's decisions and how they could hurt me."

I felt informed. It was something that stood strong in my mind to this day. "Be safe," a statement I felt was restricting to me, was actually a caring gesture. It was a prayer. The statement and the restriction to not ride my bike to Crenshaw Boulevard was for my safety. My dad wanted me to be safe from other people. All this time, I only heard "Be safe," never pondering that the safety might not be in my control. I thought about my safest space. I asked my father if I could ride my bike to the library in the opposite direction of Crenshaw Boulevard. He obliged. I learned that day that my safety was my parents' primary concern. My restrictions from going places were not denigrations of my decision making skills but instead assessments of the poor decisions others make. Thus, the pertinence of establishing a safe space in the world for me to travel became necessary. I had to ask myself, and now I ask you, **"Where is your safe space?"**

"Where is your safe space?"

I saw the library as a great place to learn. Not only was the local library in a more affluent region, the books took my mind to the safest place I have ever known, the universe of my imagination. Located in the View Park community of Los Angeles, the library brought me very unique interactions with many different people. I loved seeing people read and write. Everyday people came to the library to expand their knowledge and imagination. Someone new lived in the library, inside every book. On days I found myself alone between the bookshelves, the voices of great minds speaking to me through pages and pages, numbered with the words of another imaginative universe. Where to next? My bike could not take me to these places, but my mind could travel through the entire universe in seconds. The human imagination is the greatest resource on Earth. Through cultivation of the imagination, a parent can take their child to new worlds. Simultaneously, the destruction of one's imagination can shame a child into deep corners of the universe where stars do not shine, thus making the forming human being an unknown individual lost in the abyss of universal darkness where our eyes have no use.

People beyond our household see greatness in us when we often cannot see our inner spirit ourselves. The expectations others have of us often reflect the acting character we hold to be true, today or tomorrow and futures all. Thus they place that character into the bodies of others to assess who we will become. The communities we live in often assert those notions and communicate their expectations, not only in their verbal commandments, but also in their interactions with us, or lack thereof. The community outside also influences our thoughts. Your self-esteem can live at the feet of your community. The notions your mother, father, and guardians put in your mind are directly applied on the streets of your neighborhood. There we see what rings true or false. There lives the judgment of right and wrong. There lives the impact of our decisions to accept others for who they present themselves to be. Moving throughout the community, we build a catalog of reputations. The reputations live within our actions. Speech, gestures, and attendance act on behalf of our thoughts. When learning from the teachers of our community, we must decide to hold these notions as truth, dare, or false. The social hierarchy of your community becomes your omnipresent reality.

In regards to restriction, the community can enforce the lack of freedom to roam mentally, spiritually, and physically. The community enforces the same restriction of movement DeGruy witnessed in a bank. For the young student in attendance at a privileged school, we can see the treatment of him being different than that of a student attending a non-affluent institution. The peer, a troubled individual named Tyler, misbehaves during classroom instruction at the privileged school. He is offered a chance to redeem himself by acting accordingly. Tyler, not having his father at home, seeks attention in school, and misbehaves in class to garner attention. With an engaged parental community and caring educators, Tyler is sent to the school psychiatrist. In that space, Tyler is now being aiding by a professional designed to serve his mental and emotional health. She teaches him how to overcome his challenge. Tyler begins to self-regulate in order to behave better. Tyler's parent is informed on how to help him accept his father's absence. The community comes together to assist Tyler to become a greater human being.

In a non-affluent school, Tyler would have a different experience. The classroom disturbance would result in him being sent out of class with no destination. The teacher, being much more stressed, would aim to create the most peaceful experience possible. Her concern with dealing with attention-seekers would be much lower, for many students are now dealing with absentee parents, and everyone needs more attention. In an overcrowded classroom, it becomes the norm for various forms of attention to be sought after, but as one human being, she cannot manage a disturbance once it distracts her from her duty. The second time he is sent out of class. Tyler will be sent to the Dean of Discipline. With less funding than the affluent school, Tyler would have no option of seeing a psychiatrist or psychologist. Thus he would not learn to manage himself appropriately. Tyler instead is now suspended from school for mismanagement of his behavior, a skill he has not been taught. Becoming a threat to enter the school-to-prison pipeline, which is a socially-recognized pattern of increased prison time for students from poverty of the mind, body, and soul that receive fewer second chances due to a family, community, and school having poor resources. Additionally, harsher penalties and increased suspensions assist in the school-to-prison pipeline due to underfunded staff, faculty, and administration. The increased stress for exceptional performance from an underserved and impoverish school increases the stress of the school's leadership (staff, faculty, and administrators). Students in the non-affluent schools are at risk for harsher sentences from the school and prison system for committing the same disturbances as affluent students.

In second grade, I lived in Queens, NYC. I attended the local elementary school, Roy Wilkins elementary, P.S. 136. My teacher, Ms. Trumpet, was a great woman. She impressed my grandmother so much at the time that my grandmother gave Ms. Trumpet the permission to physically punish me if need be. As an energetic child, I was not bad but like all atomic beings, I was in constant motion. When my work was finished, I could be seen flying around the classroom from one side to the other. I was also an intellectual student who loved to get ahead. I would ruin the academic experience for many of my peers who did not read ahead. My grandmother instilled in me the need to be brilliant. She claimed all the best men knew much more than the rest. Reading already intrigued me, so I took my self-education to the next level every day. Writing became interesting to me once I learned cursive.

The ability to write without lifting my pencil as much fascinated me greatly. I remember I came to class and Ms. Trumpet grew furious when I wrote my entire assignment in cursive. She asked me before to not do so because it was difficult to read the handwriting of a 7 year old, let alone the handwriting of a 7 year old's cursive. I conveyed to her that I needed to practice, and that school is the best place to develop this skill. She demanded I rewrite my assignment in legible print. I refused to oblige in front of the whole class and began to deliver a dramatic speech as to why I should not have my educational advancement be held back.

"I am on time to class every day. I have given my all. I look to get ahead. Education is the key to freedom, Ms. Trumpet. I have a dream that one day, all kids will write in cursive. We will be able to write freely, to speak our minds and to boldly go where no kid has gone before. I will write in cursive. I care not what you think!"

She crept up to me with the power of a mother. She grabbed my hand and walked me to the front of the class. With my hand in her palm, I was at her mercy. With the quickness of an eagle, she slapped my hand. My eyes watered instantly. The classroom glared on in shock. Both Ms. Trumpet and I both knew she had this right. I knew the punishment was fair. She placed me in the corner and murmured, "Never again. You write in print." I stood there the remainder of the class period. I knew she held me accountable for my actions. I knew she would slap my hand every day if she had to. I wrote in print and spoke with the same confidence but in a favorable manner to Ms. Trumpet. I never challenged her again after that day. I knew when she hit my hand and spoke to me in the corner that she loved me. She did not send me out of class, but instead made me an example in front of all the other students. It was an opportunity to be a role model of excellent behavior in her class. She and my grandmother spoke about the incident. My grandmother smacked my tush. These women loved me and pushed me to step into my greatness because they wanted me to associate pain with poor ideas. It wasn't excessive nor did it make me cry, but it made a point. It was a fine point indeed. The community accountability did not look to have me marked as a troublemaker who would enter the God-forsaken school-to-prison pipeline. Instead, the teacher chose to build a strong relationship with my grandmother and to acknowledge our household's vibrational energy wave toward confrontations with children. Ms. Trumpet embodied my family's beliefs and sense of righteous actions, and committed herself to the dream my grandmother held for me. My community became my village, and it takes a village to raise a child, as stated by African proverbs.

My intelligence and abilities were never in question. My imagination and desire to write in cursive gained ample support from both my grandmother, who taught me to write in cursive, and Ms. Trumpet. She wanted to make sure I grasped the content of the academic tasks at hand. In developing my handwriting, the challenge proved to be no easy feat. My confidence in my academic performance affected my confidence overall. I had confidence in Ms. Trumpet's classroom but I learned, although confidence is great, there is more to it than being bold. I learned there are a time and a place for bravery. When wrong, it comes across as arrogant. When right, it's honored. Thus, I learned to manage my actions and passion. I earned student of the month for two months straight afterwards. I learned to love knowledge and understand more about when it is the right time to apply it. My grandmother valued it very much and told me to write my first book in cursive. The practice would better my skills. I needed to learn to be patient. She often communicated how she was patient for me to learn. I should be patient with Ms. Bell to teach when she engages a student who does not process information at the same speed as I. In fact, my grandmother began giving me books to take to school so I could read when I finished my work, instead of spreading my thoughts across the class.

Teachers, whether employed as such, living as parents or community members, will make a difference in your thinking, if you allow it. With each of us having a unique perspective on life, we develop a unique perspective on learning. The education of life provides many lessons. No two people see the same highlights in a movie, let alone in life. We often do not agree what occurs within a two-hour film; yet, the director and editor for the film predefine the perspective of sight we have. With the perspective being in our hands throughout life, we do not see the same truths. Thus the truth of the world remains different for each of us, which is exactly why people debate the ending of the movie *Inception* to this day. Was the dream over or not? The director wrote a short commentary about the ending and his intent that clarifies this ending. Discover the truth or you will not know. I believe it was real life, but my truth is not yours. We continue to discuss what remains valid. Therefore, the depictions of life and the real applications of the movie to understanding the power of an idea that consumes the human mind can serve to be the greatest advantage or hindrance to your existence. Freedom of thought is not the right to think whatever we wish. Freedom of thought allows the truth of many to enter so we have the freedom to decide our universal truth will be.

The dialogues you engage in teach us your perspective. If you control the dialogue, you control the perspective. In a classroom setting, the formal teacher controls the dialogue. She becomes a community leader. The dialogue follows her guidelines. The information from the books provides one perspective. The teacher provides another perspective, assuming she has information not conveyed in the textbook. The textbook provides one scope and understanding of how something works. In science, every notion, whether proven right once or a million times, still remains a theory. In history, the story told is that of the victor, not the loser, the oppressed, or the forgotten. School conveys a discussion in favor of the winner. If you want to win, write your own story. The world needs your perspective. The world needs your truth.

    The current perspective in history for African Americans ranges over three specific points in history: slavery, Dr. Martin Luther King, Jr., and the 44th President, Barack Obama. The rest of minorities receive no recognition in formal history classes conveying "American History," thus controlling the conversation about racial presence, oppression, and perspectives. As the saying goes, out of sight, out of mind. What we do not see, we will not think about. You don't know what you don't know that you don't know. If forgotten and left to the winner of imperialism, many stories will remain untold. As long as your story remains unknown, it shall remain misunderstood and not relevant. The conversation of history being passed down from parents and community members to children serves as a great source of empowering stories. Presenting narratives from various perspectives on history, science, and academic subjects provides various perspectives to minds. This conveyance allows for multiple understanding and the students to derive a truth within themselves versus accepting a single-story perspective. For news in present day U.S., we seek multiple sources. In research papers assigned in class, multiple sources serve as requirements in order to convey our notions. Yet, the multiple sources to create validity in school are not provided. They must be sought after. You will not find what you are not looking for. Thus, one textbook usually determines the completion of information gathered for one to develop knowledge. Inside of a collegiate course, you cannot expect to see multiple perspectives, but just the one of the professor. There is too much knowledge for one person to convey in less than 15 weeks – 10 for Drexel. The professor will never talk about every page in the readings assigned. The professor will get to the focus of the article and discuss her favorite parts. She thinks this is the best way in a two- to three-hour time span to engage as many of the readings as possible. Sometimes all of the reading will not be engaged in the course.

You need access, as a student, to the knowledge so you can learn more about the topic than the course structure will allow. You will receive more information than can be discussed. Determine the value of it. What is not discussed can be a great reference in an upcoming assignment or answer to a question on the final. Study what you value so the motivation to learn comes easily.

You will grow more interested in school once the relativity of these perspectives strike familiarity to your current life. The perspectives most closely tied to you create a mental environment that welcomes your vibrational energy waves to interact with the information and develop. Your curiosity will grow once the relativity of information directly addresses your future ambitions. In a diverse community, multiple perspectives from the source of information may arise. Allowing yourself to understand the material from different perspectives allows you to strengthen your argument. Dialogue and debate do not have to force you to change your mind, but to strengthen your reasoning to pick the most righteous arguments.

Lastly, develop your own truth. For example, the planets are named after Roman gods. Take the planet Mercury. Students regurgitate the names of the planets, but never gain an interdisciplinary understanding of the names or the history of the significance to the names. Mercury evolved from the Greek god, Hermes. Hermes evolved to be from the conceptions of the Egyptian god, Tahuti. These gods are known as the gods of information and communication. Tahuti serves as the messenger most close to god, often serving as the right hand to the leader of the gods, as a messenger between the Earth and heavens. Mercury thus serves as the closest planet to the sun. Christians praise God on Sunday because the sun served as the ultimate representation of enlightenment. The sun feeds humans energy and vitamins through melanin and to the plants through photosynthesis. The sun becomes visible every day as the earth rotates around it, providing light for the entire masses of the planet, allowing us to see all the beauty that surrounds us. This lightening process enlightened us to the reactions and things we can see now that the sun shines bright. Thus we seek enlightenment through that which we can see. What we see becomes images in our mind. Tahuti serves as the god of enlightenment by communicating knowledge both ways between heaven and Earth. He represents the ultimate knowledge of the light traveling from the sun to Earth. As each civilization rose and fell, the planets gained different names. The Roman names stayed prevalent in Western enlightenment, allowing Mercury to be the name of the planet closest to the sun during our human civilization. Go to a different country and the names will be different in their civilization. The term enlightenment stems from the sun's impact and remains prevalent today in highly intellectual, spiritual, and academic communities, a blessing the god Tahuti/Hermes/Mercury used to govern. Their names, like your name, matter!

  An interesting narrative of naming is often skipped in school. The narrative of students earning their names and nicknames tells a lot about who they are. The history and significance of your name has a meaning that imposes a lot of light on the journey you are having in life. Once your truth is recognized, the narrative of your journey becomes more important. The formal education of school leaves little room for the personal experience to be conveyed. There is so much information to learn, but the teacher has little to no time to engage the person that lives inside of you. Finding your peace of mind must come from outside of the classroom.

  Often, the friends we have serve as the greatest outlet to tell our stories to. Many people write blogs to share their stories. This knowledge is endless and very valuable. The ability to control the narrative of life holds much power. Without the opportunity to convey the life we live, we leave ourselves to be explained by others. We can see efforts to tell a different narrative in the arts and entertainment industry. Moviecation is an educational term used to describe one's ability to learn from movies. I developed the term musication to convey the ability to understand the narrative of an individual experience through music. These efforts allow all cultures to say that there are more truths to hold self-evident than the single story conveyed. Many movies in America reveal different understandings. People often take movies about musicians' lives very seriously. The narratives that reflect the musical stories people identify with create a relative perspective. The relevant perspective of the music has a spiritual effect on the person's emotions, mental state, and physical balance. A song can change our mood. The mood simultaneously effects the emotion, mentality, and physical nature. The learned behavior of the music's message, tempo, and combination of effects can greatly impact someone's day. The positive effect of music to convey a story and perspective relevant to its audience has proven to play a huge part in music's creation. In the 1800s, the American slaves used music to convey travel routes of the Underground Railroad. People communicated direction to reach freedom by remixing gospel song and making new songs. Later that century, battle drums were used to keep a beat for military men fighting for the emancipation of the slaves and to unite the economic strength of the union to the Industrial Revolution. In the 1900s, music served as a pathway to racial understanding to listen to the effects of the American experience in various perspectives across socio-economic, political, and racial divides. In the 1960s and 1970s, music served as chants of anti-corporate culture and the development of the war economy in protest against the Vietnam War. In the 2000s, music served as an avenue of critique of the variances of the socio-economic experiences. Throughout the history of time in human civilization, music has served as a spiritual tool in religious practices. Lastly, music has always been a great way to get the party started. The use of musication as an avenue to convey vibrations to the physical mind has worked very well. The vibrations from amplified music set the tone mentally. Physically, human beings are comprised of 70%

water. Therefore the vibrations from amplified music create water vibration waves in our bloodstream. The reason "we can vibe to this jam" is because the music's vibrations physically alter us with a favorable vibration. The reason why many people cannot study with music or resist dancing to a good song stems from the feeling we have when music is turned on. The impact of music is a learned behavior of vibrations. When coupled with poetry in rhythm, the power is gigantic. To understand humanity and know how society will respond to a major act of turmoil in politics, analyze the top five most popular songs in that era. The top songs serve as a global mental response to the present-day society and culture. The songs of the time set the tone and mindset of the people. Protestors against police brutality sing Bob Marley and Kendrick Lamar songs. These artists' lyrics set the vibrational energy waves of many people at one time across the globe.

     Teachers sing a song to students every day. The consistent impact of stating a child's name, nickname, or not speaking his or her name at all affects the students' self-esteem. What we are called, we often become. That is why our name means a lot. It is what we are called the most. The voice's vibrations enter your subconscious mind as affirmed notions, ones we focus on, accept, and transform into. Students contribute to many affirmations of the mind with nicknames. Oftentimes, we meet adults who are still marked by their childhood experiences. The permanent effects of self-perspective cannot be forgotten, but they can be overcome with positive reinforcement. The teachers of life hold that responsibility. The responsibility of leaderships falls on you to name your children with positive intent. Call life-learners pleasant and positive names. Since we all learn all the time, treat everyone with positivity.

     Even in play, poor attributes can be attached. Too many teachers-of-life call the youth, "bad kids," "knuckleheads," or worse. Many verbally strike others with words of foul play. The school's campus provides an avenue for the multiplication of learned notions of self. The school environment can serve as a place of happiness or depression, if not both, for all in attendance. The teachers have to reinforce the infinite possibilities of intelligence within each child. Genius is not an esoteric gift granted to a few. Genius is a result of the long-time effort of consistent and persistent action towards one goal in one subject. To have a great classroom environment, the classroom must have individual, small group, and large group activities.

Individually, a child will learn. Sitting in silence of thought or in self-engaged conversation allows the student to get comfortable with his or her own thoughts. Our own thoughts often scare us more than anything else. The student must work through internal concepts to master material of all kinds.

Secondly, a small group of five or less, preferably three, has a guided dialogue. The three-part conversation forms a triangle. Three specific triangle options usually appear in one of the three Triangular Formations: (1) a United triangle (equilateral), (2) an Egyptian triangle (Scalene), or a (3) Titans triangle (Isosceles). (1) A United, small-group conversation allows each person to bring equal value to the conversation. Each person fully expresses his or her opinions. United small groups may not have everyone speaking in equal portion, but the equality rests in the equal expressions of ideas based upon how each person wants to speak. (2) An Egyptian small-group conversation has one person expressing their idea the most. Someone else is second, and the last person is third in expression. In order of importance to the discussion, the purpose of each small group member differs. The shortest side, referred to as Osiris, is the starter of the conversation and the guide. The base of the triangle, referred to as Isis, takes the conversation from its beginning into the grand conception of the final stages of the academic dialogue. The hypotenuse, referred to as Horus, thrives as the ultimate nexus by putting the dialogue into an understandable format, often explaining the concepts discussed to small groups of peers, the entire class, or the teacher. (3) Finally, the Titans small group is constructed by two individuals who contribute the most valuable information to the conversation with the base participant serving as the spokesperson for the small group or a conceptual nexus. Each small group type promotes excellence of thought through various forms of intellectual engagement. The dynamics of each triangle differ, yet the general process of beginning the conversation, evolving the concepts, and finally creating a nexus between the thoughts yields the desired result. A teacher must recognize and appreciate these various small group types to allow free learning dialogue to take place. **Equality of the mind's expression and actualization weighs far more heavily than a social equity of participation though speaking in equal proportions.** I would encourage teachers to assign small group styles and components to have a more micromanaged group effort if they find this valuable for the community style of the classroom.

You are you because of what you do every day. #Habits

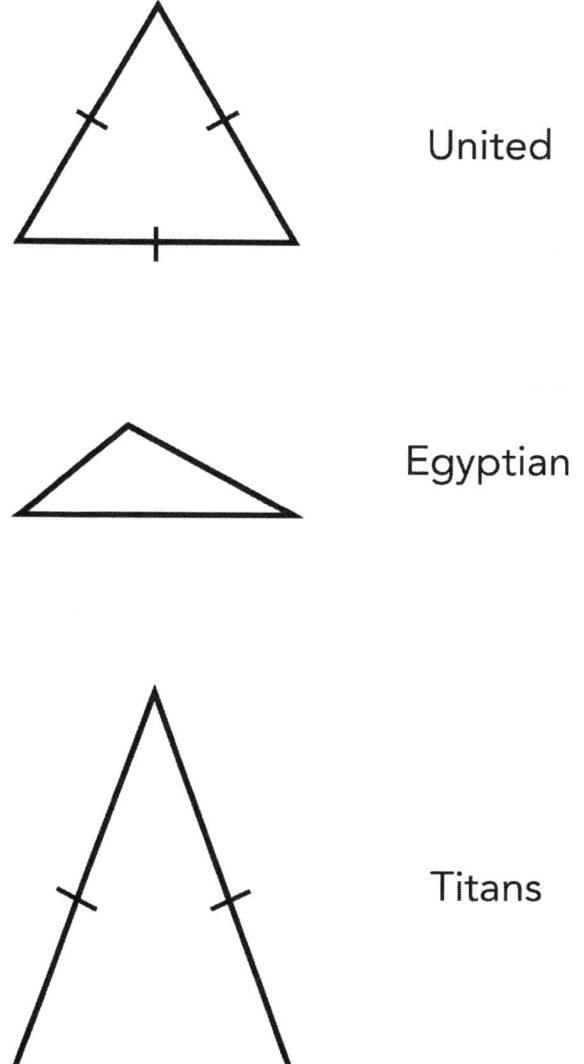

Large groups are less effective groups, but have a different impact that can still enlighten. Large groups have more than three people. The large groups create a dynamic that is less personal between the members. Factions can be created, as well as couples. Nonetheless, an equal approach of engagement in these circumstances can exist in order to be fair to all students. A true fairness would allow for each student to do what is best for him or her to achieve the fair goal without hindering one another. With unfair opportunity for participation, imbalances in preparedness and opportunity will arise.

    The goal of group interaction is to foster creativity and community. Community calls for collective action. Unity is established in many group formations besides United. Unity happens when the balance and freedom of expression are valued in each person participating. Thus people learn to serve a grander purpose in the world through community actions. Unity creation yields the highest amount of RIM, which occurs for many actions through the interactions of teacher-lead classroom engagement.

    In the Triangular Formations, solitude, or large-group learning, the students must reflect. Reflection promotes thoughts within self about self. Reflecting refers to a light experience. Light travels in a straight line. It holds all the colors of the rainbow, and this appears white, a collection of all color. When it hits a mirror, glass, or water, it beams in a straight line in another direction. The direction depends on the angle in which the light contacts the clear force. Nonetheless, the light shines in another direction or back in the same direction to which it came. Reflection, as a thinking concept, requires us to conceive our perceptions about where the light is coming from. Light is the information and experience gathered. We reflect by processing the information and spreading it back to the world. Thinking is enough, but the reflection is stronger in greater forms of expression. The reflections of a professor shine brighter than the average individual because the professor can spread the information to many more people than the average citizen. Authors and speakers also have reflections that shine brighter. Nonetheless, we are all born ignorant. Thus, we have to realize Malcolm X was right when he stated, "There was a time when you didn't know what you know today." It is important to understand that the ignorance of one is a teaching opportunity for another. We must serve as the teacher to inform others of the information they have not yet been exposed to. It requires patience for understanding. It takes time for people to understand. The ability to have patience to teach someone something new serves as a great motivator for the student to learn more. It encourages them. Thus the process of RIM takes place. RIM is the greatest key to enlightenment before actualization. Reflecting allows one to take knowledge and critically think about it in relation to what they already know. The process of another person joining their journey of enlightenment inspires the student to learn more than what they already know, thus motivating the student to achieve at the highest level possible in future educational environments. Understand that reflection processes the past. Inspiration encourages the moment. Motivation empowers the future. Providing RIM to another human being is an example of love. The encouragement to grapple the unknown and make it truth will provide a great avenue of respect for the learning process.

All learning is not polite. Tough love exists, as all people must learn through failure. Failure will provide a scar to serve as a reminder of what not to do. Knowing the wrong steps makes the right steps easier to see. The light at the end of the tunnel requires us to walk in the dark. The universe is mostly made of darkness, but the stars scattered throughout make it possible to know there is much more to learn than what we know on Earth. It is because of the light that we are aware of the darkness we live in. Tell someone your truth, but let him prove it to himself. The wise will heed the word of others who hold scars of truth, yet the curious mind will always travel the darkness to learn the lesson firsthand. One scar tells one story. The darkness waits with many wounds to inflict, many scarred stories. Understand that failure is neither an end location, nor is it forever. Failure is a moment, not a life sentence. Failure is but a bump in the road to enlightenment. **Teachers must respect the curious and serve as the wise to guide students through**

the darkness. Additionally, teachers must respect the various journeys and conceptions RIM will bring about. We all find different truths in darkness and in light so it is up to the teacher to appreciate the different results that may come about from a student's travels down the same path of knowledge, requiring a great dialogue of notions conceived from engaging the material at hand.

Paulo Freire's Banking versus Problem-Posing Education supports this theory. He holds two truths in education of how a teacher may engage students. One is entitled the Banking Concept; the other is called Problem-Posing Education. Let us understand the two approaches to understand how every human being can be a "banker" or a "poser". (1) A banker is a teaching human being who deposits information. To keep ideas simple, let's look to the traditional form of teaching. A teacher deposits information into students' minds. He or she asks for students to memorize and regurgitate information back to them in the form of examinations and quizzes without any critical thinking. (2) A poser presents a world problem. The problem is relevant and current to the community of students learning. The posed problem requires the student to acquire information and deposit it into their minds, then to invest that information into further information acquisitions. Next, the critical analyzing of the information allows the student to invest that information into a dialogue to exchange information between each person while also critically analyzing the new information. It creates a full Circle of Thought as the inputted information gets processed and reassessed with every outputted statement, thus creating a critical dialogue on how to solve a current problem facing the community. The two differ because of the critical thinking process. Friere suggested these two learning situations occur in the world but banking dominates and creates an oppressed group that feels limited in mind. For even the brightest minds in a banking education may only be able to communicate what was communicated to them, thus eliminating innovation and creativity, the birthplace of human evolution. Oftentimes, problem-posing education requires the teacher to be able to listen to students and accept the opportunity to learn from different thinkers younger than them, which is often seen as a hindrance in education. Consequently, I believe it serves as a teacher's greatest advantage to learn from his or her students, for the ability to learn is restricted from the mindset of those who do not wish for it. We always have more to learn with an infinite source of knowledge living behind the eyes of each person, be they 5 years old or 50. Learning from someone younger than you communicates encouragement for the youth to continue to see himself as a source of knowledge, thus promoting their ability to innovate and create opportunity for others. Learning is a circle. The Circle of Thought is not only singular, but also a unifier of persons all.

When learning is restricted, you become a chained elephant. One night, an elephant trainer demonstrated the thought process of a chained elephant. The trainer spoke about how animals taken from their homeland may grow weary and feisty when the uncomforting location of their new caged home becomes overwhelming. When the animals, elephants in particular, are born into this restricted habitat, the frustrations of their parents can be genetically passed down, and the mannerism of their ancestors' mindsets will also impact the newborn elephant's mentality. When elephants are chained as infants to a post they cannot break from, it makes an imprint of limitation on their minds. The limitation of physical movement becomes a mental limitation. Thus, a fully-grown elephant will not leave the post if even a shoe string ties it there or there is no chain at all because the mentality of limitation has been established strongly as a child, serving as a foundation of ability. A student may also encounter the mental limitation of the chained elephant when the student is overly banked. The student learns to not think critically and view critical thinking as her ability outside of her chained element. A mental chain and limitation becomes true, and these under educated persons become our global citizens. It is important we punch those limitations in the face so every citizen can get the full benefit of a proper education. The mental limitations provide a restriction only we can break. If we think about our minds as finite, we often see ourselves as people who may have a limit on the prosperity we can gain. Instead, I **encourage you to understand the art that is learning because it will extend the mental limitations you set upon yourself.**

    The art of learning takes place just as a picture does. It starts with a sketch. We sketch out with a pencil on the canvas of life the foundation and expectation we wish. After accepting the path designed, we begin to apply the necessary to achieve a beautiful artwork. We apply the paint. We mix water in it to make the paint applicable to the canvas. Life is a blank canvas. Through application of our paint to the canvas, we compose a stroke of color. The color awaits more applications of paint to result in a great piece of art. Juxtapose the artwork to the learning process. Before we begin learning, we must understand the intention of our learning. What do we intend to derive from engaging this material? Our canvas is our mind. The pencil is the information. Our designs serve as the expectation of what we are to learn from this information. The strokes of paint serve as the knowledge because we are applying the information to life and thus creating an artwork called life. Next, we see the result of each careful stroke unite in a beautiful creation. When we apply knowledge, we can see it come together. Our life is what we are, not what we want it to be. We can see if we followed the design or not. The imagination of what the color strokes of paint would result in can now be put to the test. We see if the painting did or did not come out to what we thought it would. We can understand if we should adjust our strategy on the next canvas or not. I often find the picture turns out to be much better than my expectations. The painting may have taken a different course because the pencil cannot mimic color. It is a precautionary tool that often limits the scope of what great artwork my life can be. Therefore I see the art of learning to be an application of excellence to my life that I cannot predict no matter how detailed my outline may be. The beauty of art is the process of realization. When people look at my life, they see proof of what I have learned to apply in it.

Understand the power of storytelling. Our lives are constantly telling a story. When we walk down the street or interact in class, we convey stories of ourselves. Our very being, attitude, and posture communicate a story. We demonstrate the experiences of life and what we have come to value in our actions and expressions. Thus, the best learning comes from understanding the process of life behind every art piece. You are the artwork. You are the gatekeeper of the story of how you came to be the beautiful display of art you are. When we see people, we judge their art. When we have the chance to hear the story of people's lives, we can understand the strokes of paint and whether or not what we see serves as a true testament of the penciled design.

As a teacher, the lives of students allow us to connect the learning process better. We can assist students to pencil and paint better if we understand the differences between prior art development and the present need. We create the nexus between what was a tumultuous past to a prosperous present. The personal stories of students can better relate to the information conveyed if we create direct connections. For example, I taught a class entitled "Creating Culture in America" during the fall of 2014. I challenged the students to listen to a Chance the Rapper song entitled "Pusha Man." The song has three phases. The first part served as a stereotypical inner-city rap song about selling drugs and being cool for the enterprise. The second phase speaks to why the drug dealer sells the narcotics, which is due to famine, family responsibilities, and financial challenges that come with living in a low socio-economic community. The third component speaks to the lack of helpful aid the entire low socio-economic community receives to combat these issues and eradicate the cycle of oppression in the wealthiest nation on the planet. At the end of the song, he proclaims to mainstream U.S.A., "I know you'd care if you were here, too." The students received a pop quiz that required them to listen to this song and answer the prompt, "Why should we care?" It forced the students to critically analyze their impact on society in order to deconstruct oppressive actions, not only as citizens of the mainstream nation, but also as urban college students who live in close proximity to similar inner-city evils. Many a time, people can keep themselves apart from the societal issues of others, even within their own country. Students felt responsible to understand. Their responses to the assignment required them to decide if they care or do not care about the experiences of Chance the Rapper and the inner-city turmoil of Chicago, Illinois.

    The ability to convey societal challenges through storytelling allowed the students to view the drug dealers of the United States as human beings. The beginning of the song highlighted the drug dealer, commonly known as the pusha man, to be viewed in the entertaining preferred fashion confirming the status quo and glorified criminalization. I noticed the students bobbing their heads in rhythm to the song, but when the transition occurred into the second phase, the students stopped. They remained still in critical thought. They neither moved nor smiled. The beautiful experiences of an artist took them to a different place through storytelling, a perspective unknown. The picture of Chance the Rapper and inner city Chicago changed as the paint was removed. The pencil shades emerged and the canvas was exposed in a raw form, allowing the layers of art to be revealed. The question of social responsibility no longer seemed like a beautiful artwork we admired from afar. I aimed to put the paintbrush of social equality into the students' hands. They grabbed the canvas and began to mark the canvas with pencils. Basquiat would be proud. The connection between our socio-political responsibility, art, and learning were united.

It motivated some students to make a greater impact on the student body while challenging students to create a designed artwork of life for themselves. After the winter term passed, I had two students, Abe and Khadija, who wished to recreate the reflective process of understanding ourselves within the framework of the world. If humanity is a giant art piece, it is important to understand how we are stroking the canvas. Each person is a paintbrush in humanity, letting our paint tell the story of our species. I communicated the concept of humanity and how the way we fit within it may be too grand for a workshop. It was perfect for a class that lasted fall term, but even in those eleven weeks, we left many conversations unfinished. Many topics never made it to our classroom dialogue. I promoted a smaller scale assessment of the Drexel campus and university community as our artwork. We need to encourage students to paint with intention on campus. We need to establish an understanding of how the university serves as a place of innovation, community, business, and human development. Khadija and Abe agreed, and they served as my student co-founders of the three-day workshop series, "Motivators: Design a Life".

The aim of the workshop series was to guide the students to construct a life with intention on campus to maximize their human capital. The gains they could make from excelling on campus required social, personal, professional, and academic excellence. To understand the university artwork in creation, the students needed to know what they were painting. The series allowed peer engagement to teach students that having a formula is required and to trust the process. Don't rush the process because the tortoise is mightier than the hare. The hare may win today. The hare is faster. The hare can move many times up and down the racetrack of life. Yet, the hare lives for 14 years on average. A tortoise will thrive for 100 years, taking in, critically, the environment around him. Thus Khadija and Abe shared their development of understanding and critically analyzing Drexel

University as a place aiming to make great contributing citizens through professional excellence and community engagement. **What impact will you make on your community?** I posed this question to the students with great intention. We experienced the wise words of leaders from all walks of life. Khadija, Abe, and I led activities challenging student to build bridges between their ideal lives, experiences, college community, and the reality they faced today. It was an incredibly reflective process questioning students' purposes in higher education. College is a great experience to find oneself, but individuals need to create themselves before too much time is wasted in college. Without creating yourself, you will not find peace within you. Don't blame the world for not having purpose when the power to establish your own purpose is your responsibility. Your life will result in an art piece of happenstance instead of intention if you continue to ask the outer world to build your inner world. Motivators: Design a Life created a thinking space to reflect upon our experiences, great leaders, and inspiring quotes with the Golden Circle established by Simon Sinek, being our vehicle of thinking.

Sinek serves as a motivational consultant for businesses and conveys three points to the success of a great business: The Why, How, and What. "Most employees know what they do. Some leaders of the company know how they do it. Few people actually understand why they do what they do" (Simon Sinek, 2014). In modern society, the wave of entrepreneurship has become the dominant form of enterprise for financial freedom. Everyone is a business. You are a business. The identity of a corporation is tied to the body. The foundation of the corporation comes from the Latin term corpus, meaning body. We, human beings, are born with a body. Corporations are all identified in two ways. The first identification granted to the business is a name. At birth, we are granted a name to be called. In the U.S.A., each corporation is given an EIN (Employee Identification Number). The social security number given to us at birth serves as our identification number when we are employed or pay the local and federal government to serve us (taxes). Thus, business are structured in the United States too emulate the human. You are a business.

    Sinek's Golden Circle applies to all businesses. From the prior information we can assess that each human being is a business within the federal government corporation of the U.S.A. Therefore, every citizen is responsible for knowing their Golden Circle. We took each day to analyze the greatest Golden Circles of the world and challenge students to brainstorm their personal corporate commitments. Upon attendance, each student was bestowed with an unruled composition book, because life is a blank page. It is with this book that your paintbrush begins to paint the campus community canvas with intention. You will not wait for words to fall on the blank page, but instead, you will create a story, person, business, and student who embrace what you are taught and will teach others by living your life lessons.

All people must learn through failure

11
ADVISING

Advisors are your personal trainers for success in higher education.

In the world of banking, there are financial advisors; people who are dedicated to helping the customer take advantage of the best offers available at their financial institution. Advisors in an education system serve as the people who assist the students to maximize their opportunities within education to the best of their abilities. In a banking system of education, we can see the advisors are restricted to offering students opportunities as transactions. This is the same way a bank teller or financial advisor will only convey information for your finances that their financial institution offers. **What is best for you and the institution simultaneously?** The institutions hire individuals who speak to the best interest of the school and you. This professional focuses on providing the best medium for your experience academically and in co-curricular activities. It takes courage to tell a student to transfer schools, utilize resources beyond the academic community, or convey that a university professor's main goal is to earn tenure through their research production. Everyone wants to secure their self-interest, and an advisor must understand the various interests of the people in the academic community. When meeting with students, the advisor must understand the purpose of each teacher, institution, student, administrators, and executives to best guide those asking for assistance. The advisor lives on the front lines of educational transcendence that students experience every day.

Thus communication becomes the primary avenue of opportunity. The advisor communicates ideas and challenges notions, developing you into the best student you can be. Advisor aim to help you actualize the your academic purpose in and outside of the classroom. Know yourself to know your wealth to best help advisors understand your desired learning outcomes.

The advisor can best serve you, the student, with love. Love will be the toughest challenge because it demands each student become a priority once we understand the student's academic purpose. You should grow intellectually. Tough love is best characterized by observing a football coach. There is a lot of passion and intensity within a designed plan of action in order to win. The love is one of a personal trainer who makes the mind of the student more fit to accomplish their goals. No lies will be told to convey comfort. We must be honest. We must be direct. We must stick to the plan. We, the advisors, will be there to periodically check in with you, the student, to make sure you are on track to meet your goals. Every day, repeat to yourself, "It's possible." If one person accomplished their academic goals, it is very so much possible for you to accomplish yours! Whether it is a specific career path or achieving a goal undiscovered by humanity. There will be a bit of mentoring in this, but the advisor can restrict themselves to specific meetings and appointments. Mentoring and going all out for the student is not a demand of the advisor. Your personal trainer does not work out with you all the time. They demonstrate and observe. You visit your trainer when you can, but your trainer is not there during the game or practice. The trainer is there when needed. Developing the student into the excellent scholar requires a breadth and depth of knowledge in every industry they wish to enter. To promote their excellence within their desired field, the advisor must know the basics of the culture within the profession and dream desired in order to best engage the student. Listening to the student speak about the knowledge gained gives an advisor insight. An advisor being willing to learn from the student will serve as a great practice to relationship building. This will take effort from you, the student, to being open with your advisor about your goals and struggles. A closed mouth does not get fed. In order to eat at the table of opportunity, you must be able to open your mouth, use your words, and communicate. As an advisor, listening to you, the student is my best advantage in helping you achieve. You say the answer to your questions many times but often desire external validation before you fully commit.

In my one-on-one meetings, I often ask the students to tell me their life stories. They convey their experiences and how they arrived at this university. It is a great reflection process and an opportunity to express who they are. Many students do not reflect about who they are and why they are here. Sean Carter once stated, "Don't go with the flow, be the flow." I notice most students ride the boat on the river of life instead of using oars to direct themselves through the current. A salmon swims upstream to determine her path. By taking control of your lives, you will arrive at your desired shore instead of one of happenstance. Listening to their story allows me to pull references from their lives to quote and mention in my advice. When students realize they have already overcome all of their worst days in life. Every bad day you have faced before, they conquered. You are undefeated when facing your worst days. Going forward in life, remember you are undefeated. Your self-confidence to achieve is your greatest asset. Without directly communicating that notion, I find many ways to encourage my students to achieve by citing how they have already achieved so much in life, even if the present challenge requires readjustment to their successful approach.

The group discussions I have with students highlight new thoughts. They are able to meet new people. I see every student who enters the student lounge. The student schedules may change, and that opportunity will change when they come into the lounge. Thus, they have a new opportunity to meet new students. A conversation I have with one student will allow another who knows me to enter the dialogue. I introduce the students to each other and allow the triangle of conversation to occur. Whether it be

Egyptian, United, or Titanic, I become whatever role is necessary for a great conversation to happen.

The value of the contribution depends on the students' self-worth, the attentive listening, and the value we express in the statement relayed. Attentive listening comes from body language, confirming to the speaker that the listener appreciates what has been said. This happens through the occasional head nod. Nodding the entire time is distracting and actually takes more energy than listening. Eye contact is the most important. Watching someone speak gives full confirmation. Blinking and occasionally smirking make the consistent eye contact less creepy. Deep blank stares will contradict the power of the eye contact so feel free to look away from time to time. The attentive listening communicates faith in one's words and rhetoric; this increases the willingness of one to speak more openly to you. Most importantly, the speaker receives appreciation and validation through attention, a need all humans value.

Life on a college campus focuses on four aspects of engagement that an advisor must be able to understand in order to provide the most valuable advice a student can utilize. When engaging students, the Box of Engagement contains four aspects: Academic, Personal, Professional, and Social.

Attentive listening comes from body language

Academic	Personal
Social	Professional

The Box of Engagement

Students too must understand the intensity of the Box of Engagement in order to best comprehend and organize their lives. When one can fit the aspects of life into an organized format, they can decide their values and life agenda more efficiently. The academic box engaging a student's life contains the classroom, tutoring, and studying they conduct in order to achieve the highest marks possible in their desired studies. The personal box focuses on a student's mindset for human development, leisure reads, romantic experiences, and self-improvement. This is the most important box of engagement because it requires the student to establish a definition of self-love and to actualize it on an everyday basis so the student can grow strong in confidence, competence, and self-worth. The professional box of engagement focuses on their preparation and experiences within the economic culture they desire to achieve in. Simultaneously, if a student works while in school, the professional box of engagement considers the influence a student worker has on their maturity and ability to achieve on a college campus. Lastly, the social box of engagement considers the remaining spaces of experiences a student has with people who do not fit within the previous spaces. Friends live within the social space, along with how a student spends. Social engagement is important for the student to have fun and find ways to engage people without a personal, professional, or academic agenda at hand. It serves as the space to see which self is presented. Oftentimes we may look to social media as an outlet to express concepts we have and speak with people about our lives, but more times than not, unless one parties excessively, there is not much room for engagement in this box. The primary amount of time spent should be personal, with an emphasis on self-love. The secondary amount of time should be on academics, for the development of educational success promotes one's ability to serve well in professional spaces when organized correctly. The professional box will soon take the most time once a full-time job takes place, for most Americans spend more time at work than they do anywhere else. Lastly, social skills to manage a conversation well and be able to entertain others are the greatest assets one can learn in the social box, but serve a better purpose when utilized in the other three boxes. The social box of engagement hardly advances one's ability to actualize their vision of life. It is the greatest inhibitor, but it does confirm one's ability to be normal. Normal should not be a goal. People should aim for excellence in all four boxes, but in the proper order. Otherwise, a social box of engagement's primary focus will allow one to be liked but not efficient in achieving their dreams.

An advisor should always understand your achievements and goals in all four Boxes of Engagement in order to properly advise you on courses and time management. The Box of Engagement will allow an advisor to understand, on a surface level, the impact of prior experiences and present-day focus. When establishing goals to achieve, the Box of Engagement presents many opportunities for the student to explain and reflect about who they are. Advisors create the safest space for reflection of self because we are straddling the lines of engagement. Our professional box of engagement is to be at the center as a circle of growth for the student to enhance their ability to achieve in life via the four boxes of engagement.

Great questions an advisor can ask you, a student, to understand your Boxes of Engagement are: **(1) What is your family like? Does your family believe in your ability to succeed here? I am sure they are proud of you. (2) What are some differences you see between your high school experience and college experience thus far? (3) How did you decide your major? What majors do your friends study? If you could make your own major, what would it focus on? (4) As a junior, tell me about the differences you experience in and out of the classroom from first year to now? (5) What are you thinking about for next summer? You should start** planning now before fall semester is over. Are you interning, traveling, or taking classes? I know you like to plan ahead. (6) What skills and passions have you developed so far in your college experience? What did you do to improve those skills and passions?

Advisors, encourage your students in college by reinforcing their commitment to excellence. After a student achieves a goal, challenge them to do more excellent things. Once you pump the ego of a student, use it as an anchor to achieve more. If they succeeded once, they can succeed again. Repetition of achievement yields the highest growth in excellence throughout life. Direct them to gain skills towards their goals. Experience is the best teacher in life. Through student organizations, many students can practice skills and develop their passions before testing the professional market. Everything matters. Every minute counts. Every decision is a life decision. Every mistake is a lesson and a blessing. **In order to create a better learning environment, we must convince our students to have faith in themselves.** We must motivate them. Through great efforts of self-love and exampling love, our students can be better than us. We have a job that requires us to eradicate our needs by making our students self-efficient in self-love and actualization of their educational imagination. Due to the social requirement of a college degree in order to pursue 45% of available jobs in the U.S.A., we have to guide students to help them achieve the basic requirements for upward mobility. Love your students. **Making your students better will make you better.**

When the student comes into your office with great inhibitions, it is important to search their dreams. On the Internet, in front of the student, we can learn how they can achieve these ambitions. Find one characteristic of one of the great people who have accomplished the student's career or life goals. Focus on it. When we state a familiarity between the student and their favorite achiever, we create faith in the student's ability to capture opportunity. We may have to convey all the hard work they will have to do to replicate this individual, but that is just true for most valuables of life. If it were easy, everybody would be doing it. As an advisor, it is important we set small milestones to guide the student's path to success. With a wide variety of student majors, we may not know every great person, but with the Internet, we can find one in less than one second. From that point, we can establish a new set of goals for the student. We create, with the student, a dream to manifest. This may become their definite desire and lead them to great heights. ==The dream is great, but who you become in pursuit of the goal is most important.== The knowledge, passions, talents, and skills cannot be lost. The value they seek lives in the ability to learn and actualize. There, the true wealth of self-education lives in abundance. Truthfully, students, you can do this for yourself. If your advisor is unwilling, it is time you take your life into your own hands and achieve your dreams by following the steps outlined in this chapter and the chapters before it.

It requires going above and beyond sometimes. I had two students approach me with a great ambition to cure cancer. I could not believe it. They asked if I had any research opportunities first-year students could partake in. I had no idea what to say. I was at a loss for words. I told them to look into a summer research program offered by the Honors College called S.T.A.R., but they wanted something immediate, not in the summer. With six months left until July, I told them I would contact some friends and see what I could do. I had a few friends in oncology research labs and asked about opportunities. They, too, had nothing available, but one had access to a listserv that listed many research opportunities. I communicated to these students that the listserv would be forwarded to me and I would send them the same research opportunities. Until I could get them some opportunity, I asked a friend if she would allow us to have a tour of the research lab she managed. I had a feeling, if they could see their destination, they could achieve their desire. Soon, an opportunity came. Then another. Within three months, both students were interviewing at laboratories. After four months, both earned research positions in oncology as data-entry interns. It was not exactly what they wanted, but they were in the building. I communicated to the students that while they were in entry-level positions, they still had opportunity. Yes, you are at the bottom of the research lab, but you are in there. Go above and beyond. Do more than asked. When you exceed expectations, this is how you achieve your desire. People appreciate those who go the extra mile. I told them I became Professor Miles because I excelled as an advisor and program coordinator. The overachievement in the position provided an opportunity to achieve my dream of co-teaching on a university level at 23. I taught my own class at 24. Do not belittle this, but see it as your first piece of gold in building your gold mine. "I am proud" of you two. Way to go!"

The dream is great, but who you become in pursuit of the dream is most important.

12
PROGRAMMING

Consistently finding ways to give students the power of understanding will improve the success of programming efforts.

The power of group dialogue knows no bounds. Everyone has an infinite source of knowledge behind their eyes. Therefore, each pair of eyes brings a new perspective to the dialogue. In programming in higher education, I have learned that opinions matter. If we, the programmers (of humans not computers) and program coordinators, create a schedule of events the students know and expect, they will show up to these events at a higher turnout. Everyone has plenty of opinions. Present an idea. Let the thoughts be known. Be quick to present the notion. Be quick to listen to the feedback from the students, staff, and faculty. Ask their opinions. Before allowing the group to respond, challenge everyone to be critical, which encourages solitude in thought and collective dialogue. Have them write down their own thoughts to respond to the topic at hand. Afterwards, have small groups speak to each other about their conceptions. Allow for differences and similarities to erupt. Bring the large group back to a discussion to speak on the various thoughts expressed. Ask participants to respond to each other. Have a list of thoughts you want to touch base on and critically challenge. When students bring up thoughts you wanted to speak on, be sure to dive deeply into those thoughts until the point you, the facilitator, wishes to achieve has been accomplished. From that point forward, if the students focus on a point you did not intend, allow further critical thought to occur. What the facilitator does not value may hold great prestige with students. Everyone can become a teacher, student, and advisor in a workshop. There are no limits to the knowledge gained and contributed.

There must be a goal for the programming workshop to achieve. **What must the students know? What can they not be without? How will the participants feel? What physical item can they leave with?** Create the topic. Create the goal. Create the process. That is the foundation of excellence within prosperous programming. For example, a program I love is the Art of Office Hours. I have facilitated it many a times. The program begins with a conversation about why office hours are important. Students then establish the answers and reasons without me having to state them. We all know the power. The students can gain insight, further explanation, develop relationships with professors, and possibly earn a letter of recommendation for future use. I made a YouTube video, briefly recapping some of those points. Watch it here: https://www.youtube.com/watch?v=D8MIRex8zuc Continually, I create a process to discuss the manners and culture of a proper office hour session. There is a lot to engage in 15 minutes, but without taking the right steps, a student can disrespect the information and knowledge gained, created, and disseminated by a professor. We conclude by asking students to demonstrate office hour tactics and a one-sentence summary of the lessons learned within the workshop.

Another workshop activity I love is the "Silent University." Students surround a large piece of paper. Eight students hold seven markers total. For 15 minutes, in silence, the eight students draw their ideal university. For 10 minutes afterwards, we discuss it. Many a time, students forget essentials, such as administrative duties and libraries, but have a huge concentration on social engagement spaces and entertainment. The university looks more like a playground, but it conveys where they find value in the university. Academic and social experiences are the most valued in their eyes. The students explain their mentality, and I explain how a university works with the various forms of necessary human capital required to lead a high-ranking university.

Programming and workshops are the best spaces to challenge and develop a student's value of the school, society, and life. Consistency and conversation are the most important components of programming. Consistency matters because people love to know what is happening and when they can expect it. In addition, the consistency of putting the students' benefits at the forefront of the events will make them more successful in attendance. Having a lot of free, tasty food helps, too.

This creates an opportunity for students to feel special. The deliberate space of engagement to create and develop them in an intellectual format they can dominate encourages leadership and being outspoken. Students need to know how to self-advocate and stand up for themselves. It is the only way to not get bullied through life. The domination is not of others or the programmer but instead of themselves. When someone can predict what is happening, they feel as if they are in more control. The power of control reduces their stress and allows them to succeed. People always perform better in a class towards the end of the semester because they now understand the format of the class, the instructor, and the academic strategies of the course much better. They gain more competence and confidence from the increase of understanding, which promotes their ability to achieve within the environment. The same opportunity to achieve control in the programming space must be upheld. Therefore, a standard event time in the educational institution allows for the students to know when and where to show up. Secondly, the consistency of knowing the event subject, guests, and agenda helps a lot as well. Thirdly, the consistency of structure within each workshop promotes the students to understand how to succeed in it. I always promote reflection as a strong base. It will challenge the students to think inward for answers. Thus, the answers to the workshop are inside of their minds. No matter how trying the challenge is, the students will know they have the answers no matter how long it will take to find them.

In regards to conversation, the students need to feel as if their ideas hold great value. Conversation allows for the students to develop their ideas. Equal opportunity to speak is more important than having an equal time limit for everyone to convey his or her thoughts. Some people speak more than others. It is not about a socialist environment of equal speaking time. Equal thinking time and equal opportunity to speak matters more so than everyone speaking one time or two times each. The conversation will allow the programmer to learn from the students while simultaneously facilitating their intellectual development. The beauty of the exchange and open-minded conversation, often restricted in banking method-style classrooms, promotes a free learning environment of equal human beings, thus prospering the learning process and environment to encourage the advanced critical thinking and reflective techniques of the people involved.

Students need to know how to self-advocate and stand up for themselves

13
MENTORSHIP

Mentorship is about getting ahead of the game

Mentorship is not confined to the institutional structure of the university or the entire school system. The grand majority of mentors come out of pure positive relationships that people develop across academic disciplines, interests, and necessities. Mentorship knows no age restriction but usually has a transfer of wise to unwise. The core reason mentorship exists is for us to love each other with the intention to transfer a skill. The mentor loves the mentee and wishes to extend the lessons learned in the mentor's life to the mentee so the mentee can avoid the mistakes the mentor learned through life experience (self-education). The mentee respects and admires the mentor and wishes to learn from the great amount of life experiences, and communicates their affirmation of the mentor's achievements consistently by following a similar path of greatness or even outperforming the mentor's achievements.

Shared experiences validate the mentorship. The experience of being able to learn from life and reflect upon it in a wise manner is a skill. The need to convey the lesson to others to give them a higher foundation of excellence also serves a natural requirement in mentorship, which is to be unselfish. In order to adjust to life's achievements, we have to know what others have learned so we don't need those experiences to learn the hard way. We learn from our mentors' experiences and thrive by not making the same mistakes or choosing the best option to succeed, like them. Therefore our hard lessons will be unique to us and propel us forward to our dreams manifested. Learning from failure is not bad. Learning from the same failure is bad. You do not want to repeat the same mistake over and over again. You are not learning if you commit the same mistake. You are insane. The definition of insanity is repeating the same action over and over again, expecting a different result. Repetitive mistakes are a decision. Repetitive mistakes are a lifestyle. Repeating the same mistakes over and over again shows you have a lack of confidence in yourself to achieve. You do not believe you can really do better so you continue making the mistakes repeatedly because you have a false sense of control in knowing what the outcome will be. You can change it. Ask your mentor, how? Life will forever be challenging. We must adjust to the challenges, which may require us to change how we operate and approach our lives. Your goal should be to learn from your mistakes and move forward to new lessons in life. There are many lessons in life to learn. There is always something new to learn. We cannot sit in the same lessons of life to master the same challenges that have always existed. We do not want to sit in the same class over and over again. Why do you want to make the same mistakes over and over again?

 We must master growth. Growth comes from a mentor who has excelled beyond our achievements into challenges we have not yet faced. We learn from their experience and use that information as words of wisdom to make the best decisions for the challenges we face. Their wisdom of experience, reflection, and conveyance will propel us faster to our dreams. We can even progress faster in life than them once we learn to put their advice in action.

 The care a mentor exudes places our dreams at the forefront of their agenda during the times we need them. If you see your mentor once a month, we know, for that hour, the mentor will set aside their duties to focus on us. You may meet over lunch and see your mentor has eaten all of her food because she listened to you talk the entire time. You may also see she has not eaten much because she has contributed a valuable amount of time to answering your questions and concerns about challenges you face. **The mentor questions our decision-making and suggests positive adjustments of enhancements.** Their wealth of knowledge sees red flags in our decisions. They coach us through like a personal trainer to master the challenges of life. The mentor limits the Google search and serves as a resource of life knowledge. They limit the Google search because they give us a small direction within our efforts of where to look to find the answers. The mentor does not know all, but they understand how to find all. They know of other resources, be they human or technological, to access to find out more about the path to success. The mentor got to where they are in life because they are resourceful. Your mentor should be where you want to be in life or at least at the next stage of life professionally, personally, or academically.

    The mentor knows his passions, talents, and skills for which they are most purposeful. Within that confine, the mentor is best used. Talk to a mentor for what they are best at so you can emulate their best skills. The mentor may be a renaissance person but is most likely a professional with a specialty. I, Professor Miles, am an educator. I know the higher education environment very well. I am an expert in college access, retention, graduation, and community building. I have served as a professional and personal mentor in higher education since I was 18 years old. In eight years, I mastered the ability to help people get into and graduate from top universities, state colleges, Ivy-Leagues, and leading STEM (Science, Technology, Engineering, and Math) institutions. I have developed strategies of success for the transition from college to career by creating workshops, speeches, and YouTube videos on the intangibles of college, career, and life success. I educate people on the hidden curriculum and how they can create a prosperous life despite the many challenges that you face every day. I am a professional educator. I stay in my lane, and my best gifts are within the industry of higher education, career development, and self-education. I am passionate about my mentees learning from school, professional experiences, and personal development.

I know many academic disciplines on an introductory level, but once I have done all that I can for a mentee, I direct him to his next mentor or challenge. Every mentee should also recognize that the mentor is not permanent. It is a role to be played. You may have one or two that last years. Those mentors will be your greatest friends. Some people are here for a season. For most mentors, they will have a temporary position in your life. Once you achieve your goal, the have completed their purpose in your life. Your mentor is meant to be in your life at certain stages. Everyone you meet is not meant to be in your life forever. Actually, the majority of people will let you evolve to the next level and then move on. It is not bad. It is not good. It is, what it is. Listen to an expert about their expertise.

Never forget the opportunity to learn from experts whenever you can. **Who are your mentors? Who do you go to for advice in your life's work and personal mission? Your major? Your career field? Your dreams? Your goals? Your ambitions?** You don't know everything. We can put the minds of all seven billion people on this planet together and still not know all of Earth's secrets, let alone the secrets of the entire universe. It is difficult to know everything. Mentors are better than a Google search, which can provide you with a wealth of options that will drive you crazy. It is just information, not a story. You will not be able to decipher it all without some guidance as to what is valid and valuable. The mentor communicates how to implement the information. The mentor tells us what we don't know. Mentors are human and do not know everything, but the mentor does convey more than we know in their specialty. They have wisdom. The wisdom is important. Wisdom is more precious than anything you can desire. Google gives us information. We use that information and turn it into knowledge when we use it once or twice. The knowledge, when applied and reflected upon, should be given to another student of life who can utilize the wisdom.

      Challenging situations in life continue to arrive over and over again. The situations cannot be avoided. New situations will arrive, causing us to use our applied information and garner wisdom of our own. We build our wisdom from other people. The stories, lessons, and experiences of others serve as a foundation for our knowledge. The experiences they have, when conveyed to us and utilized properly, can propel us forward in life to not make the same mistakes or to make the same great decisions. It will grant us more achievements. Your mentor is a really good friend who will specialize their help to make you grow your ability in one specific area of your life. Having multiple mentors will allow you to grow in multiple aspects of your life. This is how we surpass our mentors' excellence in life. This is how we succeed to new heights. Be great! You already are.

You know what I don't know that I don't know that I don't know

14
REFLECTION

Think about you. Write about you. Discuss with you. It's all about *you*!

Silence. When you are in the silence of your minds, you can find many answers to your life. You should focus most on being away from people. Other people can often destroy your silence. When you are alone, you can focus and reflect upon who you are. To understand yourself, you must be comfortable with being alone. You see who you truly are when you spend time alone. Away from your influences and your friends, you gain an understanding of what you like to do around your friends and what you prefer to do alone. You will understand you versus you in a group setting. I traveled all the way across the country five times in my life. It was a definite challenge to maintain friendships. I always had a chance to move to the beat of my own drum. I was able to set a standard for myself and start anew. I could pick my friends again. Most importantly, I could reassess who I was. I had to reflect upon myself moving across the United States to see who I truly wanted to be. I had internal creations in my mind of who I was suppose to become. The books I read gave me great insight and new thoughts while I developed who I am. Books like "Think and Grow Rich" by Napoleon Hill, "Leave It To The Apes" by M.B. Watson, and "The Greatest Salesman in the World" by OG Madino, help me to develop my self-confidence. These books were next level in my self-education as I learned to create myself and thought about who I wanted to be everyday.

The mind must move and think. Direct your thoughts. Your mind is always taking in information. Everything you see, hear, taste, touch, and smell is being entered into your memory bank. It is stored in your subconscious as something to recognize, respect, and replicate in your own life. What the conscious mind focuses on is what you will become. In reflection, we can center our thoughts on the information gathered throughout the day, discussion, or decade. We critically think about who we are and who we are to become. With the mind constantly taking in information, we want to process that information in a positive manner and control the emotions we want. Happiness, joy, excitement, and positive passion are feelings that we must attach to our greatest desires. In order to make information valuable to our conscious minds, we must reflect on why the information we gain is important. Secondly, we must associate positive notions and feelings in order to do so.

When we think about the importance of silence to reflect, we must think about how silence and reflection have created the universe's greatest beauties. The sun is a great light that reflects light off the moon and warms many planets. In space, no one can hear you scream. It is an entire universe of silence because it is in silence; we shine bright like the sun does. These two entities, silence and reflection, work together to create the beautiful light we need in our dark minds. We must look to the example of God's work above and use it as an example of the actions we must replicate below.

Thinking is therefore our greatest asset. By reflecting in silence, you can find the answers to many challenges. In a classroom, we often ask for silence when someone is talking. The real advantage available to the classroom rests in the listeners who have the opportunity to reflect while one-person talks. Thinking about what another person states in class or in conversation is reflection. When people tell you to "think before you speak," they are encouraging you to reflect more. Reflection has existed for a very long time in the universe. When we reflect more in our actions to shine bright like stars, we will blossom into a better light for others to see the world through our perspectives. One thought begets another. Control your thoughts. You cannot control anyone else's decisions no matter how hard you try. Stop it. Focus on you, boo.

Thinking is the human advantage, so we must use it to enhance ourselves. When I complete my day, I think about everything I am thankful for. I reflect on my blessings, privilege, and opportunity. On every phalange in my hand, I state something I am thankful for. On my right hand, I state the positive materials, experiences, and accomplishments achieved in the day. I usually give my thanks to God in the beginning, and then recite my thankfulness in the following manner: "I am thankful for writing more of my book today. I am thankful for being able to positively influence my students. I am thankful for my job at Drexel University. I am thankful for the apartment I live in." I give thanks for each phalange in my hand. On the left hand, I state the positive materials, experiences, and accomplishments I am thankful for that I have not yet achieved. The subconscious mind does not know the difference in what is real or fake. Therefore, I trick my mind into assuming I have achieved my goals already. "I am thankful for earning my PhD! I am thankful for founding my own university. I am thankful for the midnight blue Range Rover with deep peanut butter-colored leather seats. I am thankful for educating over a million people of the." These thoughts and visions of the now and future allow me to place my mind into a great place of peace to reflect upon what I have and what I am striving to achieve. God does not give us anything we do not ask for. Everything we want in life takes a direct and focused intent. The purpose of free will serves to control our desire to do the best we can to accomplish our dreams. God may give us dreams based upon our experiences. Those experiences serve as messages we must decode.

As humans, we do not appreciate the given. **We appreciate what we work hard for.** We have to work for our mental desire. Reflection allows us to do so. If we are not in the right position, we cannot see the light. The light is the message. The moon reflects the light. The moon is in the right position to see the message. The moon reflects the light from the sun. The sun serves as the ultimate source of light in this solar system. Therefore, Earth must be positioned properly to gain light and warmth from the sun. Every night comes before sunlight and every day filled with sun comes before a night of darkness. Yet, the moon is still there. The sun is still there, even when it does not shine or reflect light on Earth. Before we illuminated the night sky with electricity, we had to sit in the dark of the earth. We had to survive the darkness to see the sunlight. The sunlight did not disappear; we turned away from it. The Earth rotates away from the sunlight. The moon circulates so it is not always in a position to reflect the light of the sun. I speak of the cosmic structure we live in to show how reflection works as an analogy to the experience of life.

    We close our eyes to recreate a darkness we can control. In the darkness, we have no light. We must think about what will bring warmth like the sun's light. What actions, accomplishments, and focus must we achieve in order to bring light into our lives? There is more darkness in the universe than light. The darkness scares us, but in that fear. We find evidence of our true light. In reflection, we find our light source, the source of the direction we should travel. Our light. The light is the knowledge that directs us to the path we should travel to achieve our destiny. The destiny is our decision to be a light for others. Based upon our gifts and choices, we create a destiny that will illuminate. The illumination will be your life's work. We see what we want to see. What we want to see is based upon the choices we have made in life. We are exposed to what we wish to have and to hold. The exposure of life lets our eyes see it and fixate on it.

We appreciate what we work hard for

I was a popular kid in college. I knew a lot of people and a lot of people knew me. I often walked down Bruinwalk at UCLA and had my eyes fixed on my goal. It may have been class, a meeting, the gym, or my dormitory. My mind was closed off to anything that was not my goal. Walking down Bruinwalk, the main pathway at UCLA, I did not see many people. I saw my destination and me. When I was walking to the gym, I noticed two types of people: the person I wanted to be, and the person I did not want to be. You can imagine the people who stood out. Overweight people and athletes served as my motivation. I said to myself, I do not want to be fat. I want to be fit. I have discipline and focus. My ability to sculpt my physique is my responsibility and my healthcare. I will achieve it because it will shed light on my health to make my health the best it can be. The beautiful women I saw on campus who were running to maintain their health stood out to me. The athletes and bodybuilders on campus who earned the greatest physiques on campus stood out to me. I saw what I wanted to see: my goals. I want to look like an athlete so the people maintaining a great fitness level became illuminated in my vision. Many a time, while walking with this focus, I had friends and associates who would wave to me, but I would not be able to see them. My focus was not on people who do not fit my vision. I could only see the motivating factors in my mind. Especially with my headphones on, nothing fazed me. I WAS focused on my goal. I only saw people who supported that mission.

In reflection, focus on your goals and motivation. Simon Sinek's Golden Circle is great for this. You must recreate the focused mindset that you wish to have with your imagination. When reflecting about our preventative healthcare, we have to envision where we want our bodies to be. We must see it in our minds. In our minds, we must envision our bodies becoming what we want them to be. In reflection, we can think about the process of cardiovascular exercise, calisthenics, or weight lifting as means to gain the physical fitness we envision. Reflection is a meditative practice of understanding what we have done and will achieve. It allows the mind to develop itself into a machine of excellence. It will allow you to understand yourself, your practices, and your best habits. By understanding our best habits and practices, we can manifest our goals and achieve our greatest desires. Physical fitness serves as an example of what we can achieve professionally and academically. It demands discipline and perseverance over years in order to gain results. What you envision you can become. It requires performing consistent action to manifest. Whatever your vision requires, you must achieve. Your plans may change, but the goal must be decided upon with a relentless intent to be accomplished. Reflection will not only show you the best of yourself but the worst of yourself. It is the best time to critique yourself. Through critique, you can self-assess who you really are. Only in honesty with yourself can reflection truly shine light on a better understanding of what you need to improve you.

     Reflecting with others also illuminates who we really are and seek to become. Reflecting with others may shed light on areas of life where we are blind. You may not be able to see what others can see. If I were meant to have your vision, I would have your eyes. I cannot see what you can see. You have a unique and specific vision to see in this world. Therefore, I will come to you and ask you to reflect upon my actions and abilities in relation to my goals. Tell me your truth. Tell me where to improve. Oftentimes, reflection requires speaking to someone who has a different expertise. Reflection requires humility. Reflection requires receiving critique and empowerment. I took my plan of how to become a great educator to a leader in finance. I knew every detail of how I wanted to achieve my goal and why it was necessary for me to help the world through education. I see educators helping thousands and millions of people accomplish great tasks and improve the human capital of many underserved people in the United States.

This finance expert called herself Amoré. Amoré told me that I know the answer, but I am not living the answer. I went into a rant of how I have lived my dream of educating students at Drexel, UCLA, Penn, and high schools on both coasts in the United States. She did not demean those accomplishments, but held me to the standard for which I came to achieve. Becoming one of the greatest educators alive is no easy task. It is something that requires great skill, knowledge, and applicability. The best educators do not teach simply through books and discussion. The greatest provide a means of action for people to put their education to the test of life.

Amoré told me I have to be able to improve my financial understandings in order to impact students to the best of my ability. I have to improve my understandings of the financial market and the state of the institutions I work with. Their academic development is a great advantage when the resources are in place to aid that development. By only speaking to the knowledge people needed to learn and earn, I would miss out on the financials they need to have in order to truly possess the resources to manifest the educational development of the students. I sat down. I looked at her seriously. I thought to myself, she is right. I have done a lot of work to earn my master's degree in education, teach honors seminar courses at Drexel University, and speak on educational topics that benefit the higher education industry. I have committed to a lot in my field and the people who I believe will benefit from my efforts. Nonetheless, I can still improve my specified skills. I made it to the top of this education mountain just so that I can realize I am at the valley of the next mountain I need to climb. I am better for what I have gone through, which makes me a perfect candidate to achieve an equal opportunity education in the United States.

Through dialogue and reflection with Amoré, who could see my life through a different pair of eyes, I realized I have more to learn in order to earn my definite purpose: creating an equal opportunity education. I have to be willing to allow others to give me constructive criticism in order to reach my goals, no matter how much I reflect alone. I have to reflect alone and with others. The best part about reflecting with someone else is engaging people who have tangible ways to benefit your improvement. The greatest aspect of reflection is improving.

Reflections also needs to be written down. The vision in our minds must be seen. We must see it to believe it. We must write down our goals. It is important we specify the details of our mission. It will show us the progress and the regressions we make in our attainment of our definite purpose. The reflection is mental and physical as we write down our aspirations. The mental is the idea and the physical is the paper and ink that hold your ideas. The mental and physical divides within humanity are meant to unite, but it takes a deliberate effort. Your physical components are a reflection of your mental state. In your understanding of the moon and sun reflection relationship, the body is the moon and the mental state is the sun. The fit body shows a health-conscious mind. The health-conscious mind has a routine. It holds value in discipline and the ability to overcome resistance. The resistance of exercise, especially in lifting weights, proves one has the ability to commit and preserve. The persistence of a muscular physique reflects the discipline, focus, and routine commitment of the individual to the idea of improving their health. The true power of reflection rests between the mental and physical components. If you commit your mental focus to reading and applying best practices to achieve your dream beyond your physique, such as completing your college degree, the possibility of achievement will be much greater than a healthy body: it will also be a healthy spirit and mind.

The commitment to make a difference is the best commitment one can make. Making a difference in people's lives matters most, for pieces of paper explaining one has a degree of knowledge in a subject does not prove her capability of applying that information to good use for the greater service of humanity.

     Reflection promotes your ability to analyze your human capital. Understanding your human capital allows you to position yourself to make the best positive impact possible in the world. Your service to your fellow human being creates a reflection process in others. Your example of improving yourself and applying those improvement techniques to the world allows others to reflect about their place in society, thus creating a community of reflective individuals, all because you focused on your journey. It begins in the actions of one to spark the reflection in another's mind. With motivation, on a daily basis, we will begin to live what we think about most. Reflection allows us to live our thoughts. Action in front of others presents an example of thought executed. It presents a thought lived out. People will think about your actions. They will reflect about how you achieved your goals and live the life you dreamed. For the great minds to come, those persons will inquire about how you came to be who you are. For those who are common of mind, they will assume you achieved your goals due to some gifts from God no one can replace. For those poor of mind, they will assume negative connotations of you, for your presentation of thought exudes a critical reminder of what they have not achieved. For those looking to transcend to a phenomenal state, they will honor your efforts and serve you to observe you and become an apprentice. The apprentice will reflect daily on the actions you perform and emulate your best self, just as children do. They perceive you as a future version of themselves and will want to attach themselves to you, just as your children will do. By being around you, they will learn what they need to know themselves in order to earn the life you live. Most likely, it is a specialty you possess, a specific quality you have that makes you different than anyone else. That specialty creates a magnificent appeal. Your unwavering will power to influence people by manifesting in your dreams into physical form is actualizing your imagination. Your mental visions live on. The relentless desire to achieve your goals creates a presence many people cannot deny. That notice is not by mistake. Someone building to become a phenomenal individual will attach himself to your excellence and learn what you learned to manifest.

Life is about creating yourself more so than finding who you are. You find your gift and create yourself like water and clay. Find your gift: the clay. Add the water: your habits. From there, you will build a great statue. These words ring true for the person who reflects on a daily basis about who she is becoming. It is important to know that you must determine who you are. Life does not happen to you. Life is reacting to you. Do not wait for the universe to tell you who you are. Instead, command the universe to become want you want it to be. The universe uses no words, but rather straight action. Become who you are to be and the universe will follow suit. As you make new decisions based on your reflections, you will see different opportunities come about. Reflection allows you to find the light source. The aim and purpose of reflection is to not be the moon. Instead, you must recognize your habits and daily actions serve as a light in the world, much like the sun, shining bright over your values and ambitions.

For people who spend a great amount of time after school and work watching television, I expect those people to shed light on the entertainment industry. Watching television will make one a confidant in the entertainment industry. Unfortunately, the skill of watching television will only take one so far. The true talent goes to the producer, director, actors, cinematographers, and participants who create their dream in collaboration with others. They literally shed light upon your life by having lights illuminate your living room to convey their dreams. Watching television is watching other people create their lives. You will not find yours on television. The people who are on television do not spend a great deal of time watching television. They spend a majority of their time developing the skills they need in order to remain relevant in their industry. The industry of entertainment is cut throat. The entertainment industry reflects life's harsh approach to society. In society, we see people remain popular as long as they can give to their fanatics in a more valuable way than anyone else. Reflect upon your life right now. **How are you giving to society?** You already are. Every day you act. Everything is an action. Laying down. Watching TV. Actions. **What do you do for society? Volunteer? Employment? School organization?** By giving to others, you teach people how to shine bright like stars do.

Do not be a Negative Nate. Instead, aim to be a Benefiting Ben. Be great. Be exciting. Benefiting Ben gives to people on a daily basis. Benefiting Ben knows that he may not receive compensation in a direct manner. Instead, Benefiting Ben sees his gifts to society as the gift itself. By giving, Benefiting Ben receives. The pleasure Benefiting Ben receives from giving to others gives him an excitement in life no one can destroy. The gift of handing a homeless man five dollars when the homeless man asks for one dollar can excite your day. I know you have the greatness in you to give to others. Spending time listening to others, family and friends, complain about their lives and challenging them to find the positive in their experience helps a lot. Destroying the pessimistic bubble in others' views of the world serves a great benefit to society. The news and social media spread so much hatred at an alarming rate that we forget to love each other with positivity. Our perspectives of the world become filled with fear and negatives. The Negatives Nates cannot rule the world forever. Instead, it is time the Benefiting Bens rise up and take the world by storm, a sun-lit storm that warms people's heart.

Life is about creating yourself

The ability to be present in other peoples' lives, allows you to understand the process of turning yourself into gold. Gold is the most sun-reflecting metal on Earth when we take care of it. At first, the metal seems shiny but bland. We attach some heat to it. It makes a nice piece of jewelry for us to wear. The Negative Nates appear to be an old material that does not resemble gold. We take the scrap metal of the Negative Nates. We ask them questions about the positives in their lives. **What positive experiences did you have today?** Of course, Negative Nate has no answer. Everything was bad. Nothing went right. Negative Nate disregards that he woke up today. Negative Nate disregards the home he has. Negative Nate disregards the electricity running through his home. Negative Nate disregards you sitting in front of him, listening to his troubles and smiling, happy to be in his presence. The Negative Nate does not appreciate the free blessings he has received in his life, including the people. The perspective that he has focuses on the negative aspects of life. The Negative Nate's mental focus shines light on the negatives because his mind is dedicated to them. Negatives occur naturally in life, but the effort to focus on the negatives makes experiences in life negatives. We can turn anything into a negative or a positive. Positive thinking is more challenging to create in the beginning, especially if the Negative Nate complex has existed within you for decades.

It may take years of effort to turn our mind into a Positive Paul. The Positive Paul sees positivity where there is negativity. The Positive Paul reflects in the moment to see how he can grow from this position in life. **What strength will I gain for overcoming this pressure to fail?** Positive Paul looks to see the blessing and lesson in life, for learning what not to do is powerful. Thomas Edison learned 10,000 incorrect methods to develop the light bulb. He only needed to get it right once. In school, you need 90% or higher. In life, you need one time to get it right. The more you know what not to do, the more you achieve. Life becomes a clear path to produce the best in us.

The Opportunistic Oprah reflects on life in a similar fashion to Positive Paul but sees more than just a positive gain from life. Opportunistic Oprah will see the challenges of life and recognize the positives plus a gain. She constantly thinks about how the moment will positively impact her future. In fact, the Opportunistic Oprah recognizes the 24 hours in a day and sees each hour as an opportunity to be positive in the world. She has 24 hours to positively progress to her dreams. Who knows what hour her big opportunity will come? 4 o'clock? 6 o'clock? 8 o' clock? The Opportunistic Oprah sees the diamond in every piece of coal. She sees the gold as a refined necklace. Her eyes are sculpted into a frame that sees the best in the worst situations. She sees the best in the common situations. She sees the best in the people she meets, and treats those people with dignity and respect. She takes full advantage of herself to make herself the best self she can be. The opportunistic Oprah has missed an opportunity before. She will be ready for the next opportunity. She will be more than prepared to make her debut. She will be fantastic at life because she has mastered her habits. She understands her purpose in life. She is now a bright sun, shining in the universe of darkness so others can feel her warmth. She creates opportunity for herself and is gracious for each breath, moment, and chance to live life the best way she sees fit. With constant reflection on your life and how you can make your life a positive experience, you too can be an Opportunistic Oprah. The choice is yours.

==If you choose your destiny, you must choose yourself.== You must choose to put yourself first. Understand what you need to do. Write every day about your dreams and make yearly, monthly, weekly, daily, and hourly goals for yourself. I believe the Opportunistic Oprah within you sees and understands the logic of an applied definite purpose to be the best person you can be. The Positive Paul does not ignore the actions of life, but chooses to see it in a positive light. The Negative Nate sees the world in a negative light, so he grows fearful and worrisome. Benefiting Ben give to others so others have no problem giving to him. Control your mind with reflection and act as a bright light of hope to yourself and others. Be the hope you wish to see for yourself. No one will save you from your life but you can save yourself from yourself.

In the movies, we see the angel and the devil sit on both shoulders. The two always have our face, yet they wear different clothes and have wings made of skin and feathers. **What mindset will you choose?** Choose you. Choose the best you. Be great! You already are. The power of positivity is already inside of you. Choose it. Be it. Love it. Reflect in a positive manner every morning and night. Take a second to tell yourself that there is a positive in this moment. If you cannot find a positive in this moment, remove yourself from the situation. Don't quit, but recognize that you might be too deep into the rabbit hole to see the light. For example, turn off the television. Learn to read and use your imagination. Write every day so you learn to express yourself. You must fight and press toward your inner best self. The Positive Paul and Opportunistic Oprah thrive by making time to check in with themselves every day.

This will shape your mind into a force that can fight any outside intruder who lives as a Negative Nate. Society's opinion of you is not who you have to be. Society might forget you even existed, but you won't. You know you. **How many people on television look like you?** A few. Truthfully, no one looks exactly like you. **Your fingerprints are different. Your energy is different.** You create a feeling in people's hearts no one can replicate. Yes, you make people smile. You make many people smile. When they smile, it is because of you. No one is smiling to make you feel better about yourself. No one is creating a fake friendly approach to you. No one in modern day U.S. society cares to be fake on a consist basis. We have full-time actors on television giving their lives to being fake characters. Even then, they are not these characters all day, no matter how easy it is to binge-watch Netflix.

People always want to be accepted for who they are by people who truly understand who they are. The biggest barrier to allowing this great congruity comes from us not becoming our best selves. We aim to become the best normal individual in society. We boast and brag about other peoples' accomplishments (television, entertainment, sports statistics, fantasy leagues, YouTube stars, etc.). We do not live out the John Wooden meaning of success: "Success is knowing you did your best to become the best that you are capable of becoming." We want people to accept our mediocrity. We settled in life and want others to accept our poor efforts. That is a lot to ask for. I would much rather accept someone who is a go-getter and tries their best at life. The greatest people around are the people who are happy to be who they are. You do not like the people who complain about their major for five years or the individual who complains about their job every day. If you are unhappy with your efforts in school and your work life, you have to change it. It is in your control. It is your responsibility.

The following sentences are hogwash: "I can't change majors. It is too late. I won't graduate on time." I am an advisor. I am a full-time educator. I have heard these statements a million times! The translation is, "I will not change my major. My friends and family will think I am crazy for starting all over. I think I am crazy. I want to graduate with my friends. Graduating on time unhappily is more important that graduating with a degree in a field I am actually interested in." Whatever is required is the mindset you should have. There are multiple ways to handle your academic insecurity. You can intern places where you learn the traits of what you are actually interested in. There are many clubs and organizations you can join that focus on your passion. Lastly, you can change majors, be an academic rebel, and love yourself for choosing you. Life will be challenging. That never changes. If life is not challenging, you are spiritually dying inside and need to revitalize yourself with an espresso, play some Miles Davis, and create your definitive purpose. It will boost your confidence to seriously reflect upon how you can become your best self. It is what the world deserves. We deserve your best. Becoming your ideal identity makes everyone around you happier. Your friends do not matter unless they travel with you on the journey to the new you. **We all evolve.** We are not trees stuck to the same forest. We are eagles, soaring high above the treetops, looking to create a nest of creativity and ambition in the tree of our choice.

When you are scared to fly to the next tree, jump and go for it. By falling, you will know a better way to fly. The pressure to fly might take you to new heights. The clouds may become your next resting spot. Go for it! You can do it. You are great! You must believe in your ability to do things you have never done before in order to accomplish what you have not done. Imagine in your mind when you reflect. Close your j/eyes and see yourself succeeding. **Aspire for more and never for less than what you want.** Do what ever is required to achieve your aims. Life is a long time, but it is not guaranteed you will be here tonight. I have dead friends and family members who suffer from terminal illness. Life is not infinite but your imagination and abilities are. There is infinite growth and possibility for you in this world. Be your best. Life is a lifelong test. As long as your heart beats in your chest, you still have a purpose on Earth you must achieve.

15
IMAGINATION GAP

The difference between who you are and who you want to be, in your life.

In order to attain your goals, you must realize the presence of the imagination gap. The imagination gap describes the gap between who you are and who you want to be. In order to truly understand the disparity of the imagination gap, we must first understand the achievement gap and the opportunity gap within higher education. These two gaps prevent one from obtaining a creative imagination and the ability to dream big.

The achievement gap speaks to the educational disparity of one group of students not excelling in school at the same rate as other students. The National Center for Education Statistics states the achievement gap for Hispanic students remains the same on average, according to their 2011 executive summary. There is a gap of 26 points between Hispanic students and White students in grades 4 and 8 within the United States. Although the Hispanic students are performing better cumulatively over the past decade in both math and reading, the gap continues to stay the same. Eleven states in the 2015 report decreased the gap in math and reading performance for students in grades 4 and 8, but six states increased the gap. The achievement gap has concerns in regards to gender, race, and socio-economic classes. The Hispanic-White achievement gap serves as one example of how students in school do not perform to the same level as a result of community, school, and home intellectual training and support. The achievement gap highlights the differences in the performance of students across many demographics.

Therefore, the opportunities students have to be supported with proper resources to advance their education are limited. In regards to socio-economic differences, students from low SES backgrounds (poverty, lower middle class, and blue collar) tend to perform at lower rates than students from wealthier homes. The difference is huge. Laura Perna and Joni Finney, professors of education at the University of Pennsylvania, wrote in "The Attainment Agenda" (2014) that **higher education degrees would be required for 63% of all employment opportunities by 2018.** The opportunity gap continues to prevent many students from being able to fill these positions due to the lack of resources and poor preparation public K-12 schools provide. It makes it difficult for these students to excel in higher education. Therefore, the lack of resources in the foundational learning in communities, schools, and families creates less opportunity for these students to excel academically and professionally. The opportunity gap is the achievement gap once we realize the academic achievement affects educational opportunity, a valuable resource. A resource is any product or service made purchasable, such as a higher education experience.

In combination with the achievement gap, we can see how the opportunity gap affects students' abilities to achieve their dreams, let alone fill the growing number of employment opportunities that exist within society for higher education graduates. The United States is a large player in the knowledge economy; the creation of research and technology creates a huge advantage for the nation. Our economic system does not focus on the creation of basic human needs such as education, food, shelter, and clothes. Our nation's economy focuses on the ability to advance humanity through technology and the actualization of our imagination. Creating products and services that have not been seen anywhere else on the planet allows the United States to remain ahead of other countries economically. We do not maintain in the U.S. We advance! We advance through our actualization of our imagination. The imagination has no limits except for the human being who possesses it.

The human being's imagination is a victim of out of sight, out of mind. That speaks to the notion that if we cannot see it, we cannot believe it. Therefore, it does not exist. Thus, the imagination will not be able to envision what the person has not been exposed to before. Children tend to repeat the actions of their community and parents more than anything else. It is rare you meet a military person who is the first person in their family to serve. Usually someone in her family has served before. In regards to college, most college students are not first-generation students. Their parents and grandparents have gone. Many of the Ivy League institutions have a legacy check box when applying. It can be seen as a rite of passage for families to create a pipeline of academic excellence at a specific university. The opportunity to excel is greater for children who have parents that are college graduates. Expect your children to do what you do with your life. You set the bar. You are what they are. They are what you are. Important information regarding the process of application and achievement can be passed down within the family. The child can imagine herself attending college just like her parents.

The opportunity of seeing someone's family accomplish something in a prior generation serves as a great benefit to a child. Normal is determined by what we engage on a consistent basis. There exists no normal life for all children. **There is no life without challenges or problems**. There exists a normal life for children everywhere. The environment a child finds himself developing in determines his normal. Normal varies for many children within one city.

I once moved to live with my grandparents in Queens, New York when I was six years old. It was a hot August day in the city. It was a new experience. I felt embarrassed to live with my grandparents. In my neighborhood in Hercules, CA, everyone had both of their parents living with them. As I went outside to play with other kids, I did my best not to mention that I lived with my grandparents. After the summer days came to a close, it was time to attend school. My grandmother introduced me to James, who was just a year older than me and lived down the street. James and I were very similar, my grandma told me. I was completely unsure as to how. We looked completely different. On the first day of school, my grandma walked over to James's home, which were located just steps away on my street. We rang the doorbell. An older woman screamed out from behind the door, "Just a minute!" I thought nothing of it. She answered the door, and she was James's grandmother. She smiled and hugged me, greeting me with affirmations of my handsomeness in my school uniform. She claimed James was not ready yet to walk to school. She asked me to run upstairs and speak with her mother to see if James' older sister Jamiese was ready. My grandmother and I walked upstairs. Jameise's great-grandmother answered the door. She called for Jamiese to come down. Jamiese escorted us to school, since she was in 6th grade, James was in 3rd grade, and I was in 2nd grade. All of us lived with a family member who raised one of our parents. None of us lived with our moms. It was the new normal. It was intimidating to experience living without my parents. Now I understood how we all had something in common, even though we did not look the same. When I knew living with your grand or great-grandparents was normal in this section of Queens, New York, I felt comfortable in my experience. I was not alone. I was normal. The experience of having extended family raise me was normal. There were many of us experiencing this.

Most of what we see in the world is in our brains. My feeling of being an outcast of the community was made up from most of what I created in my own mind. My imagination created a gap of difference between myself and the other kids. I did not speak to other kids about the imagination gap, the difference of who I am and who I thought the community kids thought I was. The imagination gap can be one of challenges, for it may only be a difference of what we think others see of us. We compare our whole lives in our heads to what we see others do. If this was basketball, we judge the game performance of our competitors to our entire practice and performance. Yet, we do not know what they experience as normal in their practice. In this case of community children, I assumed I was the only person who lived with his grandparents. I created a gap of difference in my imagination between myself and the other kids. It affected my confidence and my ability to interact. I had nothing to be ashamed of. I now had wise grandparents raising me. I found positives in my experience. In addition, I discovered how normal it was for others to also live with their grandparents and great-grandparents. We were not a majority of the neighborhood kids, but we did not have to be to feel unity. Our select experiences made us great friends. Our normal was similar.

Our perspective of how we see the world truly matters. The people around us shape our normal perspectives. The people around us often determine our perspectives of experiences. My living with my grandparents went on to be a negative one for weeks until I met James and walked to school with him. We talked about the positives of living with our grandparents and why it made us feel good to have wise people who loved us and cared for us. It also gave us more responsibility to be a young man of the house. We matured faster than our peers because we had more mature people, our grandparents, guiding our life decisions. The pattern of perception from that day forth became one where we looked to find the positives in our experiences. When I viewed the positive experiences, my grandmother could tell and fed into the positivity. She introduced me to the community. Her being a great community activist and leader in turn lead me to become a leader of elementary students and known in the community as well.

I decided to have faith in my grandparents, which set up more opportunities for me to see the positives in life. From that day forth, I found more positive experiences I could engage. I listened to other people who also seemed to genuinely care about my existence. People who expressed a faith in me to excel gave me confidence to achieve in my endeavors.

As a result, I developed grit to achieve. I developed an unwavering faith in my ability to achieve and to work with people who had genuine hearts. I became a magnet for attracting people similar to myself in mindset. They were adults, children, and teenagers who had faith in their skills. Faithful people do not have hope. The hopeful acknowledge doubt and focus on their aspirations with question. Those who have faith use the emotions and motions of positivity to create the normal experiences they want to have. The faithful believe in their abilities and appreciate the value of the assets they have right now. The most valuable assets people have are other people. The mind is the greatest force on the planet. A brain serves a magnetic force to whatever it focuses on. The negative focus yields negatives turnouts. The positive magnet yields positive turnouts. Having faith in your positive outcomes creates more positive outcomes than negative ones.

You attract what you are. The opportunity gap and achievement gap affect mostly the low-class citizens. Therefore, we can make a logical connection of financial welfare to one's ability to achieve and gain opportunities. The financial wealth in the United States is completely dominated by the top 20% of the nation. The top 1% possesses a little less than half of the wealth in the country.

There is no life without challenges or problems

We always assume the best opportunities are with the wealthy. People love to engage others who are like themselves. Therefore, the wealthy engage each other and use money to multiply their profits. Money makes money faster than time makes money. The lower and middle class trade time for money. The wealthy, via stocks, 7702A accounts, and diverse portfolios are able to master money and make the dollar their slave. The middle class and lower class slave away at employments to make a fraction of the income the wealthy earn. Time, the most limited commodity on the planet, is already taken away from most. With less time, parents of children in middle- and lower-class neighborhoods cannot adequately assist their child's ability to achieve, in comparison to the top 20%, who have the opportunity to hire tutors and highly-trained teachers from great preparatory institutions to assist in their child's achievement. Finances are linked to achievement and opportunity in a positive manner.

In order to close the imagination gap, we must provide financial literacy, fiscal management skills, and financial opportunity to the middle- and lower-class. The achievement gap and opportunity gap will close with more financial support. The more financial support a child has in the foundation of their life, the more they will expect from others. The student's self-expectation will also be higher than his lower- and middle-class peers due to the normal engagement of wealth opportunity in his life. The student will imagine greater riches and achievements than his middle- and lower-class peers and have the financial support to actualize those ambitions.

Monetary capital serves as the great economic equalizer. The education necessary to manage and compound one's income also allows one to increase opportunity. The increase in financial security improves one's confidence and thus increases their social capital as well. **Wealth is a mindset.** Wealth serves as the confidence one needs to achieve their dreams. In the mind, it comes down to our human capital, the value of ourselves in regards to our human capital, and the efforts we have put towards our dreams. In the world, monetary capital serves as the road to achievement. Our human capital provides a vehicle, but without the infrastructure, it is difficult to travel to many places our heart desires. The roads we see available throughout our life journey limit the human imagination. At the same time, with a wealthy mindset, the roads can be plenty and provide great opportunity to achieve our ambitions. The world is much bigger than our neighborhoods, yet many of us never travel beyond our city or state. Most individuals never live out of state once in their lives. We remain in our comfort zones. The imagination gap requires you to travel. Traveling is a metaphor of exposure. The more we are exposed to in life, the more we can imagine.

    Have you ever watched a scary movie and then have a nightmare that night? Our imagination knows no bounds. What we see is what we get in our imagination. The scary movie enters our subconscious and we become engulfed in the images and feel the fright throughout our body. We internalize what we see. The imagination gap requires individuals to imagine a greater today. Tomorrow lies in the sand with yesterday's adventures. Today lives in our hands. We must imagine a great day every day for it may be our last. Therefore, we will live the greatest day we possibly can so others can see the great value we have in our day.

    Overcoming the imagination gap requires you to change your perspective on life. Life is the best-case scenario. Don't waste it awaiting the worst-case scenario. People are attracted to people who think of best-case scenarios. The mind will focus on the best-case scenario and create it. **What is your best-case scenario in life?** Make sure you eradicate limits! **What is the best-case scenario for you if you wanted to make one million dollars annually? What does that lifestyle entail? Scale down from your goal: year to month to week to day to hour, what do you need to do in order to achieve it?**

What career are you aiming for? A lawyer, you might say. That is an impressive career. What lawyer do you want to be like? Michelle Obama sets a great standard of achievement. She is a corporate lawyer and attended Harvard University for law school. For undergrad, she went to Princeton University. Kenneth Chennault attended Harvard Law School. Barack Obama and Hill Harper also attended Harvard Law School. All of those individuals are in different careers. Harvard Law School is not the goal. Harvard Law School is a gas station on your life journey. As a pit stop in your life, it is important to understand the many directions one can take in life. Which road will you drive down next? School should not be the goal of your imagination. It is a gas station. Fill up and get a tune up if needed. Unless you want to enter the education industry as an administrator, executive, or teacher, you do not need to see school as your definite goal. Instead, imagine yourself making the impact you want on the world.

What did you do today that made the world better? What will you be remembered for? Does your estate and family have a legacy? What do you think of it? It is important you pass down generational wealth and not generational debt. Beyond your surname, you, too, have a name. Its memory will exist after you die, just for a moment, or a year, or ten, or forever. The people who live on in my memory are Eron Mull, Dr. Huey Percy Newton, El-Hajj Malik El-Shabazz, Ralph David Albernathy, Melvin Beaunorus Tolsen, Johnnie Cochran, and A. Moore Shearin, and I hope they rest in peace. Each of those individuals will forever be remembered in my heart. Their imaginations knew few limits. They pursued life with a tenacity to accomplish their dreams, although they died at various ages. We are alive today and we can die today. We never know when our last breath is going to be taken. Every day is our last day. We die in sleep each day, resting in the dark, awaiting the sunshine of a new day. We are never left a day without having to realize darkness is always here and light will eradicate our fear. One day, the darkness will consume us all in death. Those left in the light, living, when we perish, will have memories of our existence. **Tell yourself, write it down now, what we will remember about you?**

Now, it may seem easy to say, "Create your legacy now." It is difficult to acknowledge that we have been building a legacy since the day we were born. Even more challenging is the fact that we are only as good as our last performance. The last image people have of us is what they remember us for. First impressions matter as the ultimate comparison of our last performance. When recapping a basketball game with my friends, the summary of the game, no matter how epic it is, follows a very similar routine. Russell Westbrook had an epic dunk over the center. Westbrook completely destroyed his confidence. In the second or third quarter, it got closer, but then my team began to pull away. Now, it's close in the end, and I have no idea how they let the opposition come back from that big lead in the fourth. They leave him wide open. The forward goes to contest the shot, but Westbrook stays focused and hits the shot. It was a momentum killer and then they won the game. They won the game. They won the game. Did you get that? Results matter. The end of the game matters. Stay strong and focused all the way through. The imagination gap requires us to think of a dream and chase it with all we have and more for the rest of our natural lives. We must follow all the way through.

Stay focused. When learning what our dreams require to achieve, we should get more encouraged to achieve. The encouragement stems from the need for us to grow as individuals to become better. As Eric Thomas stated in his famous Michigan State speech: "The most important thing is this: to be able at any moment – to sacrifice what you are, for what you will become!" His words ring true to our lives because we often are scared to upgrade. We upgrade phones, computers, and clothes, but we rarely take the challenge to upgrade our lives. We live our lives using others peoples' dreams to remain stagnant instead of using the upgrade in material to upgrade ourselves mentally and spiritually. The goal of imaginative destination will have a gap between who we are and who we need to be. It is not easy to be our imagination. In order to achieve our ideal self, we have to increase our confidence, physical health, and mental tenacity. The spirit must toughen and take risks. Trading in your old self for your upgrade will allow you to attract people who are similar to your upgraded self.

     Enter into a parking lot and look at the cars. Notice how the luxury cars are parked closed to each other. The same goes for cars of all monetary values. Enter a school and look at how people of similar socio-economic classes socialize with each other more. As you upgrade, you will gain new traits and new friends. It is up to you who you engage with, but constant engagement with people will allow you to pick up their habits and trains of thought. People who associate with each other tend to act like each other. You will speak in similar fashions and have an exchange of mannerisms. This is a great occasion if you truly wish to be like the individuals you are surrounded by. If no one in your circle behaves in a manner you wish to emulate, you need to diversify your social circle. You can be the smartest and most dignified person in one circle and the tyro in another. Having various groups of individuals you interact with will make you an eclectic person who can manage themselves in multiple environments.

     Have the intent to understand people from different walks of life. The only way to accurately understand someone is to ask about her journey through life. Listen! Repeat interesting facts. Uplift them with affirmations. Understanding others allows you to learn more cultural capital. The cultural capital and willingness to listen allows you a pass to travel the world. Be brave enough to travel the world. The largest regret among college students is not traveling abroad before they enter the rat race of a 9-to-5-work life. With the poor management of personal finances, many people never leave the nation. This is a sad fact, for the world has much more to offer than the U.S. can provide, although I do regard this nation as the greatest for opportunity. It has the most billionaires. The history of humanity leaves more buried treasures and insight in the eastern hemisphere. Exposure to different perspectives opens up the eyes of individuals who can now see themselves differently. In order to imagine more and on greater levels, we must expose ourselves to great treasures and new sights. New locations provide new thoughts.

We think differently in different spaces. Have a conversation with three people. Sit in a circle. Then sit in a square. Then sit in a triangle. This is a simple exercise I perform in my classes to create new energy flows. Nothing happens by accident. Everything happens with intentionality. Every day, wake up and exercise. As your blood moves faster and you become alert, you are intentionally working towards your upgrade. Write down what you need to accomplish today. Analyze the time it will take to succeed. Stick to your timetable and begin immediately to achieve the necessary tasks on your To Do Well list. This will allow you to lessen the imagination gap, the difference between where you imagine yourself to be and where you are today.

If you are unsure how to achieve your goal or feel inadequate to truly chase it, increase your confidence. Reading books on people who have an expertise in the goal will be the best first step. Secondly, you will need to listen to audios and videos from experts on how to best prepare and actualize your imagination. The upgrade begins. Consider the information to be the download of your new software. You will restart your life every morning so you will need to download the latest version of yourself each morning. Reading in the morning will be your best bet to achieving the excellence that lives within you. Be great! You already are.

Knowing you are great, reading about great people who have achieved great deeds you aspire to achieve, will increase your ability to make the right decisions at the right time. Having the information allows you to create opportunities when they do not arrive at your doorstep. The information is key. Putting it to use is the knowledge. Passing it on to someone else makes your knowledge wisdom.

Take notes on the wisdom you gain from reading books and listening to audio on YouTube. If you have no clue what audio you should listen to, start with general instructional inspiration. The best speakers that give you specific instructions on how to achieve your goals in an uplifting manner would be Myles Munroe, Eric Thomas, Tony Robbins, and Professor Miles. We all have different styles and expertise. Our commonality rests in our unwavering passion and pursuit to help others enjoy the success we have. You will not find four other people on this planet that can deliver instructions and inspiration to succeed like we have.

While taking notes, understand your dream goal and upgrades are now physical. Your thoughts exist on paper and are real. You can burn it up, but it still lived. Once the pen touches the paper, the idea has come to life. In fact, the idea lives way before that. Once we think it, it becomes real. Your thoughts create physical changes in your body. When you get scared or startled because of something you thought you saw, your thoughts alter your physiology. A great idea will make your skin hairs rise and send chills through your body. Thoughts give us feelings. If you can feel it, it is physical. It is alive in you. Make you imagination, a reality. Fill the gap!

Wealth is a mindset.

16
Resources

The greatest resource in the world is you.

The greatest resource in the world is you. You are the best resource you have. Nothing is better than you. No one has your fingerprint. You are unique. We cannot make another brain that works and thinks likes yours. It is yours to keep, cherish, and develop. Computers were made to mimic the brain, but the computer can only be as great as the brain that controls it. If you never search for something on Google, than you will never find it. The information in the world is endless, but if you do not put it to use, the information will be donated to the library. You have made a better decision. You decided to read this book to elevate your ability to learn to earn your own opportunities. Through learning, the application of information to create knowledge, we prosper. Only through dexterity do we reach prosperity. The greatest resource is YOU. There is no greater being more important to your life than you. All the gifts in the world from God rest in your mind, but you must create the heavens in your mind. Do not throw your talents away. Use them and supply those talents with the skills you need to master life. Do not let life master you.

If we take away everything you have, what will you have left? Your brain! Your thoughts are yours and unique. Ever feel like you are the only person who thinks like you? You are. You are an insider and an outsider. Get inside your brain and make sure you place physical proof of your great ideas outside of your mind so the world can flourish. Every component of your mind, body, and soul needs to be in its best shape in order for you to be at your best. Consider your mind, body, and soul to be colleges on a university campus. Colleges are the different schools that house their own faculty. Universities are the colleges that have graduate studies (Masters and Doctorates of Philosophy) available for students to enroll in and achieve. A college can stand-alone. A university is usually comprised of many colleges. In this case, you are a university with three colleges named Mind, Body, and Soul.

Let's compare the human body to the RCM model of institutional finance. Remember the RCM model of finance is best understood with a simple breakdown of percentages. 20% of the funds go into a subvention pool for the institution serving the entity as a whole. Another 20% goes towards the home school the student is enrolled in. The major selected by the student identifies as the home school. The last 60% of the tuition goes toward the teaching school. The purpose of RCM encourages individual college houses to seek entrepreneurial marketing and recruiting techniques to increase enrollment.

The human being has a similar make up. It is divided into the mind, body, and soul. The subvention pool is the body. It serves as the overall infrastructure of the being and receives 20%of the power in our lives. The spirit serves as the home school, receiving 20% of the power in our being. Lastly, the mind serves as 60% of the being, for the mind can decide to not follow the natural guidance of the spirit, which directs us on the path God plans for us. The mind also decides what the body does, and the welfare of the food and products taken in are immediate reflections of our self-value. The resource of the mind stands as the greatest of all because it allows us to heed the word of God through our spirit and use the temple of our body to actualize the ideas we have. Thank God every day for the tripartite being, a being that can create our imagination.

Creating your imagination requires building skills and refining your talents into profitable measures. Attending college has been seen as the greatest avenue to enhance one's skills. I disagree. It is a great source of information. It does not guarantee one can effectively apply the information learned. Nonetheless, college and universities allow for individuals to interact and form bonds. These bonds allow harmonious experiences to exist. From these harmonious experiences, a group of individuals can accomplish a lot. College knows the unity of minds allows for a great advancement of society through individuals and collectives. Thus, tuition is charged to students. The cost to attend college can range from $10,000 to $60,000 as a sticker price. Staying on campus can increase the cost even higher.

There is no greater being more important to your life than you.

To obtain financial aid, one must be in dire need of assistance. People who are in the lower class have a great chance at receiving need-based assistance. They have a low chance of earning merit-based scholarships, because the best education is provided for people of the upper class and strategic middle class. The upper- and middle-class students who receive most of the merit-based scholarships have a low chance of earning the need-based aid. Thus, everyone has a gap of finances needed in order to pay their tuition. We find ourselves in an awkward predicament of having to pay the financial gap. For the upper class, the funds are available and paid appropriately. For the middle- and lower-class, loans fill the difference. Loans for middle-class families are easy to get. They are the prime market for college loans. They have the decent credit and collateral assets that allow the federal government and private banks to see a high chance of them being able to pay their loans efficiently. The lower-class community students will find limited access to federal loans due to their economic birthplace and their parents' credit scores, most likely not being sufficient enough to co-sign the loans. Lastly, the lower class rarely has a solid opportunity to earn a private loan due to these same circumstances.

The challenges of financially affording higher education continue on campus. Not only with housing, but also with the need to purchase books. The price of the books continues to rise, and the responsibility always falls upon the student. The sticker price of higher education is much different than the total cost we pay. Add tuition, $44,000, plus housing, $16,000, plus books, $2,000, plus living expenses and experiences, equals a higher education cost of around $62,000. That is incredibly expensive for one year. The price of college is absurdly high. That is the cost of many private colleges around the nation. That price mirrors the cost of out-of-state and international students attending public institutions.

Earning financial aid as an out-of-state and international student is very difficult if they want to go to state colleges. The challenge comes from many of the state-appropriated funds to assist students financially from the domestic state. Luckily, opportunities for financial support on a federal level extend beyond the boundaries of the state with assistance like the Pell Grant. Whether one attends private or public institutions, the Pell Grant can help. The government also offers the lowest interest rates for school loans as well. One can consolidate their loans and have an interest rate of 6-9%. Private loans can be as high as 22%. According to the rule of 72, we can use math to see how long it will take for your loan to double. 72 divided by the interest rate of compound interest equals the years it will take for your student loan to double. If your loan has 9% interest, the rule of 72 states that 72 divided by 9 equals 8 years. In 8 years, your student loan, no matter how much your loan may be, will double. That's frightening for people who have $100,000 in student loans by their second year of school.

The opportunity to learn places a great pressure on students in school. This pressure applies to middle-class and low-income families most. Students accrue more debt than money they have ever earned in their life by the age of 19. That is ridiculous! The will to learn has to be coupled with the opportunity to earn. Improving one's knowledge is incredibly important, but life is not a paper test. We must understand that life is full of lessons that rely upon results, results that impact human society in better and faster ways than anyone else can within your industry. That produces influence, power, prestige, and financial stability. We must have a will to learn to earn. Learning to earn requires going the distance. The distance of education is a lifelong pursuit. It challenges students to consider their financial impact on themselves and their parents (co-signers of the loans), and to decide what will be the greatest investment in their life. We must understand the value of a college degree decreases as we continue to live. It is our skills and ability that conquer opportunity. Knowing your passion and purpose first, then utilizing college to maximize your opportunities to succeed makes the most sense. Use college to improve upon the skills you value, even if you do not have a career goal in mind. Know who you wish to emulate most and find a major on campus similar to your role model's expertise. When you analyze the schools you attend, you must calculate the skills you learn.

Additionally, interacting with alumni must come into play. The value of alumni comes in the opportunity to engage people who have the skills you wish to obtain. The skills one has obtained in life will be their greatest assets. A college degree matters for the first job out of college but, after that, work experience is the greatest advocate. The skills you learn from being involved matter. Being engaged on campus can serve people better than the best grades because managing people as a student leader serves one well in the work force since most jobs require interacting with others. Grades increase your opportunities, but they are not the sole deciding factor. Managing a budget for a school serves you well in all industries. All industries are businesses, so managing money is necessary. **You are a business. Manage your funds**. My friend Mo served as the Budget Review Director for UCLA and went into a managing position for corporate Target, Inc. immediately after graduation since he gained experience being the lead manager of a $200,000 allocations budget for the university student organizations. Accounting and budgeting are important skills. His major was English.

     Use school as a resource to impress upon people the intellect you have and be coachable. The ability to allow people to help you develop is a rare trait. We think we know everything but Erykah Badu once said, "A wise man knows that he knows nothing at all." It speaks to the notion that the more we learn, the more we realize we have to learn. You learn best when you put your thoughts into actions. Read well into the minds of great people and use their experiences as a fortune telling of the great decisions you can make to improve your own life. That is cheap mentorship from the greatest minds on the planet in a book.

     Mentorship is one of the greatest assets if you apply in your life because of the principles they tell you. They gained these principles from living through their own experience. It serves you well to intern for free at places you can gain great access to great minds. Having high-quality mentorship is more valuable than today's dollar. It is a long term investment for people who serve 4 times more than they are paid. That is true work ethic. Dollars of today hardly live past the effort it took to earn them. Thus, the dollar is here today and gone today. The impact you can make on someone can last months, years, or a lifetime. The currency of tomorrow rests in the skills you learn today. Life is results-based, not test-based. Learn to earn the lifestyle you truly desire. Learn to earn the skills it takes to achieve your ideal lifestyle. Learn to earn the knowledge necessary to avoid careless mistakes that may set you back from your ideal lifestyle. Learn to earn to the respect of those who can serve you well by aiding you to achieve your ideal lifestyle. Learn to earn the various forms of income it will take for you to live each day like it is your last. Learn to earn the respect of the mirror so you bask in the glory of your accomplishments. Learn to earn the best route to success. Learn to earn your lifestyle by not negotiating the greed and need of your desires with others. Learn to earn the power of the hour, all 24 of them, and how to manifest your best self 24 hours a day. Learn to earn the will to succeed, no matter what it takes. Eric Thomas once stated that we must be "able, at any moment, to sacrifice what we are, for what we will become." The person you are today is not the person you want to be in the future. If it were, you would have your ideal lifestyle and be eating the delicious fruits of your labor. Instead, you desire to learn to earn your best lifestyle and accept you are not as great as you want to be at this moment. Life is an endless progression. The efforts of your parents and grandparents will not go to waste. Their foundation will be put to good use if you double their efforts. That is the least you can do: double the success they have attained.

Utilize the Internet to find a path to greatness for yourself that your parents would be proud of. The Internet will give you great access if you search the right words. The best thing to do is to find a role model that achieved the lifestyle you wish to imitate. If it is two, three, or four individuals you wish to combine, search them all, one by one. If they have written books, read those books. Apply the lessons they teach in those books. From there, it is greatly important to focus on their path to success. The path you create requires you to Follow One Course Until Successful (FOCUS). Success may be the riches and honor you aim for. Success maybe understanding one path to find that the lifestyle you truly desire requires more actions today than that which your role model took in the past. Today is a new day, and you are a different person in a different experience. The course of action you take will always lead to the same goal: the ideal lifestyle you have imagined.

The better you define the lifestyle you are aiming for, the clearer your choices in life will be. I challenge you to answer these questions every morning before you begin your day:

1. What is your ideal lifestyle?
2. How much does your ideal lifestyle cost?
3. How will you earn this ideal lifestyle?
4. What will human society remember you for?

These questions are the most important questions you can ask yourself. The first challenges you to focus on a clear goal. You must learn from yourself what your ideals are. We should all acquire our ideal lifestyle. Life is nothing but a shame-filled experience if we do not. Most people can drive down a road and pass every street without turning. They follow the road already paved for them and never seem to make a decision about where they should go. They eventually run out of gas and boom, there they are, stuck on the road, realizing they have never actually reached a destination. In fact, they never put a destination into their GPS, and they received exactly what they aimed for: nothing.

The second question highlights the cost of your lifestyle. If you place in your ideal lifestyle that you live in a really nice loft downtown, how much does that cost? If you live in Los Angeles, CA, the renting price of the loft may be close to $3,000 a month. If you live in Philadelphia, PA, your loft may cost $2,100 a month. We need specifics in our mind. Details are important. Driving down the road west because it is the general direction you want to go to get to the California beach is not good enough. Pick a beach and enter that into the GPS. You may end up at the wrong beach if you do not have a specific one. A beach in San Francisco is much different experience than a beach in San Diego. With no specifics, you will reach your destination, but it may not be what you desired. Be specific! Your ideal lifestyle is nothing to be coy or vague about.

The third question requires you to earn your lifestyle. Nothing is achieved without giving. We must give in order to receive. Learn what you need to know in order to earn the lifestyle you deserve. You deserve the best of you, and the world needs the best of you. Living your ideal lifestyle and being a role model for others is a must. Your children will look to your life and see what they can be. Thus, you must have a relentless desire to achieve your ideal lifestyle by any means necessary. The dreams and achievements your ideals will bring to the world are necessary. We need them. I dare not think of a world where OG Mandino, Malcolm X, Bob Johnson, Napoleon Hill, and Kenneth Chennault did not give their best to become the best that they are capable of becoming. That is success. Being your best is what you owe you and the world. Don't let the world suffer today for what you were afraid to accomplish yesterday.

The fourth question focuses on what the world will learn from what you are able to earn. You will have a legacy. Each of us will have words said over our body. The people who knew us will have something to say. Your actions every single day determine what people think of you. You are only as good as your last performance. The world is your stage. **What will people see you do today?** The concept of living everyday as if it is your last means to spend your days becoming the person you want others to remember you being. To be remembered as the person who did not hold back in life. To be remembered as a person who conquered her fears. To be remembered as the person who shed tears of joy more than tears of defeat. To be remembered as the person who climbed the mountain of her dreams. To be remembered as the person who cultivated a great team, family, and company. That is life. That is ideal. That is happiness. Progressing to your best self is happiness. You cannot accomplish everything in a day, but you can be much closer than yesterday, and have the willpower to be the person you always wanted to meet.

You are your greatest resource. Develop you. You will always have you. The lifestyle of going home to watch other people live their dream on television is a holiday treat. Don't let it be a habit. The habit of watching others live their dream will sacrifice your dream coming alive. Take advantage of today because it will never come back. Thus, we have to make the opportunities that we want to happen, happen! Being active toward achieving your dreams will allow more opportunities for you to achieve with the wealth of mind you develop.

A wealth of mind, attracting the greatest resources we can possess, an unwavering will to succeed, an ideal goal to achieve, a willingness to learn, a desire to earn, a healthy mind (water, natural foods, exercise), and a positive mental attitude. The positive mental attitude looks to develop a positive outlook in every experience, whether or not the experience works in his favor. A friend of mine, Jordan, made the best experience he could, every single time he could. Kevin Durant is a great basketball player in the National Basketball Association. His childhood coach died at the age of 35. He wears number 35 every day to honor his late coach. His reason for success in basketball comes down to his desire to honor his coach. That experience of death has served as a positive reminder of his need to achieve. He has the will to achieve for his coach. Durant maintains an internal burning desire to honor the life of his coach. When loved ones die, we grieve because we miss their life more than for the death itself. Honor your fallen angels. Honor the lives of those dear to you than have dies by becoming great!

Maximus Araelis once stated, "It is not death a man should fear, but fear never beginning to live." It is our resistance to ourselves we often run away from. We must not resist our desires to live the lives we wish most. Our loved ones, past and present, wish nothing but the best for us. We know what is best for us. It is our responsibility to achieve our dreams. The comfort in our own skins we gain from executing our dreams allow the best of us to achieve. The best of us lives in the progress of our lives, especially when we progress towards our dreams with a relentless desire to achieve it, no matter the cost. We will be able to rid ourselves of the old habits and become the new.

    Thus we will resist the plights of others that aim to prevent our evolution. We will live our days in true passion. We will not seek the validation of others in order to make decisions towards our dreams. Mentors and experts within our passionate pursuits will grant us great advice. The decision is, and will always be, yours to make and live with. After careful reflection, you will be able to decide the best course of action. You will FOCUS on your actions to validate your decisions. Confirmation from others about your journey is great, but not necessary. If others were meant to have our vision, they would have our eyes. The light of the sun shines differently in my world than it does in yours. The achievements of my life do not compare to the achievements of others, for no one can understand my passion. They will only be able to appreciate the comfort I have in my own skin from living a life I envision.

    As others aim to oppose you, understand God only places these people in front of you so you may grow strong mentally, physically, or spiritually. Everything happens for a reason. God places no challenge before you that you cannot conquer or learn a great lesson from. The ability to have a positive mental attitude so you can create the blessing or the lesson in every interaction we have on Earth promotes destiny. The destinies of life lives in your mindset to be unwavering to distractions and to be the angel on Earth you were meant to be. Earth angels, human beings, are designed to be lovers. It is not punches that we throw, but more so overcoming resistance. Body builders grow muscle in the gym. With each repetition of the weight going in opposition of its natural movement, we tear our muscles. The muscle tears occur when we are faced with resistance heavier than our strength could endure. The muscles do not like defeat. With proper diet and mental fortitude, we find ourselves, in a week's time, lifting the same weight again. We have taken time to let ourselves recover and fed protein to our muscles so they may recover and be stronger than before. This time, the resistance is not greater than our muscles, and we overcome the opposing weight. The competitive nature within us allowed time to recover, readjust, and face the same opposition again, until we conquer it. That ability of bodybuilders to build their muscles highlights the great mental fortitude it takes to achieve any feat. They show what daily, consistent, and persistent action can create. Overcome the resistance. Do not let weights burden you, for they will not ease up. You will not get stronger until you push back. Press forward in your efforts to become a victor, not a victim. **You must be obsessed with improving yourself.** God's greatest gift to you is you!

Progressing to your best self, every day, is your key to happiness.

17
WEALTHY EDUCATION

A wealthy education allows for you to take what you have learned in one space and apply it to another space.

Welcome to the last chapter of the book. You made it. Most people do not finish a book. Most people do not read more than one a book a year. Read a book a week in one field for a year and you will become an expert in that field. Books serve as a great source of mentorship. Books hold the knowledge of life. Knowledge is a two-part word. Know – what you know is based on things you have assessed and come to understand after applying information to your life.

I refer to the diamonds of transcendence as a diagram that conveys how wisdom is created. Information fills the bottom of the diamond. The diamond is then filled halfway with knowledge. Wisdom is the top half of the diamond. Wisdom is much greater than knowledge. When you take knowledge and you pass it on to someone who can positively apply it to his life, your knowledge is now wisdom. The wisdom is applicable to more than one person. The knowledge applies to you. The wisdom applies to many. My mentor John Jacobs came to my high school every Friday during my first semester of senior year. I was writing my personal statement for UCLA. He read my personal statement every Friday for months. He critiqued it over and over again. It was horrible. My personal statement got such a bad review. He once marked a big red "X" on my statement. He turned the paper over and told me to start it over again. I was two to three weeks away from submitting my application. I was devastated, but also extremely excited. I loved having a strong-minded, confident person telling me how to succeed, especially when they had achieved my goals already. He mentored me on how to get into college and be successful in the process. Jacobs had already graduated from UCLA. He imparted his knowledge upon me so I could become wise in the college application process. His knowledge is my wisdom because his techniques of college application success transferred to me. A wealthy education is applied information that works well, not just for one person, but for many.

Regardless of what someone is able to teach you, it is incredibly important you remain motivated to succeed, because it is motivation that permits you to listen to mentors. My motivation to gain entry to UCLA provided me the discipline I needed to achieve the perfect essay. Motivation continues the drive. When you are faced with adversity and the world tells you that you can no longer succeed as you wish, your reason to excel becomes your motivation. When Jacobs turned my paper over, the one I worked on for months, I could have quit. Sitting in the college office, with a college graduate, working on my college essay, I could have quit when he said, "Write your paper over again. This essay will not get you into UCLA."

Never Give Up. Never Give In.

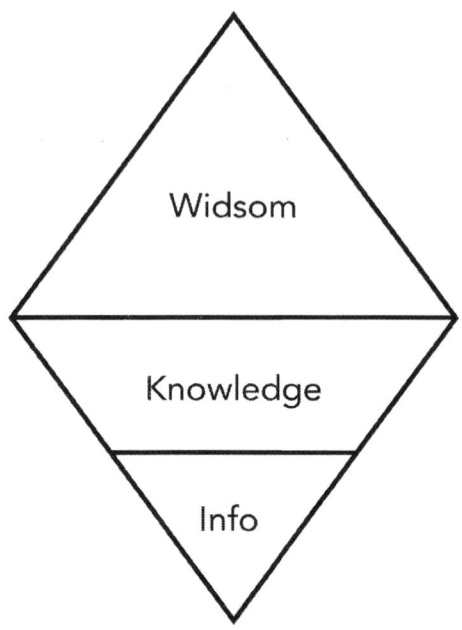

The Diamond of Transcendence

      Instead of letting his professional opinion deter me from goal, I became curious as to what it took to write a great personal statement to enter UCLA. The UC (University of California) application process was no small feat. My essay for UC-Berkeley and UCLA had to be the same. As an applicant, you apply to the UC system and select the institutions you wish to review your application. Thus, my essay had to be perfect for UC-Berkeley, UCLA, and others. I was granted entry into both institutions. My motivation to succeed, guidance from Jacobs, and curiosity to inquire from multiple sources gave me the tools I needed to enroll in UCLA.

My passion drove my ability to learn transferable skills that would increase my ability to write a great personal statement for UCLA. I did not know everything, so I had to reach out to Jacobs, who was more knowledgeable of the college application process. His guidance provided leadership for my passion of college achievement to gain momentum and proper technique. In school, we often do not seek advice from those who have achieved what we aim to do. In life, we should only seek advice from experts or people well experienced in a specific endeavor. It is their success we must have. You can achieve all of your goals independently, but with a team, the dream becomes much more viable. Even the great Serena Williams has a coach, family, and support group to keep her at her best. A team supports her ability to achieve her dreams. Her passion and commitment to excellence provides people the belief they need to have in her to help her achieve her goals. They give to her, not to receive accolades in her championship and speeches, but to help her win. Believe in yourself. Allow yourself to be engulfed with your passion to succeed. When others who have achieved your goals commit to helping you, listen to their word. The information, knowledge, and wisdom will help you achieve in a similar fashion.

A wealthy education allows for you to achieve your goals. A wealthy education allows for you to take what you have learned in one space and apply it to another. Transferring skills from one experience into the future to take advantage of another opportunity allows you to improve your human capital and thus makes you wealthier. You have learned to apply what you learned outside of class to your life to benefit and advance your personal passion. That is the key of life. Understand that the journey is life. Great is a destination, but greatness is a path. You cannot achieve the great destination of college access and graduation if you do not commit to the great actions needed every day: attend class on time, create great relationships with your teachers, earn your best test scores, lead in your co-curricular extra-curricular activities, and make time for yourself. Your daily habits will show you a great blanket of excellence. Thus, greatness is a lifestyle, not a one-time event.

 Being able to understand the actions necessary to achieve your goals through these self-education principles (titles of each chapter) places a student in the best predicament you can ask for to achieve. Education is an opportunity. Learning is a lifestyle. In order to master the education system present in the U.S., one must be excellent in many areas of scholastic achievement in and outside of the classroom. School teaches you many things, but it does not teach you how to be the best student. Being quiet and obedient is not enough to secure the academic future you wish. You must be a great student who is engaged in and out of the classroom, and seek help from many experienced people. Apply these techniques, and you will learn to earn your best opportunities in school, forever and always. Student leaders who represent the school in the best light will always gain more privileges, scholarships, and opportunities than everyone else. Be your best at all times, because you pay the consequences of your shortcomings, no one else. Not your professor, advisor, or parents. You are counting on you. You are the CEO of you.

 More than anything, this book is about taking control of your life. Do not wait for opportunity to arrive: create it. When you know who you are, you can make the best decisions of your life every day. It is incredibly important you learn more about yourself, your habits, and your dreams every day. When you know who you are, you can take control of your life and every part of it. School is not designed to teach you everything you need to know. You have to love yourself so much that you are willing to learn from life, the greatest teacher. Schoolteachers and professors can only teach you what they have done. No one has ever been you before. You are the first, the one and only. Embrace the journey of your life to become who you are meant to be: you! You cannot control the entire universe, but you can control you. Focus on the needs of you today, first and foremost. Use college as a platform for telling the world who you are. The first step is to know who you are. Know your self-worth. Demand nothing but greatness from yourself. If you don't give yourself what you believe you are worth, then who will?

Self-love is improving you constantly. The more you give yourself, the more you can give to others. There is nothing you can do for others that you cannot do for yourself. How you love yourself determines how well you can love others. Know thyself to love thyself. Know yourself to know your wealth.

Be G.R.E.A.T.! You already are.

B.E. G.R.E.A.T.

Building
Excellent:
Grit,
Relationships,
Expectations,
Access, and
Time Management.

-Miles Goodloe

1 Corinthians 13

Made in the USA
Lexington, KY
27 December 2016